IMAGES
of America

CINCINNATI'S FREEMASONS

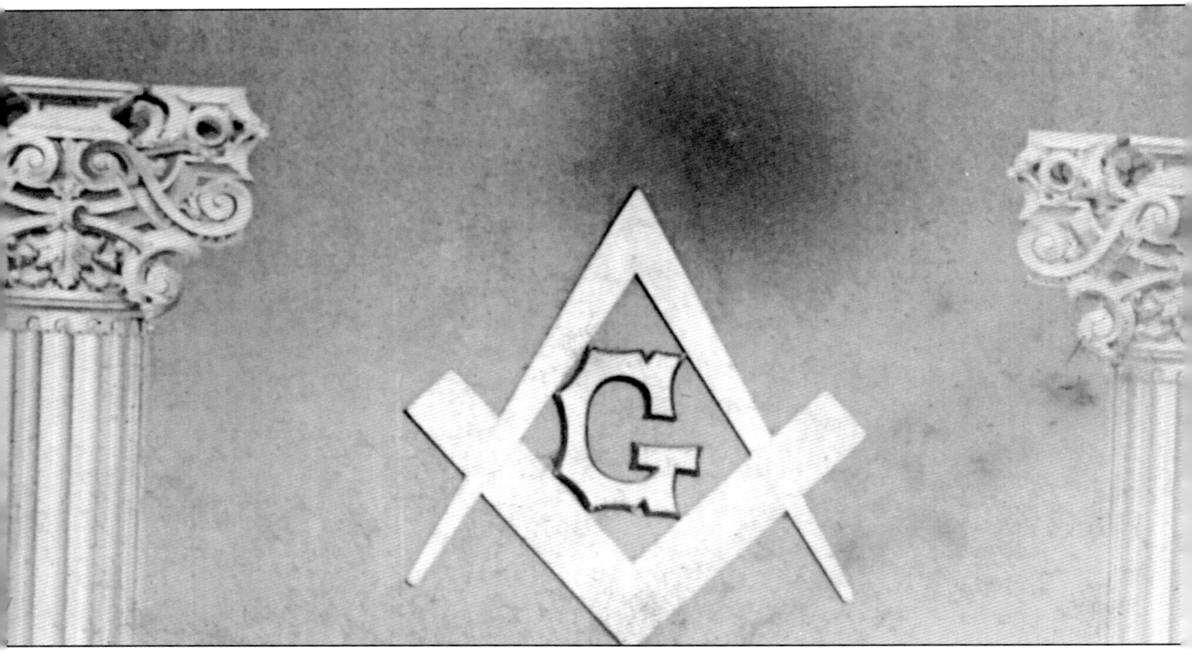

Square and Compasses. This detail from the cover image shows the square and compasses, the emblem of Freemasonry (see page 10). (Columbia Lodge No. 44.)

On the Cover: Columbia Lodge No. 44 Annual Inspection, May 26, 1923. A lodge's ritual proficiency and financial and administrative records are inspected annually by the Grand Master or his proxy. Grand Master Harry S. Johnson (see page 25), seated in the second row forward of the wall, third from the left, with the left arm of the compasses pointing to him, was in attendance on this night. (Columbia Lodge No. 44.)

IMAGES
of America

CINCINNATI'S FREEMASONS

Donald I. Crews

ARCADIA
PUBLISHING

ISBN 978-1-4671-1237-6

Published by Arcadia Publishing
Charleston, South Carolina

Printed in the United States of America

Library of Congress Control Number: 2014934402

For all general information, please contact Arcadia Publishing:
Telephone 843-853-2070
Fax 843-853-0044
E-mail sales@arcadiapublishing.com
For customer service and orders:
Toll-Free 1-888-313-2665

Visit us on the Internet at www.arcadiapublishing.com

"To all poor and distressed Masons, wherever dispersed over the face of Earth and Water, wishing them a speedy relief from all their sufferings, and a safe return to their native country; should they so desire."

Thanks Terry, Randy, Cleve, Willard, Joe, Bill, and Hiram.

Contents

ACKNOWLEDGMENTS

Nova Caesarea Harmony Lodge No. 2 is the oldest lodge in Cincinnati. What its members of the past retained has much to do with the existence of this book. This lodge's items are identified in the captions as (NCH2).

The Ancient Accepted Scottish Rite, Valley of Cincinnati (AASR) backed this project from its beginning. Special thanks to Michael Himes, fraternal secretary; and Kyle Evans, building manager of the Cincinnati Masonic Center.

Kevin Grace and the staff of the University of Cincinnati Archives and Rare Books department, which holds the John D. Caldwell Collection (UC), were immensely helpful.

Many valuable items have been provided by the Grand Lodge of Ohio (GLofOH), and great help came from Chad Simpson, director of program development; and Charles Eichensehr, grand historian.

The Cincinnati Historical Society Library (CHS) holds the Harry Hake Architectural Collection. Its staff helped me make use of this and other collections.

The Public Library of Cincinnati and Hamilton County provided many images from the Cincinnati Memory Project and permitted my use of an image from the Cincinnati Panorama of 1848.

Items without courtesy lines were either produced by the author or are in the public domain.

Thanks to Gary Troha, E.T. Carson No. 598; Rodney Gibbons, North Bend No. 346; Louis Adams, Columbia No. 44; Ronald Zemites, Oakley Lodge No. 668; Jean Watters, Dorcas Chapter OES, No. 277; Len Geshan, Yeatman–Mt. Washington No. 162; Dick Schroeder, Montgomery No. 94; Rick Long and Barrie Owens, College Hill/Harry S. Johnson No. 641; Stan Anderson, Norwood-Winton-Carthage No. 576; Tim Winkle, Alexandria Washington Lodge No. 22; the Syrian Shrine; Linda Showalter, Marietta College Library; Jaime Bourassa, Missouri History Museum Library and Research Center; Don Prout, cincinnativiews.net; Ed Robb, Shriners Hospitals for Children–Cincinnati; the Cincinnati Police Museum; and Maggie Kelley, current owner of the Hoffner Lodge.

Finally, to friends, brothers, colleagues, and family who supported, tolerated, and cheered: thank you and bless you.

Introduction

To enlarge the sphere of social happiness is worthy of the benevolent design of a Masonic institution; and it is most fervently to be wished, that the conduct of every member of the fraternity, as well as those publications, that discover the principles which actuate them, may tend to convince mankind that the grand object of Masonry is to promote the happiness of the human race.

—George Washington to the Grand Lodge of Free and Accepted Masons of Massachusetts, January 1793

Freemasonry has been part of Cincinnati from the city's very beginning. William McMillan, the great benefactor of Nova Caesarea Harmony Lodge No. 2 and namesake of McMillan Lodge No. 141, was one of the original settlers who arrived on December 28, 1788. Ephraim Kibbey, an original settler at Columbia, east of Cincinnati, was one of the first men to be made a Mason in southwest Ohio.

Freemasonry has passed through several ages in America. During the founding period (1730–1790), lodges were few, membership was small, and most members were of the upper-middle class. At this time, the philosophy of the fraternity was the philosophy of the age. The Enlightenment was in its ascendency as the fraternity came into its own. Reason, individual rights, and the blossoming of the sciences and the arts defined the mindset of the world and the fraternity. Using builders' tools and the application of arts and sciences such as geometry, logic, and rhetoric to impart moral lessons was a fitting conception for the time. Men of a particular level of success, skill, and knowledge were drawn to such an institution. George Washington and other Revolutionary leaders who were Masons were drawn to Freemasonry as much because it fit their worldview as they were taught a worldview by the lessons of Freemasonry.

The second age of Masonry in America (1790–1860) took place in the context of the industrial revolution and the country's westward expansion. Continuing to draw men of substance, Masonry reinforced standards of conduct and character. It also provided a connection to the places that people had left behind. Just as the church existed almost from the founding of Cincinnati, Masonry was a connection to moral beliefs, stability, and an image of what the world ought to contain. The best and the brightest in the community flocked to the Masonic lodge.

The Civil War brought on the next phase of Freemasonry. The war's participants came into contact with people, places, and situations they had never known before. Cincinnatians traveled as soldiers, and soldiers by the thousands came through Cincinnati. After the war, many sought the camaraderie that the service had provided. The uniformed and drill-oriented Knights Templar struck a chord with some veterans. The Scottish Rite's large and impressive costumed tales of chivalry and honor filled a need for those no longer called to service by bugle and clash of arms. The economic success of many made organizations popular that imparted their truths to a select few, even if the select few was a group growing in size as the fraternity's membership numbers increased.

The early 20th century, with all of its inventions that sped up the world, led some people to seek the peace and sobriety of the Masonic lodge or chapter. Others were drawn to emerging social organizations, such as the Shrine and Grotto. Men joined the fraternity in great numbers, and lodges multiplied. Throughout the United States, many great Masonic buildings were erected in those years, including Cincinnati's downtown temple. Norwood Lodge built two temples in less than 10 years, outgrowing its first almost before the mortar could set. Carthage, Price Hill, Avon, Hanselmann, and E.T. Carson Lodges all constructed buildings in this period.

The Great Depression hit as the 1920s came to an end, and the social order changed. Many communities saw their new Masonic temples suddenly become great financial burdens. Luckily, the thrifty Cincinnatians were able to keep the new Cincinnati Masonic Temple solvent. However, the tough financial times did end plans for construction of the fourth building of the complex, the Shrine wing.

Masonic membership boomed following World War II. Many returning servicemen had strong desires to maintain the camaraderie experienced as "a band of brothers." Society in general sought a return to normalcy after hard times. This included growing families, churches, and lodges. Uniformity across the institution was a norm, and the expectation was that rules would be handed down and followed by the lodges and their officers. This seemed appropriate to many of those who made it through the Depression and World War II, but would be less popular with the next generations.

The competition for time, a more casual lifestyle, ever increasing entertainment choices, and the lack of family or community connection to organizations have negatively affected membership and participation in many groups, including the Masons. Masonry however remains the largest fraternal organization in the United States, Ohio, and Cincinnati. Many men and, through the related orders, women and young people, continue to be part of the "gentle craft." Efforts have been taken to deal with declining membership numbers. One-day classes, in which numerous degrees are presented in a single day, have introduced some men to the fraternity. Since the beginning of the millennium, two lodges have been founded in Cincinnati, each designed to practice Masonry from a particular perspective. Some Masons, in fact, believe that the fraternity may be better off as a smaller institution, being more able to concentrate on its purpose and meaning.

This book attempts to capture the essence of this great fraternity in one place over a period of time. Statements contained herein endeavor to describe the fraternity as it exists or existed in Cincinnati, Ohio. While many of these ideas are true throughout most of the United States, some may not be. Some practices or things described here may differ with experience elsewhere.

Finally, all opinions contained in this book are my own. I hold no rank or status permitting me to speak for the Masonic fraternity. I am merely an interested member. What appears in this volume, including any errors, is of my making. Assistance has been welcomed, but judgment has been mine. This book's pages allow me to just brush the surface of the topic. In the limited space available, many lodges and many valued brothers have of necessity been omitted. No slight was intended by what is or is not here. This is an overview only. Hopefully, it describes the essence of Freemasonry in Cincinnati.

One

WHAT IS FREEMASONRY?

Freemasonry is the world's oldest and largest fraternal organization. It is an all-male society, bound together by ritual and modes of recognition and an expected code of conduct. Freemasonry's rituals teach morality, using symbolism from the stonemason's trade to instruct in the development of character. Freemasons belong to bodies called lodges. Lodges meet in buildings usually called temples in honor of King Solomon's temple, which figures prominently in Masonic ritual.

The Masonic lodge confers three degrees or ceremonies to teach candidates the philosophy of the fraternity and their duties to God, their brothers (fellow members), and the world. A candidate progresses to full membership via the degrees of Entered Apprentice, Fellowcraft, and Master Mason.

Nothing written on Freemasonry can avoid the topic of secrecy. Secrets in Masonry are relative. A building occupying half a city block in downtown Cincinnati is hardly a secret. Pins, rings, and license plates identifying members hardly involve secrecy. Secrets are mostly means by which Masons may recognize each other and serve the purpose of reminding members of shared experiences and commitments.

The origins of Freemasonry are unknown. The most common theory is that the operative (working) stonemasons' guilds in England and Scotland, builders of the great cathedrals, began to admit nonoperative or speculative members. With the end of the cathedral building, the speculative Masons became the majority, and the secrets of the builders' trade symbolically became the secrets of the Freemasons.

The philosophy of Freemasonry is firmly grounded in Enlightenment ideas dating to the dawn of the 18th century. While some learned men at this time began to refute God, others saw the scientific discoveries as proof of the existence of a Grand Architect or Great Geometrician. Some members of learned groups, like the Royal Society, were among those drawn to the fraternity.

London 1717, the first Grand Lodge, was founded by four existing lodges, coming together to celebrate the two feasts of the Saints John, the patron saints of the stonemasons. The advantages of some form of central administration and leadership became evident. Similar developments throughout the British Isles led to Freemasonry's growth, including in the colonies in North America starting in 1730.

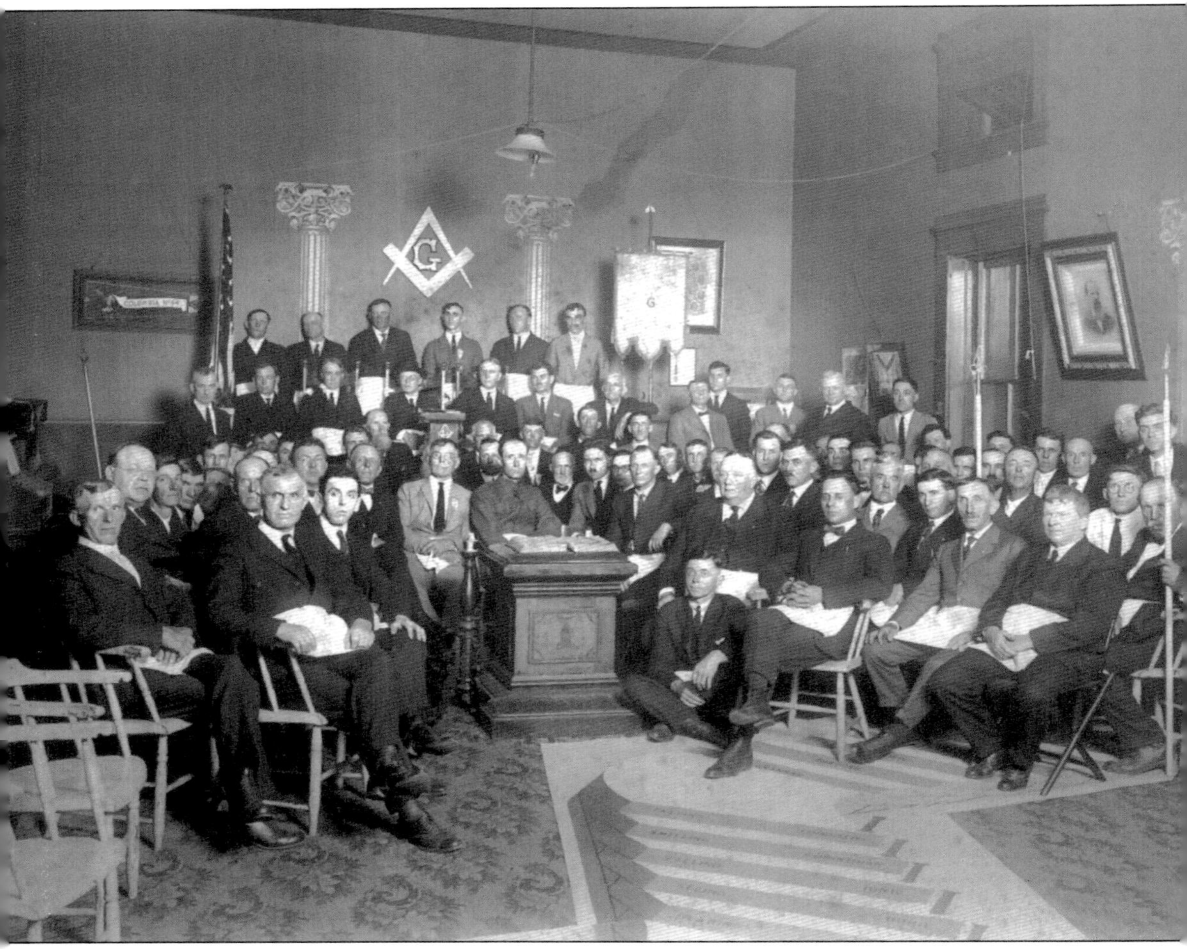

COLUMBIA LODGE NO. 44. Many items visible in this image define the location as a Masonic lodge: the altar, candles, brothers wearing aprons, Deacons' and Stewards' staffs, Fellowcraft Degree floor cloth, pillars, and square and compass stenciled on the wall. The Master's station is symbolically in the "East," representing the beginning of the day. The Senior Warden would be at the opposite end of the lodge room or the "West" (see page 14). (Columbia Lodge No. 44.)

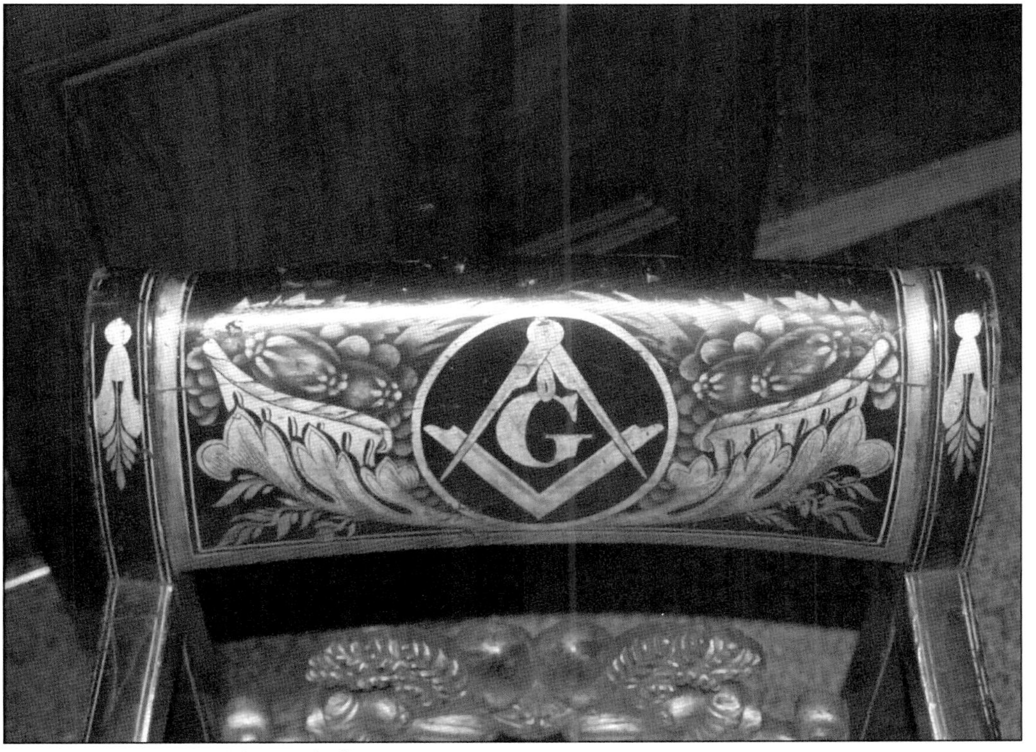

Detail from 1790s Master's Chair. This chair was a gift from St. John's Lodge No. 1 in New Jersey in honor of Nova Caesarea Lodge No. 10's chartering. The square and compasses (as it is referred to by Ohio Masons) is a universal emblem of the Masonic fraternity. The emblem can be found on buildings, clothing, fine jewelry, and inexpensive souvenirs. These builders' tools symbolize self-mastery and self-improvement in building "that house not made with hands, eternal in the heavens." (NCH2.)

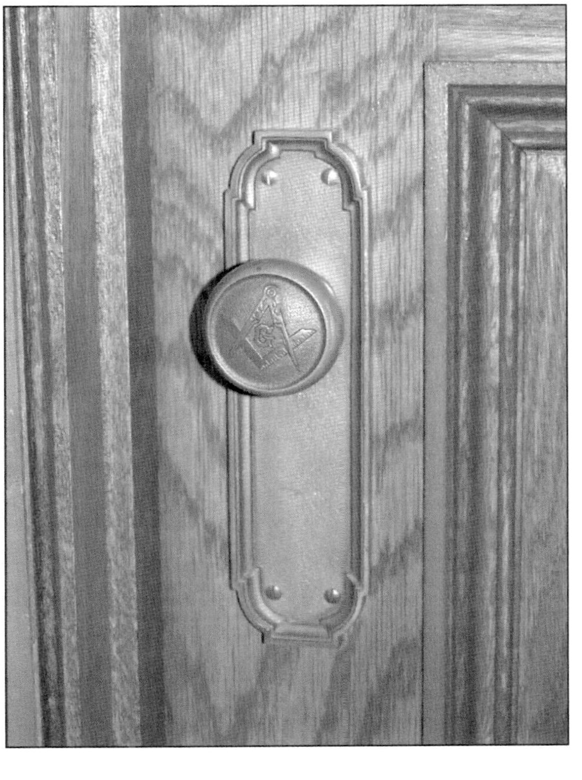

Doorknob, Fourth Floor, Cincinnati Masonic Center. The "G" inside the square and compasses alludes to God and to geometry. This is a reminder to Masons of the power, goodness, and might of the Great Architect of the Universe observable in science and mathematics.

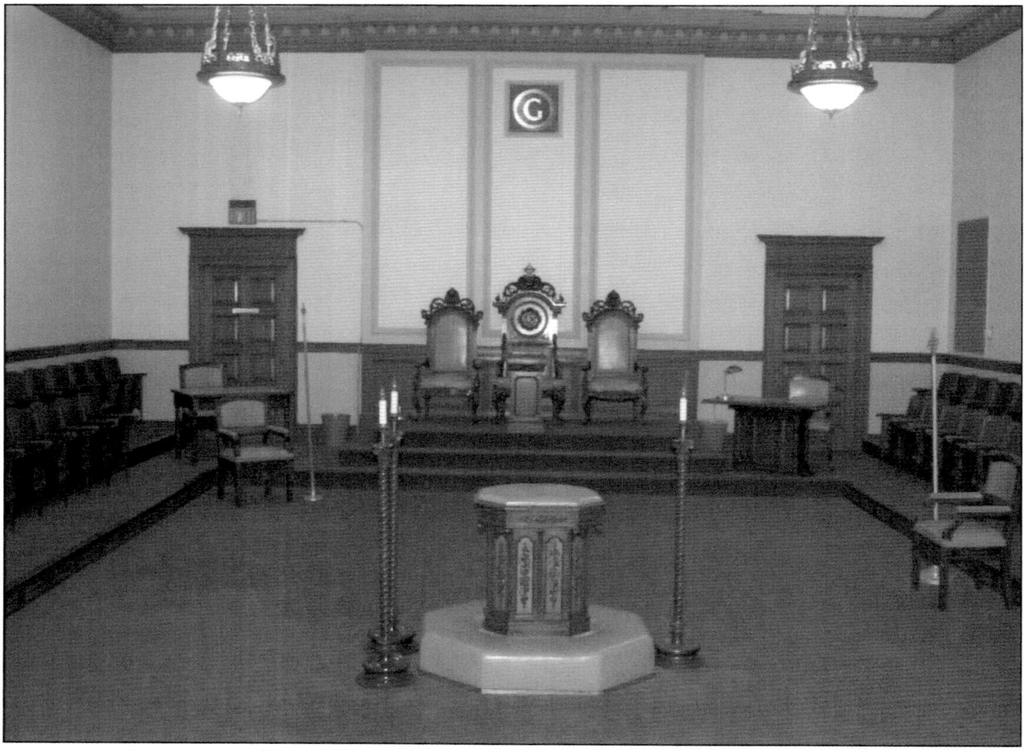

ALTAR AND FURNITURE, LODGE ROOM FOUR, CINCINNATI MASONIC CENTER. This furniture from the 1850s was originally in the temple built in 1858. An altar, lit by three candles, is located at the center of all lodge rooms. The volume of sacred law (usually the Bible) is open on the altar when the lodge is meeting. The square and compasses are also displayed on the altar when the lodge is open, symbolizing self-mastery supported by divinity. (NCH2.)

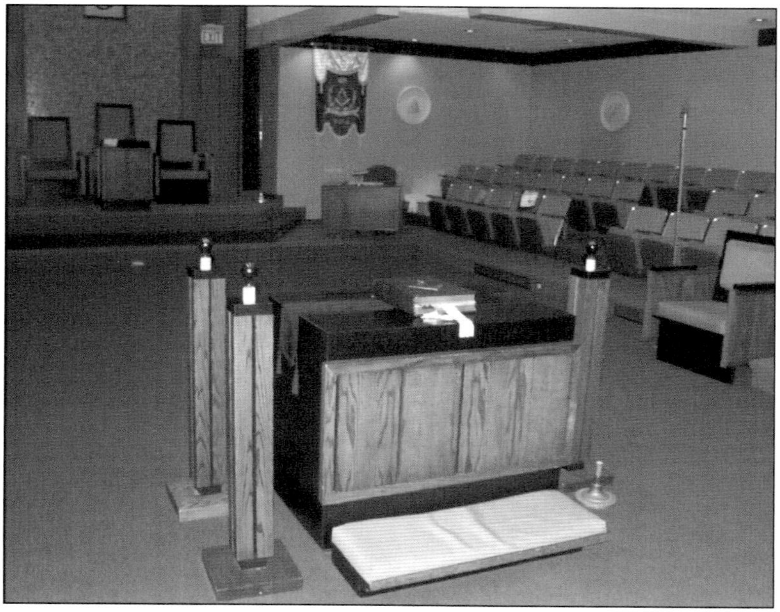

ALTAR AND FURNITURE, OAKLEY MASONIC TEMPLE. This 1960s furniture appropriately matches the time of the building's creation, as did the 1850s furniture in the image above. It serves exactly the same purpose. The traditions of lodges and their physical material have much to do with an individual Mason's attachment to and pride in his lodge. (Oakley Lodge No. 668.)

DECORATED APRON. The apron is the attire of a Mason. It represents the apron of a builder or workman. White aprons are usually worn by modern Freemasons, symbolizing the purity of a Mason's intentions. Aprons may be decorated to signify office in a lodge or other body. Aprons decorated with ritualistic symbols were common in the early 19th century. (College Hill/ Harry S. Johnson Lodge No. 641.)

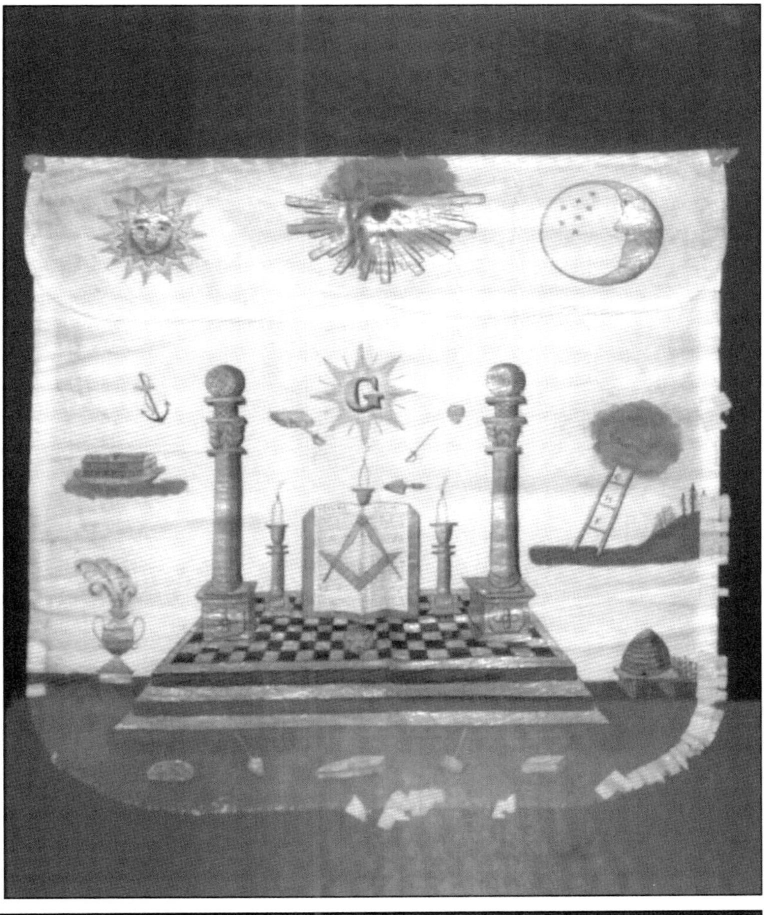

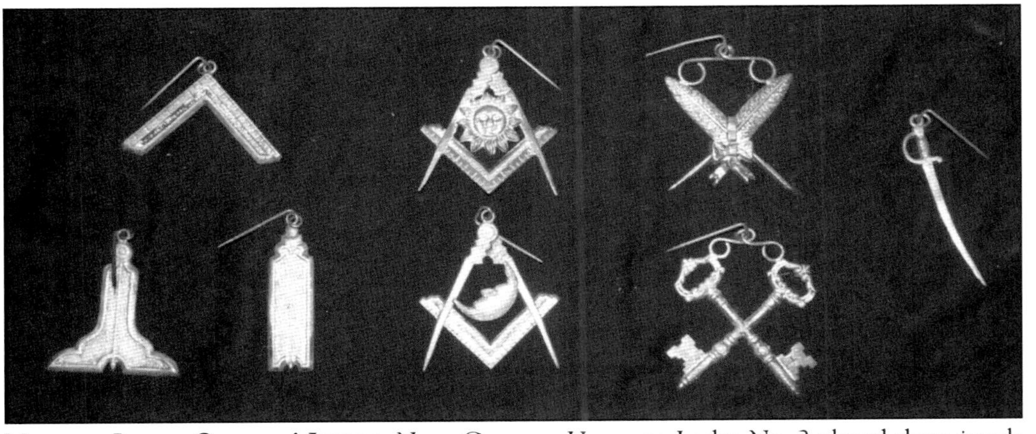

MASONIC LODGE OFFICERS' JEWELS. Nova Caesarea Harmony Lodge No. 2 placed these jewels in the cornerstone of the 1858 temple. Each piece identifies the office of the wearer. Shown here are, from left to right, (top row) Square, Worshipful Master; Square and Compasses with Sun, Senior Deacon; Crossed Pens, Secretary; Sword, Tyler; (bottom row) Level, Senior Warden; Plumb, Junior Warden; Square and Compasses with Moon, Junior Deacon; and Crossed Keys, Treasurer. (NCH2.)

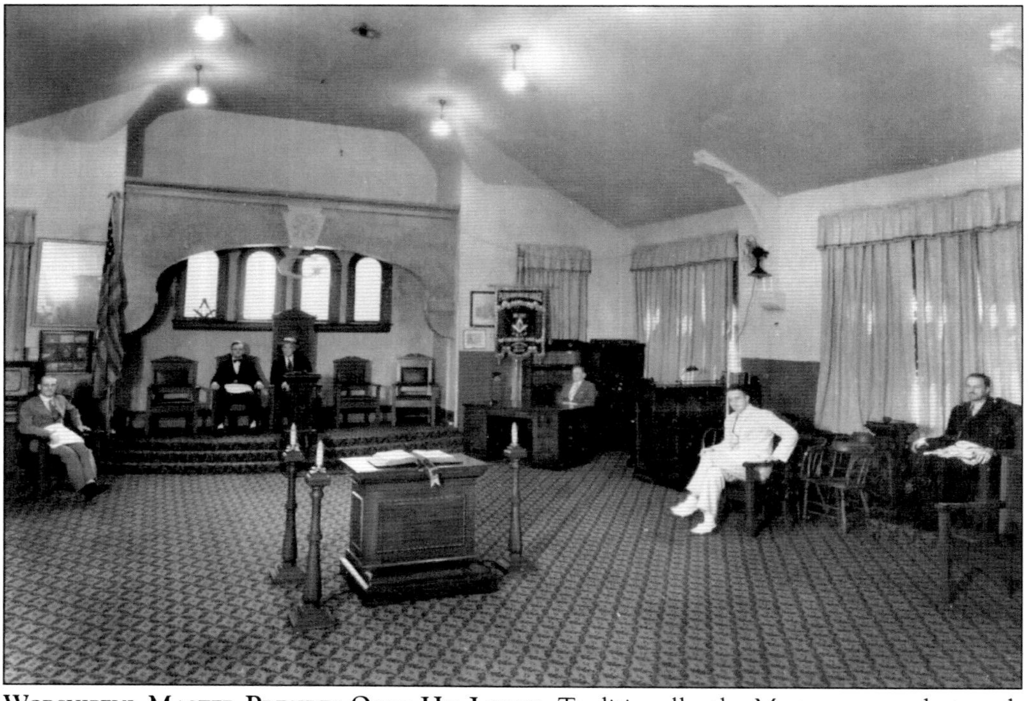

Worshipful Master Presides Over His Lodge. Traditionally, the Master wears a hat, such as this Master's straw boater (left of center). "Worshipful," much like the honorific "Reverend," refers to a duty to direct the lodge to be mindful of God in all its affairs. The officers shown here are, from left to right, Senior Deacon, Chaplain, Master, Secretary, Steward, and Junior Warden (similar to a second Vice President). This photograph shows Pleasant Ridge Lodge No. 202 in the 1930s. (Montgomery Lodge No. 95.)

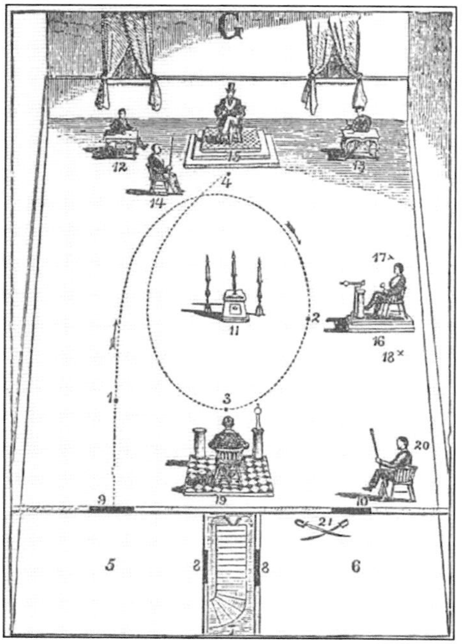

Masonic Officers' Stations and Places. This image from the 1866 *Duncan's Masonic Ritual and Monitor* shows the location of various officers in a Masonic lodge. In Ohio, they would be Worshipful Master, 15 (top center); Senior Warden, 19 (bottom center); Junior Warden, 16 (right); Senior Deacon, 14; Junior Deacon, 20; Senior Steward, 17; Junior Steward, 18; Secretary, 13; Treasurer, 12; and Tyler, 21. Additionally, the Chaplain would be on the Master's right and Lodge Education Officer on his left.

Two

Grand Lodge, Grand Masters, and Grand Secretaries

The Grand Master is the supreme authority of Freemasonry in his jurisdiction. Ohio Grand Masters, as in most Grand Jurisdictions, are referred to by the honorific Most Worshipful Brother. Lower-ranking officers in the Grand Lodge (governing body) are Right Worshipful Brothers. Brief biographical sketches of the men from Cincinnati who served the Grand Lodge of Ohio as Grand Master follow. Each Grand Master's biography includes, in the caption title, the year(s) elected Grand Master and, in parentheses, lodge membership. The three Cincinnatians who served as Grand Secretary for a total of over 100 years are also included.

The Grand Lodge of Ohio was founded at Chillicothe in January 1808 by six lodges already operating within the state. At the time, Cincinnati Lodge No. 13, operating under an 1805 charter from the Grand Lodge of Kentucky, existed in Cincinnati. It had originally been chartered as Nova Caesarea Lodge No. 10 by the Grand Lodge of New Jersey in 1791. The lodge was represented at this first Ohio Grand Lodge session by Thomas Henderson and Francis Mennesier. It would be chartered in Ohio as Nova Caesarea Harmony Lodge No. 2.

The other lodges that founded the Grand Lodge included American Union Lodge, which had been working in Marietta since June 1790 under a warrant issued by the Massachusetts Grand Lodge to a military unit during the Revolution. Erie Lodge No. 47 in Warren and New England Lodge No. 48 in Worthington were both chartered in 1803 by the Grand Lodge of Connecticut. The Lodge of Amity No. 105, chartered in 1805 by the Grand Lodge of Pennsylvania, was in Zanesville. Scioto Lodge in Chillicothe was chartered in 1805 by the Grand Lodge of Massachusetts.

Rufus Putnam of Marietta, a former general under George Washington in the American Revolution, was selected as Ohio's first Grand Master, even though he was not in attendance. He graciously refused the honor. In Putnam's absence, in 1809, the first Deputy Grand Master (second in charge) was Thomas Henderson of Cincinnati. He was the first person to preside over Ohio's Grand Lodge.

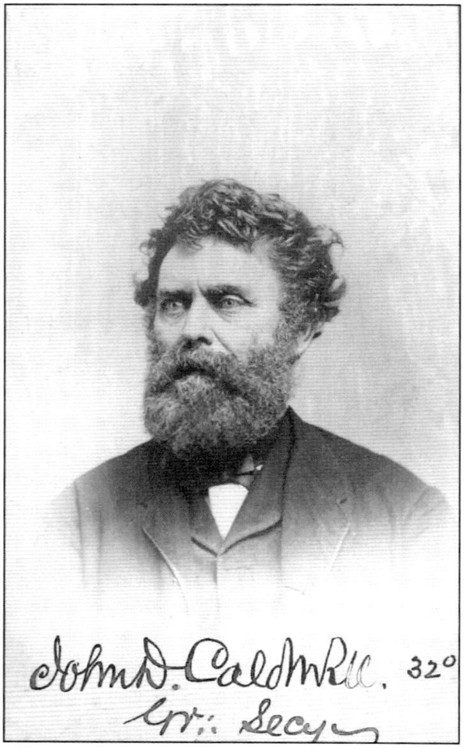

John D. Caldwell, Grand Secretary of the Grand Lodge of Ohio. Beginning in 1852, Cincinnati would be home to the offices of the Grand Lodge for more than a century. During that time, the office of Grand Secretary was held by only three men. The first of these was a devoted Mason and dedicated citizen of Cincinnati, John Day Caldwell (1816–1902), a member of Nova Caesarea Harmony Lodge No. 2. He served as Grand Secretary from 1852 to 1887. (GLofOH.)

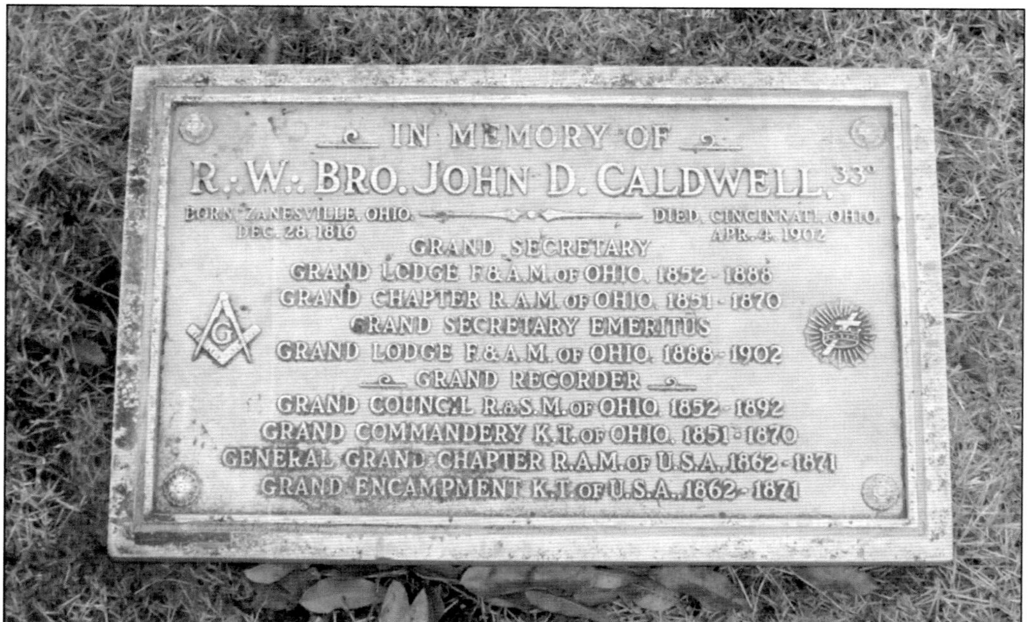

Grand Secretary of Almost Everything. Caldwell's tombstone in Cincinnati's Spring Grove Cemetery lists the six Grand Masonic bodies he served as chief administrative officer. He was Grand Secretary of the Grand Lodge of Ohio for 35 years. For nine of those years, he simultaneously served all six bodies.

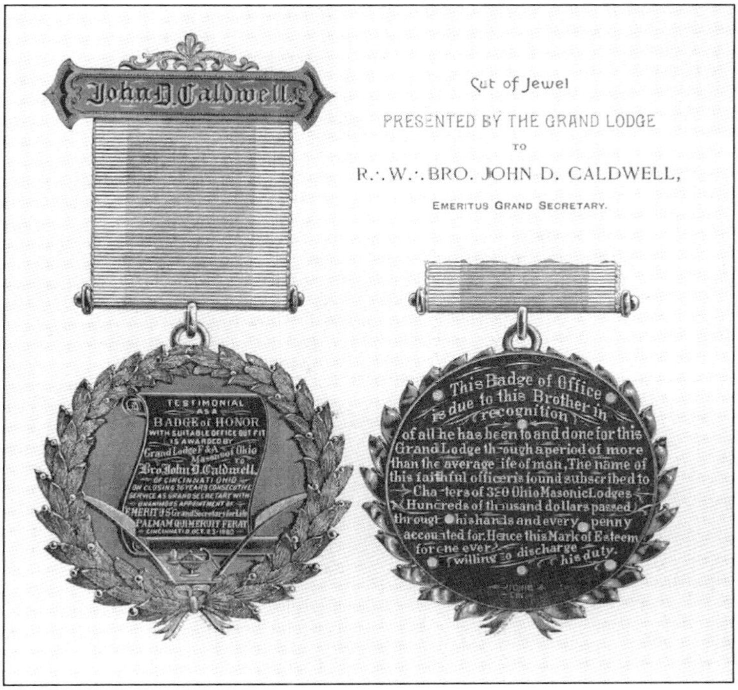

CALDWELL HONORED AS GRAND SECRETARY EMERITUS. A medal was presented in 1889 to honor Caldwell's years of service to Ohio Masonry. The medal is in the museum at the Cincinnati Masonic Center. He was further honored with an annual stipend. Caldwell donated his substantial Masonic library to Cincinnati's Public Library, walking in to the library's downtown location one day and advising them, without forewarning, that a delivery would be arriving later that day. (UC.)

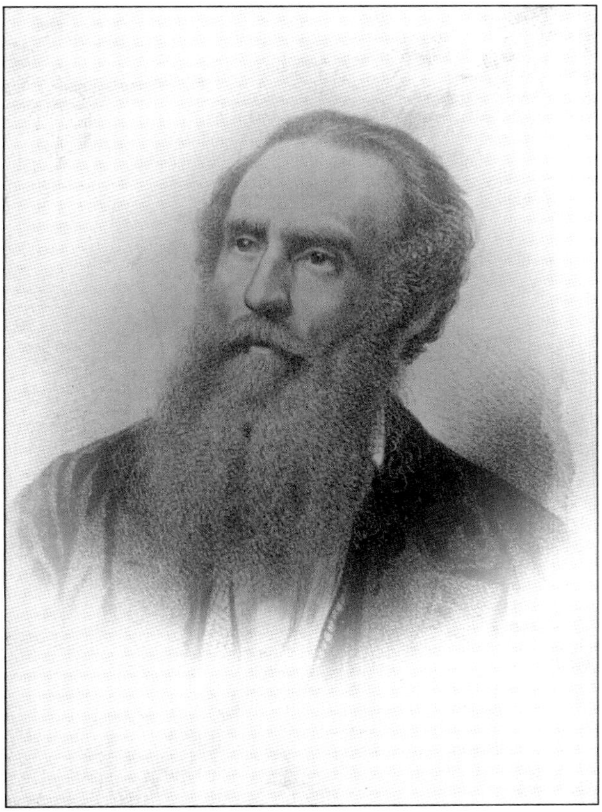

WILLIAM BLACK DODDS; 1854, 1855 (NOVA CAESAREA HARMONY NO. 2). Dodds's varied vocations included canal construction, the coal business, steamboat transportation, fireproof safes, and banking. Dodds (1808–1885) received his Masonic degrees in 1843. He was elected Worshipful Master eight consecutive years, starting in 1846, including his first year as Grand Master. Dodds was the first Cincinnatian elected Grand Master. From 1849 to 1851, he served as Grand Master of the Grand Council, Royal & Select Masters. (GLofOH.)

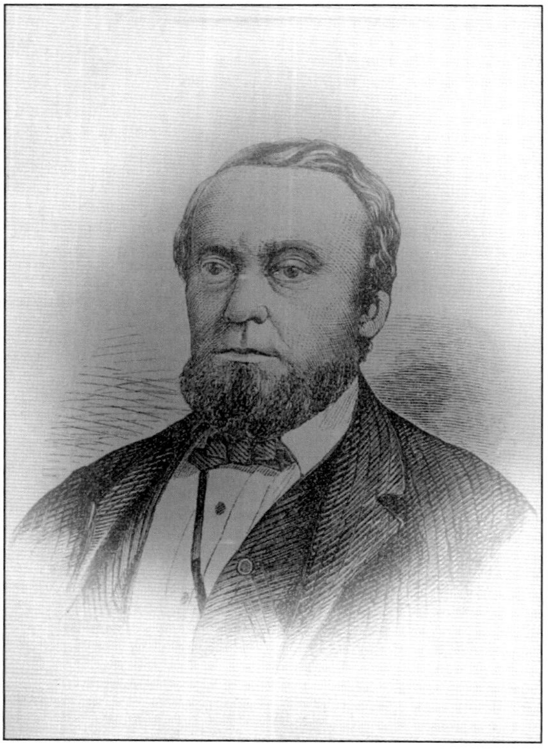

Howard Matthews; 1867, 1868 (Cincinnati No. 133). Matthews was elected Deputy Grand Master (second in command) in 1861, but he could not serve because of his duties as a paymaster for the Union army. He was again elected Deputy Grand Master in 1863 and served until October 1867, when he was elected to his first term as Grand Master. Matthews (1817–1870) was an insurance company president and Hamilton County auditor. (GLof OH.)

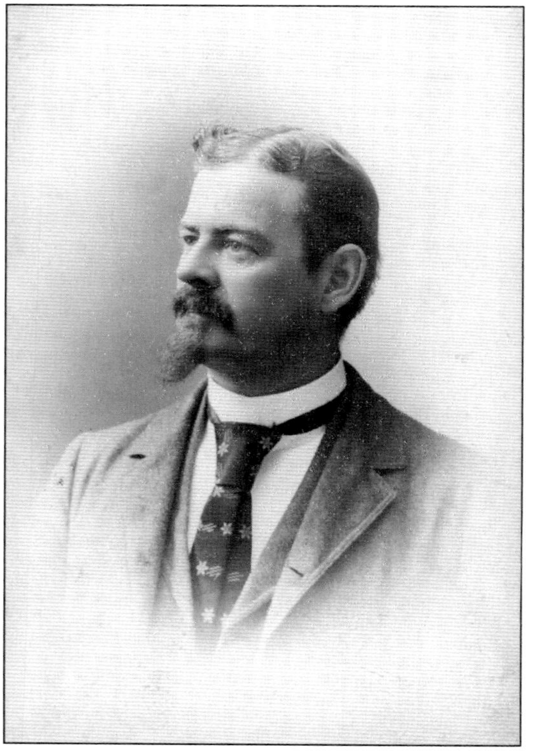

Jacob H. Bromwell, Grand Secretary (Wyoming [formerly Glendale] No. 186). While Grand Secretary from 1888 to 1924, Bromwell served in the US House of Representatives from 1894 to 1903. He was a judge of the county Court of Common Pleas from 1907 to 1913. Bromwell also served as the mayor of Wyoming, Ohio, for six years. Bromwell (1848–1924) was Grand High Priest of Ohio's Royal Arch Masons in 1895 and Grand Commander of its Grand Commandery, Knights Templar in 1919. (E.T. Carson Lodge No. 598.)

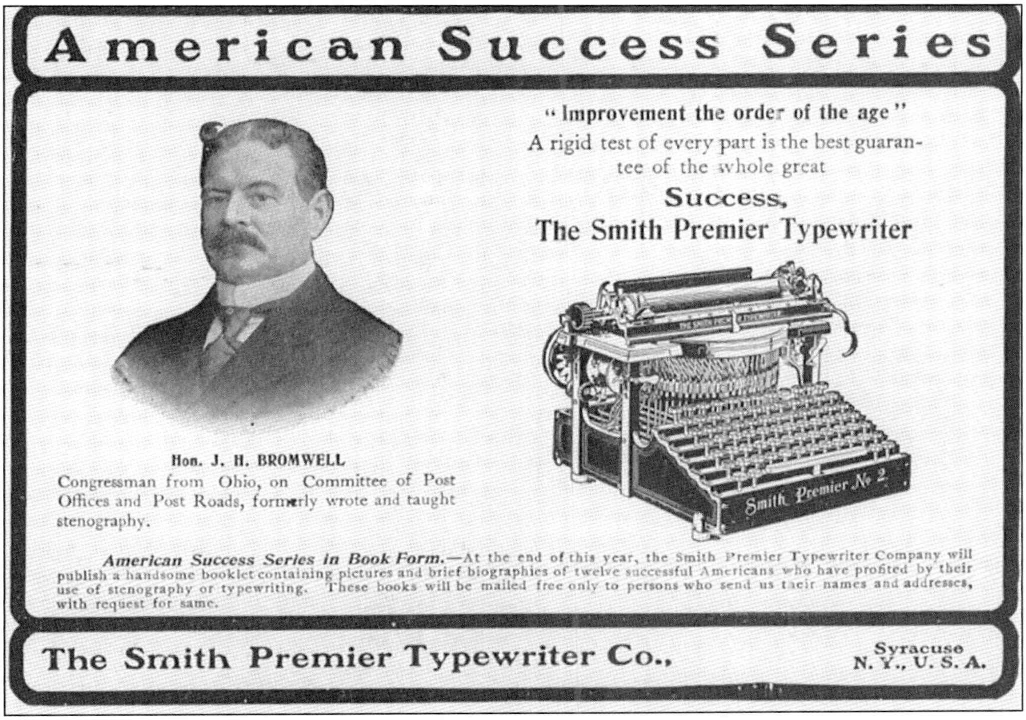

CONGRESSMAN BROMWELL ADVERTISING A TYPEWRITER. This advertisement from the August 1902 *School Board Journal* makes reference to Bromwell's earlier career as an educator. During the 35 years he served as Grand Secretary, Ohio's Masonic membership grew from 33,218 to over 180,000 members and from 408 to 601 lodges.

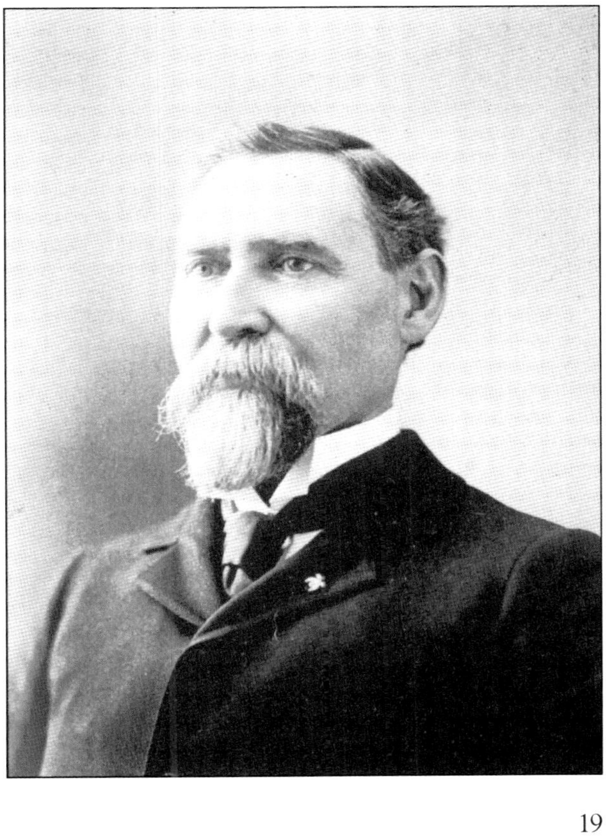

LEVI C. GOODALE; 1890, 1891 (MCMILLAN NO. 141). Goodale (1843–1929) participated in civic, business, and Masonic affairs, including as Cincinnati Chamber of Commerce president, state legislator, and president of the Bradstreet Mercantile Company (predecessor of Dunn and Bradstreet). He lost his bid for Cincinnati mayor in 1897. He also served as Ohio's Grand Master of Royal & Select Masters in 1882 and 1883 and Grand High Priest of the Grand Chapter in 1901. (AASR.)

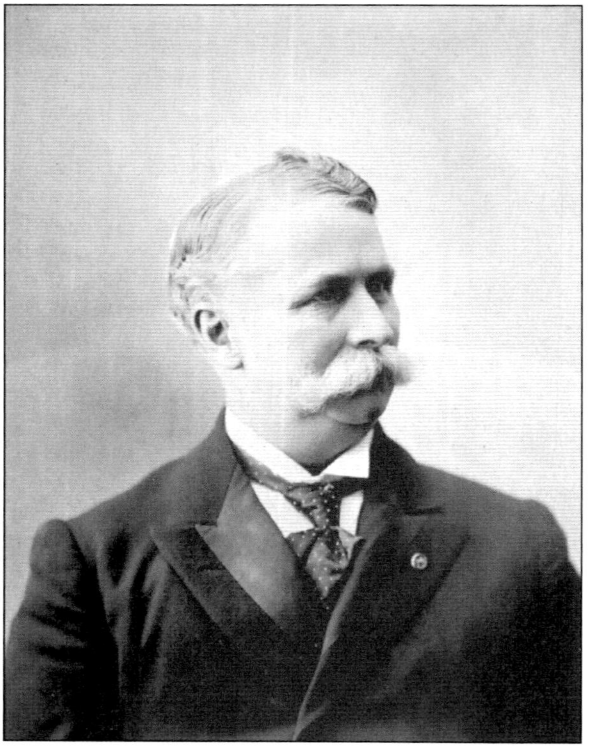

First Ohio Mason Made at Sight. William Howard Taft was not the first man to be "made a Mason at sight" in Ohio (see page 52). Asa Bushnell, later governor of Ohio, who generously provided much of the land for the Masonic Home at Springfield, was the recipient of this unprecedented honor from Grand Master Goodale on October 18, 1892. This image appeared in *Representative Men of Ohio, 1896-97.*

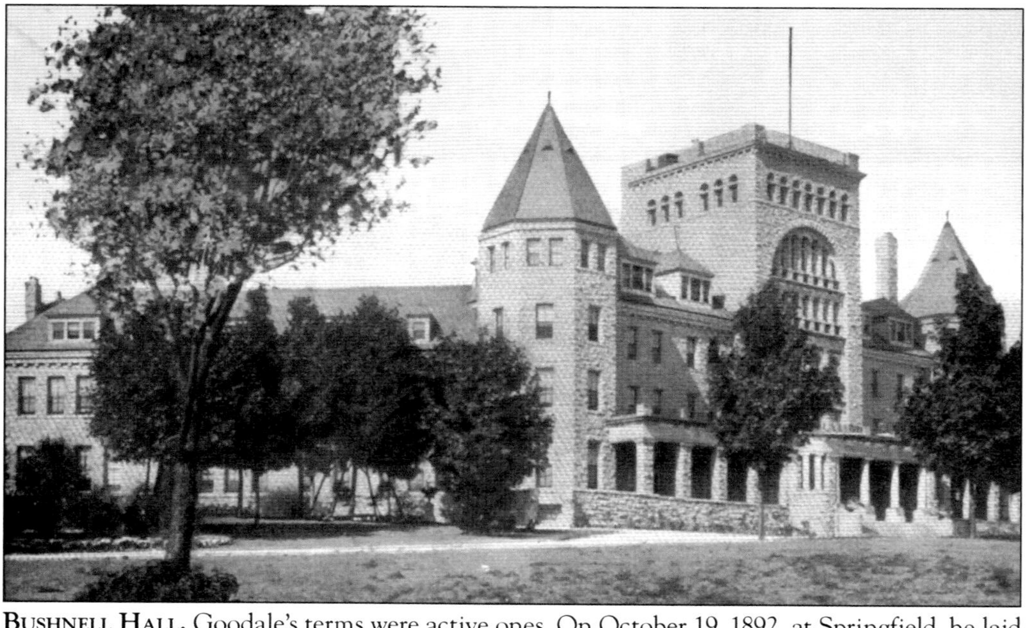

Bushnell Hall. Goodale's terms were active ones. On October 19, 1892, at Springfield, he laid the cornerstone of Bushnell Hall, the Ohio Masonic Home's first building. He was forced to deal with a "clandestine" Cernaeu Grand Lodge formed at Worthington. The first "true" written copy of the ritual was produced. And the District Lecturers (now Deputies) were for the first time directed to inspect lodges' presentation of the ritual as well as teach it. (GLofOH.)

William Bromwell Melish; 1895 (Lafayette No. 81). Melish was one of the most influential Masons in the history of the fraternity. Nationally, he led the Knights Templar and the Shrine. In Ohio, Melish (1852–1927) was Grand Master of the Grand Lodge. At 33, he was the youngest man to be made a 33rd Degree in the Scottish Rite's Northern Jurisdiction. He was also Commander in Chief of Ohio Consistory, Valley of Cincinnati, AASR. (Imperial Shrine.)

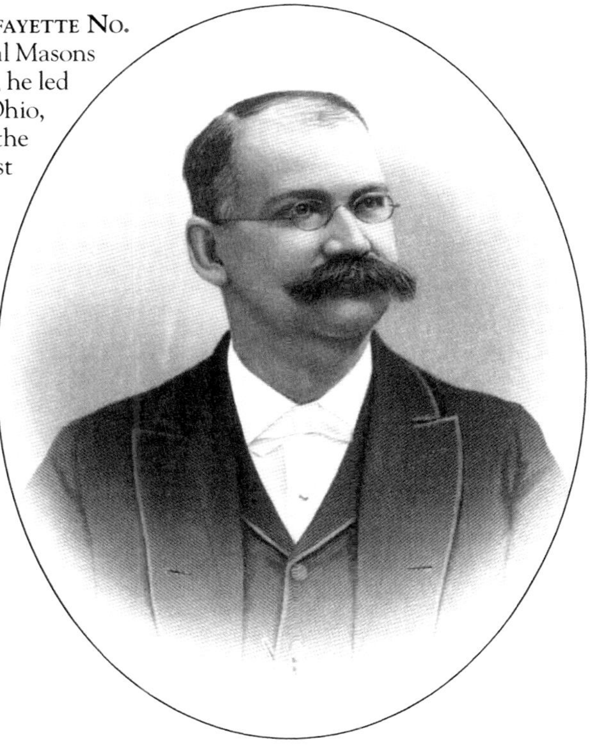

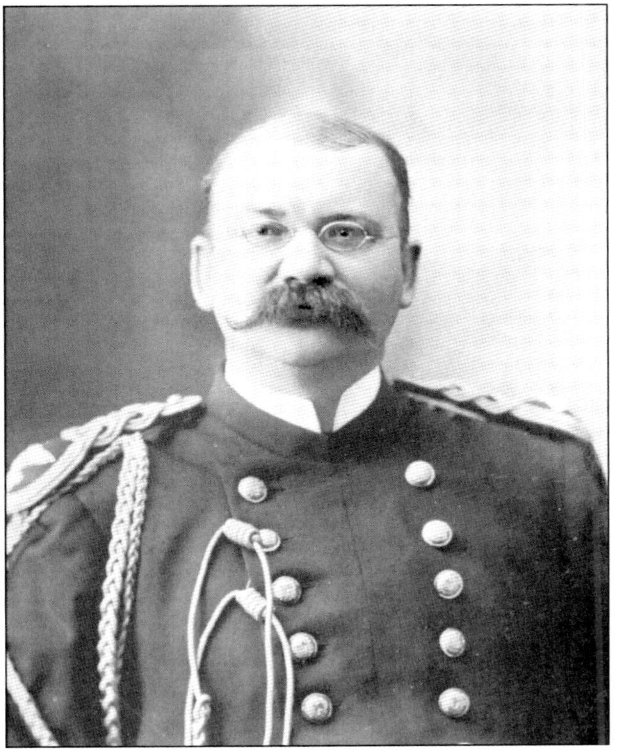

Melish's Activities Outside of Masonry. President of Bromwell Brush and Wire Goods, Melish also served as Cincinnati Chamber of Commerce president. He was appointed to the Cincinnati Water Works Commission and was a trustee of the public library. Outside of Masonic circles, he was referred to as "colonel," from his service as aide-de-camp to Governor Bushnell in the Ohio State Militia, as pictured here. This image appeared in *Representative Men of Ohio, 1896-97.*

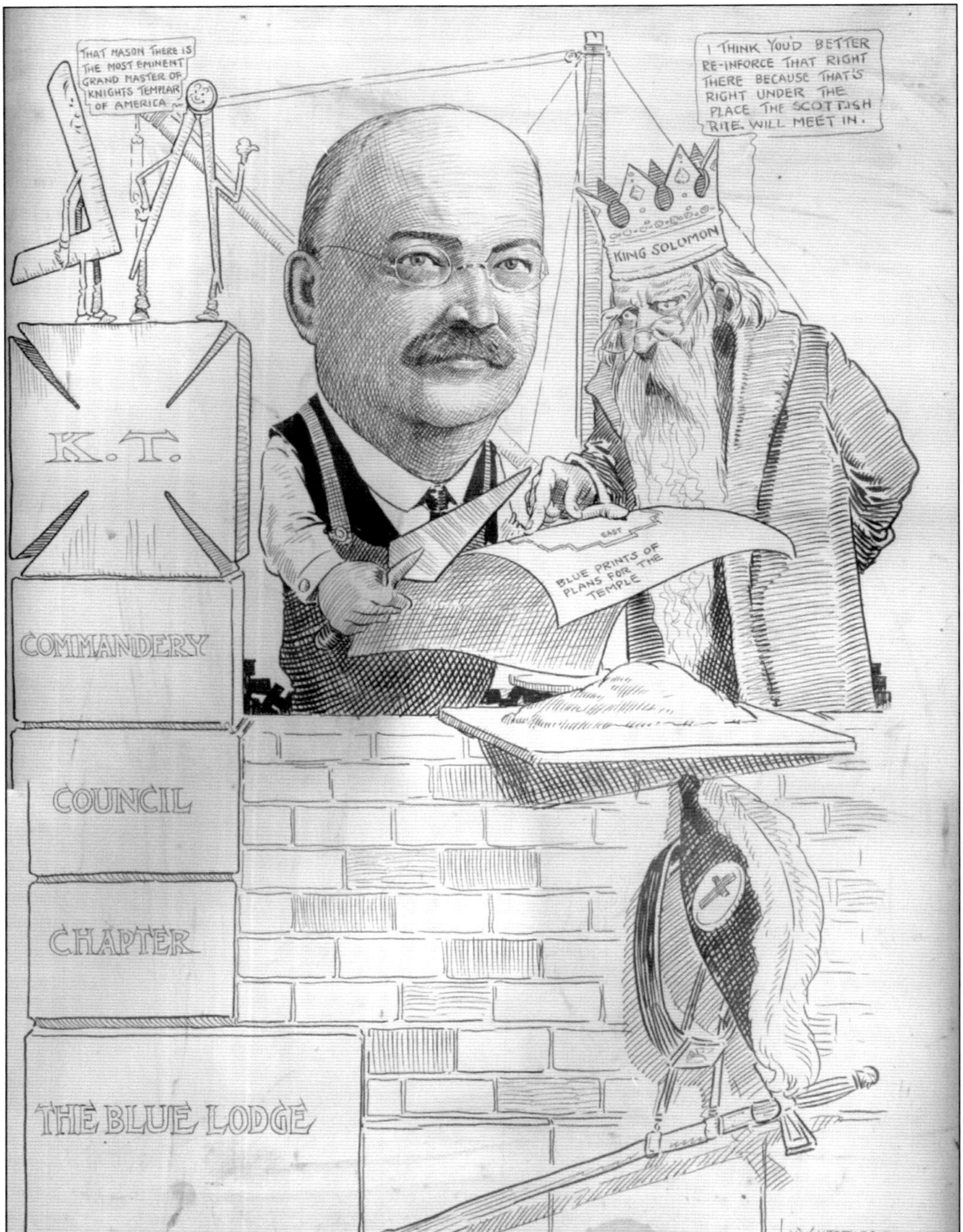

Melish Caricature by Editorial Cartoonist J.S. Whiteford. During World War I, as executive manager of the Masonic War Relief Association, Melish oversaw thousands of dollars sent to care for European Masonic orphans and widows. In 1919, he traveled in Europe to determine Masonic need. He is the only American awarded the Grand Templar Cross, English Templary's highest honor. His death in 1927 was front-page news. (Trinity Commandery No. 44.)

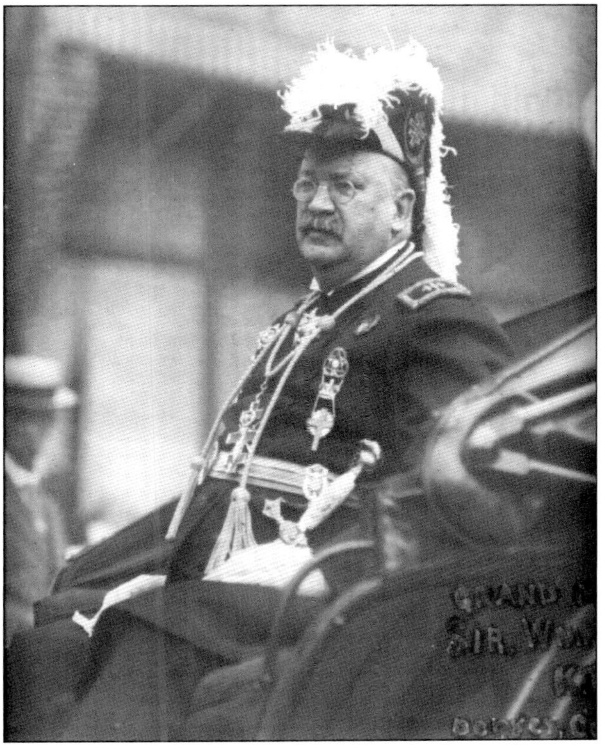

GRAND MASTER, GRAND ENCAMPMENT, KNIGHTS TEMPLAR OF THE UNITED STATES. William Melish reviews the Sir Knights at Denver in 1913. He was elected to a three-year term as Grand Master in Chicago in 1910. He was founding Commander of Trinity Commandery No. 44 in 1887 and Grand Commander of Ohio in 1890. (Trinity Commandery No. 44.)

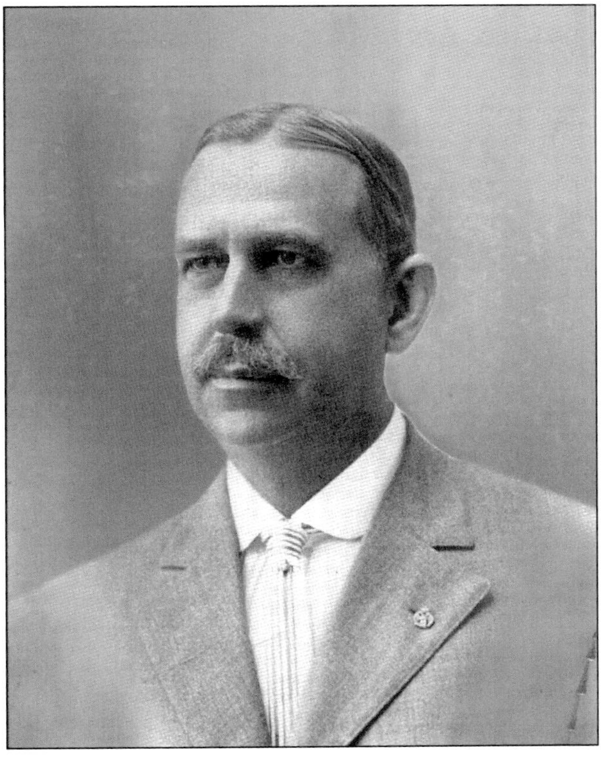

JOEL C. CLORE; 1916 (LAFAYETTE LODGE NO. 81). Cincinnati postmaster, president of two banks, attorney, and loyal Democrat were titles that Clore earned outside the fraternity. In it, Clore (1859–1926) was an officer in numerous York Rite bodies; Commander in Chief of Ohio Consistory, Valley of Cincinnati, AASR, from 1910 to 1916; and Syrian Shrine's Potentate. Freemasonry does not exist in a vacuum, and Clore's term was influenced by world events. (GLofOH.)

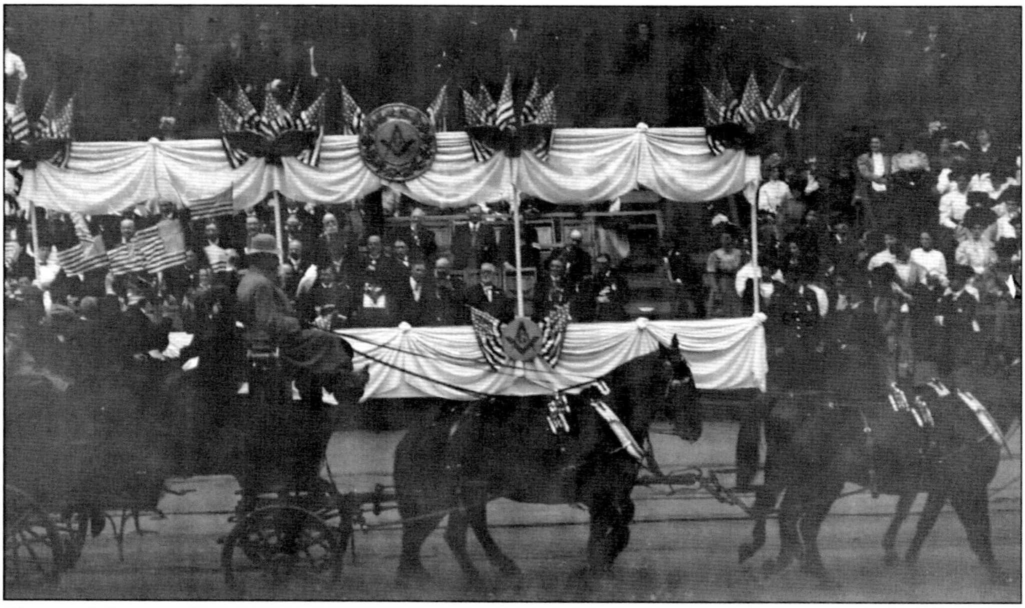

Grand Master Clore Salutes Passing Masons, June 23, 1917. On April 6, 1917, the United States entered World War I, declaring war on Germany. A massive downtown parade to celebrate the bicentennial of the premiere Grand Lodge (in London) became a great patriotic affair. Over 6,000 Masons from throughout Hamilton County and nearby Kentucky participated. Parade participants collected $2,000 to support war efforts by the Red Cross. (GLofOH.)

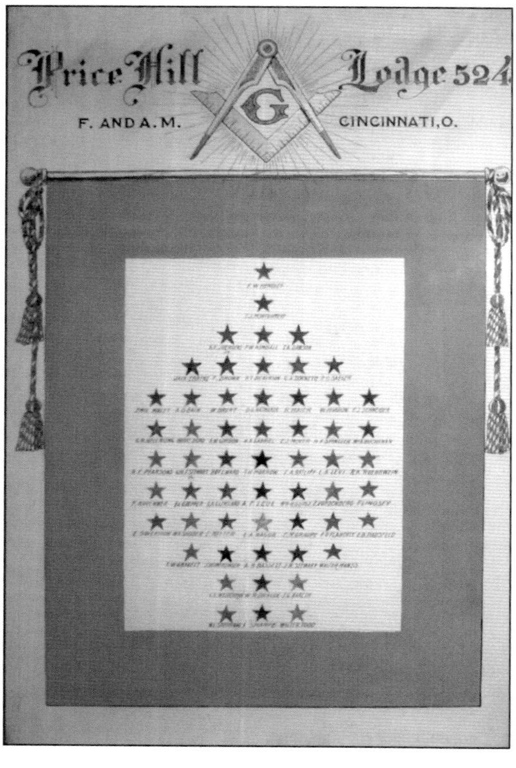

Blue Star Posters and Banners. Each star represented a member in the armed services. Ohio Freemasonry endeavored to support the war effort. The Grand Lodge offered assistance to Scioto Lodge No. 6, Chillicothe, to assist Masons stationed at Camp Sherman. Chartering military unit lodges, as was done during the Civil War, was considered, but it did not happen. The Grand Lodge invested heavily in Liberty Bonds. (North Bend Lodge No. 346.)

Harry S. Johnson; 1922 (Hoffner No. 253). Johnson (1868–1959) presided over a growing institution, with membership nearing 180,000. But growth did not come without pains. He had to deal with some social organizations composed exclusively of Masons, forcibly reprimanding them when conduct influenced by the Roaring Twenties ran counter to the rules of the Grand Lodge. (GLofOH.)

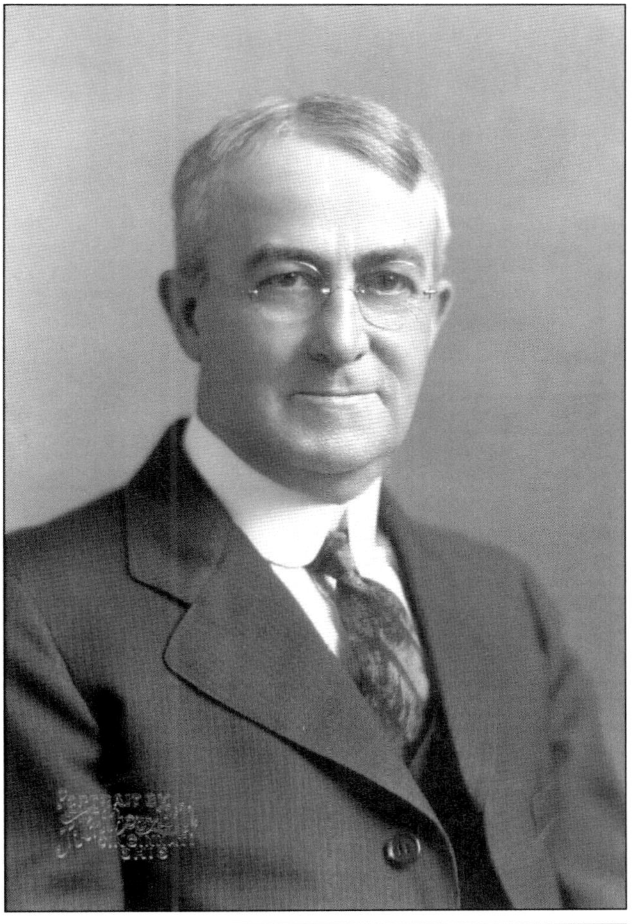

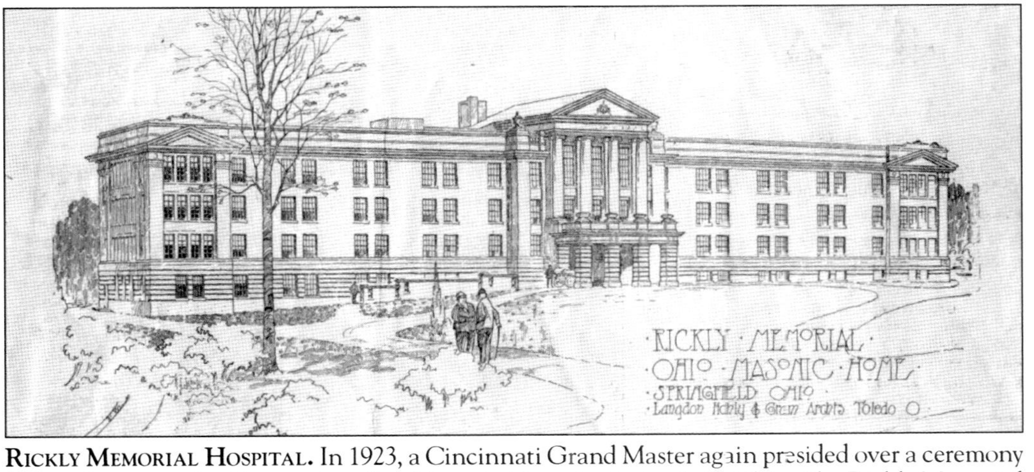

Rickly Memorial Hospital. In 1923, a Cincinnati Grand Master again presided over a ceremony for another major building at the Ohio Masonic Home in Springfield, Ohio. The Rickly Memorial Hospital was dedicated by Grand Master Johnson during the Grand Lodge session of 1923. The addition of the hospital allowed medical care to be provided at a greater level than before. (GLofOH.)

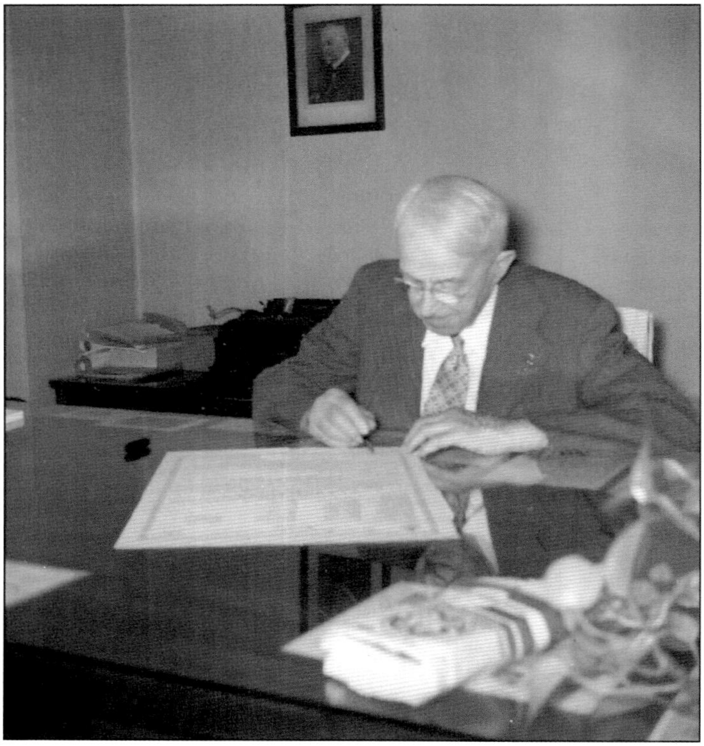

HARRY JOHNSON, GRAND LODGE FIXTURE. Johnson, after serving as Grand Master, was elected Grand Secretary in 1924. He served in that office until his death in 1959. His death ended the century-plus reign of Cincinnati Grand Secretaries and led to the removal of the Grand Lodge office from Cincinnati. Johnson's previous career was as superintendent of the Central Union Depot & Railway Company, predecessor of the Union Terminal Company. (GLofOH.)

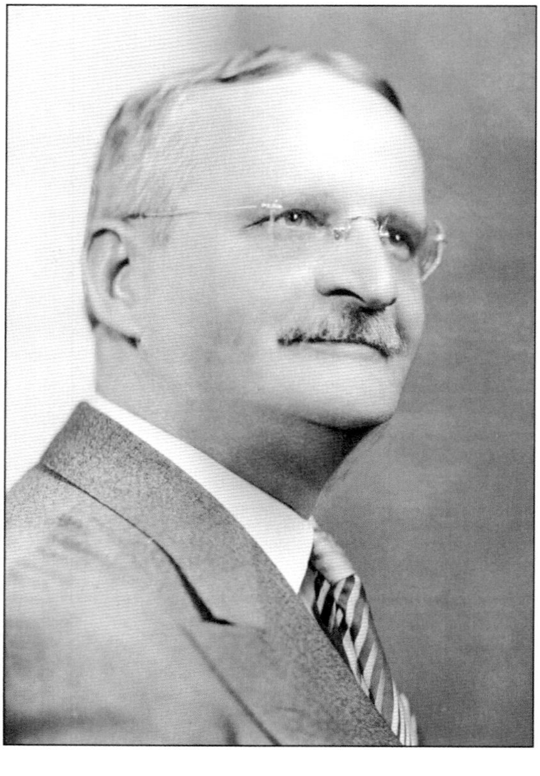

LOUIS B. BLAKEMORE; 1937 (CALVARY-CLIFTON NO. 700). The Great Depression hit Ohio Freemasonry hard, and Blakemore (1879–1971) presided during some of this era. Membership had slipped almost 15 percent since 1928. The 1938 *Proceedings* voiced concern for the suppression of Masonry in Germany and Italy. A highlight of the year was the 175th anniversary of the founding of Marietta, Ohio, home of Ohio's oldest lodge. Freemasonry was well represented at the anniversary celebration. Ohio Consistory, AASR, Valley of Cincinnati performed a play, *John Brent*, about Masonry's influence on the American Revolution. (GLofOH.)

WILLIAM W. CARLTON; 1946 (EVANSTON NO. 695). Carlton (1898–1964) was called to active duty in 1940 while serving in the Grand officer line. While away on active duty, Colonel Carlton was elected in absentia as Junior and then Senior Grand Warden and then three consecutive years as Deputy Grand Master. After his year as Grand Master, he again answered the call of duty in the Korean conflict. He is buried in Arlington National Cemetery. (GLofOH.)

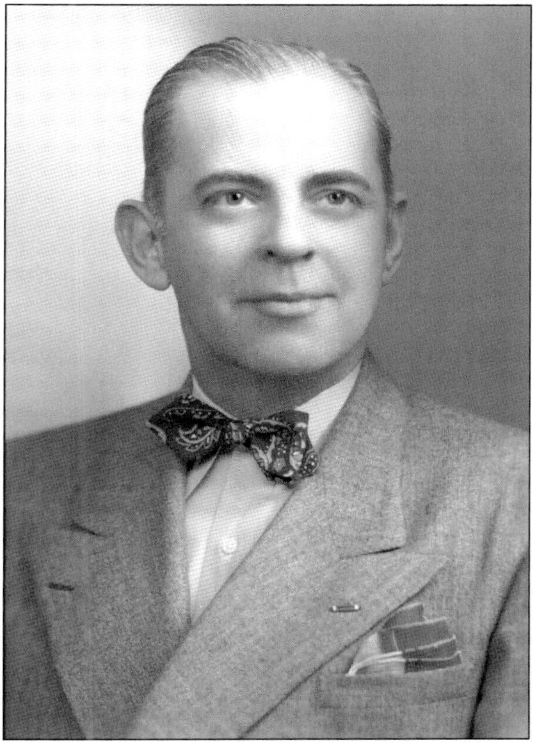

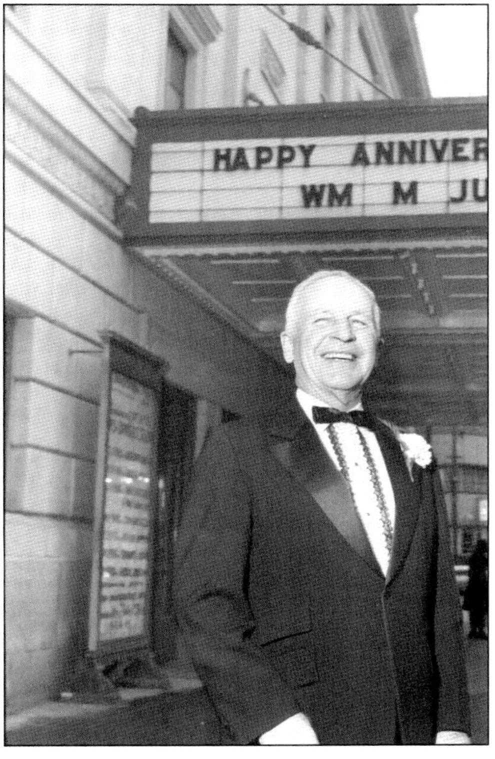

WILLIAM M. JUDD; 1951 (YEATMAN NO. 162). Judd (1896–1980) emphasized the importance of the fraternity's ritual: "the proper rendition of the Ritual, giving lectures and charges and explaining the symbolic meaning of our emblems . . . is the very essence of Freemasonry and the cement which binds us together. . . . If we ignore and disregard this important part of our work, then we might disintegrate and fall apart and become merely a social or luncheon club." (GLofOH.)

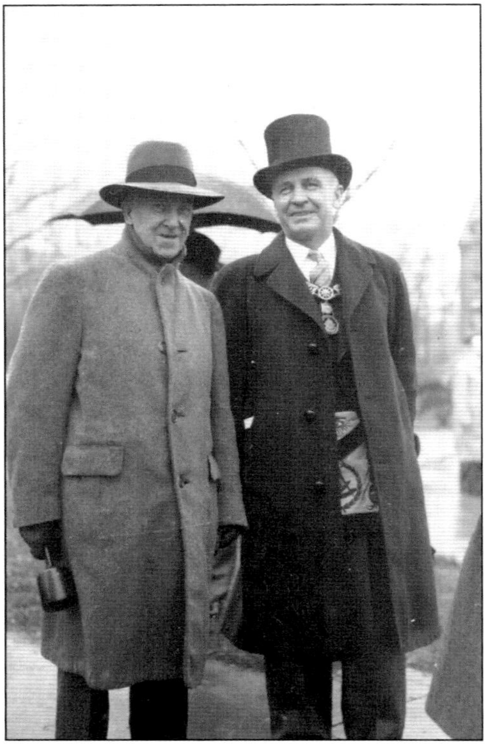

Grand Master Judd and Grand Secretary Johnson. Judd (right) recommended creating a permanent Grand Lodge office closer to the center of the state than Cincinnati. He suggested that such an action could begin after Harry S. Johnson's retirement. Judd proposed either Worthington, adjacent to New England Lodge No. 4's temple, or the Ohio Masonic Home in Springfield. Worthington was selected and served until 2012, when the office moved to Springfield. (GLofOH.)

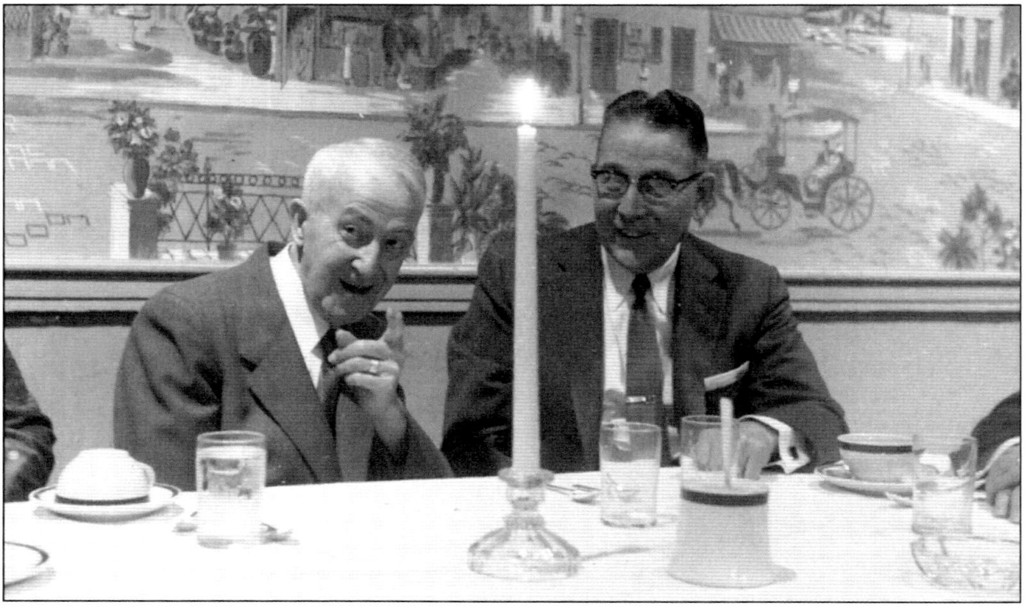

Chester Hodges; 1958 (Linwood No. 569) and Grand Secretary Harry Johnson, c. 1958. Hodges (right), known as "Dad" by everyone associated with Masonic youth groups in Ohio from the 1950s until his passing, was an ardent supporter of the Order of DeMolay. Hodges (1907–1995) served as Executive Officer for Ohio, the chief adult advisor for the young men's organization, from 1960 to 1986. He was the first Ohioan to serve as the Grand Master of DeMolay. (GLofOH.)

GEORGE DESILVER; 1965 (MCMILLAN NO. 141). For more than 30 years, DeSilver (1903–1988) served on the board of the Cincinnati Masonic Temple Company. His pride in the downtown temple most likely led to his requiring as Grand Master that a survey of the condition of all Masonic buildings in Ohio be performed. His work life began at Pickering Hardware at age 12 and continued there for 53 years. He ultimately became the company's president. (GLofOH.)

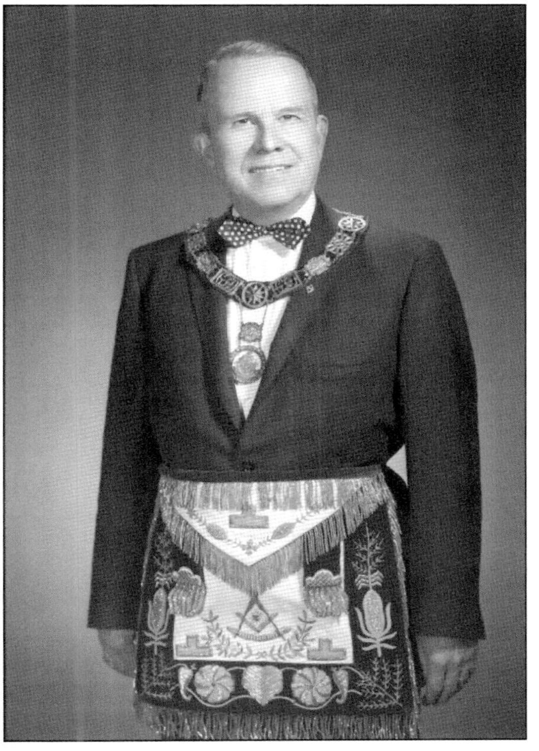

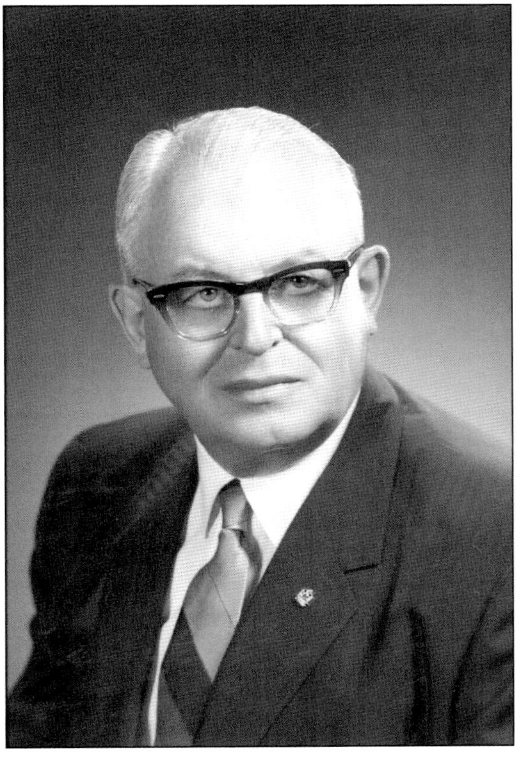

DR. DALE FOX; 1972 (LAFAYETTE LODGE NO. 81). An orthopedic surgeon for 43 years, Fox (1909–1995) was a pioneer in sports medicine. He consulted to professional sports teams, including the Cincinnati Bengals and Reds. With the US bicentennial gearing up during his term, he instituted Patriotism Week for all Ohio lodges in June 1973. (GLofOH.)

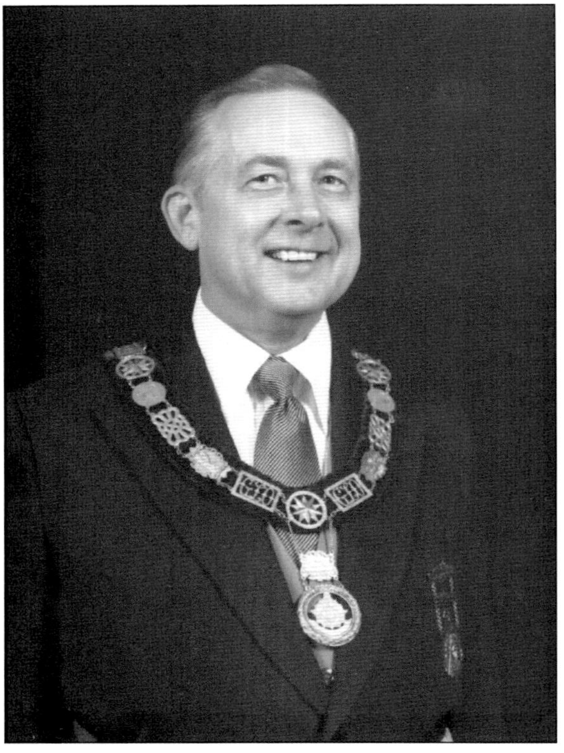

Charles A. Brigham Jr.; 1979 (Madisonville No. 419). Known in national Masonic circles as well as in Ohio, Brigham served on the board of the George Washington Masonic National Memorial from 1981 to 1994, including four years as its president. An Army Air Corps veteran, Brigham (1924–2003) was one of the many men who returned from World War II and gravitated to the fraternity. (GLofOH.)

Dr. Hilmer W. Neumann, MD; 1985 (Cheviot Lodge No. 140). A physician and authority on chemical dependency, Neumann (1925–2000) was active in and out of the fraternity. He was a Naval veteran of the Korean War, had a private medical practice, served as assistant deputy coroner, and was medical director of Marjorie P. Lee Home for the Aged. He was the first Senior DeMolay to serve Ohio as Grand Master. (GLofOH.)

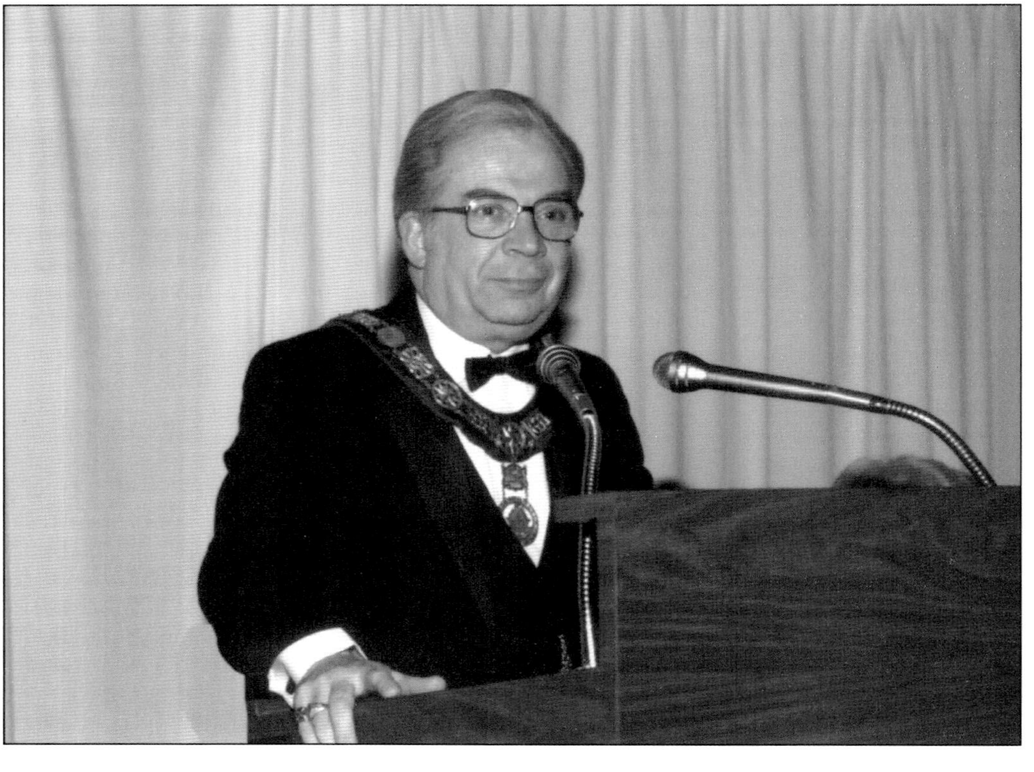

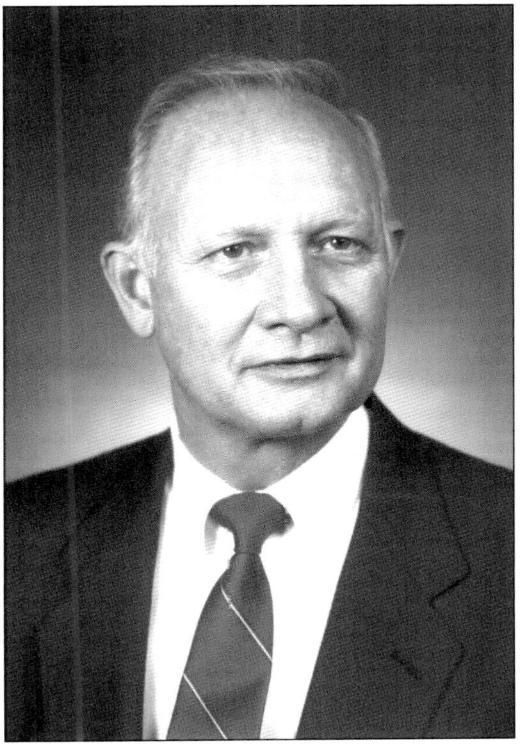

H. Ray Evans; 1992 (Queen City Lodge No. 559). After four years in the Air Force, Evans (1932–2013) served over 27 years as a Cincinnati policeman. He was the Executive Secretary, Valley of Cincinnati, AASR. As Grand Master, Evans represented Ohio Masonry at the dedication of the Gettysburg "Brother to Brother" Masonic monument and at the bicentennial of the laying of the cornerstone of the US Capitol. (GLofOH.)

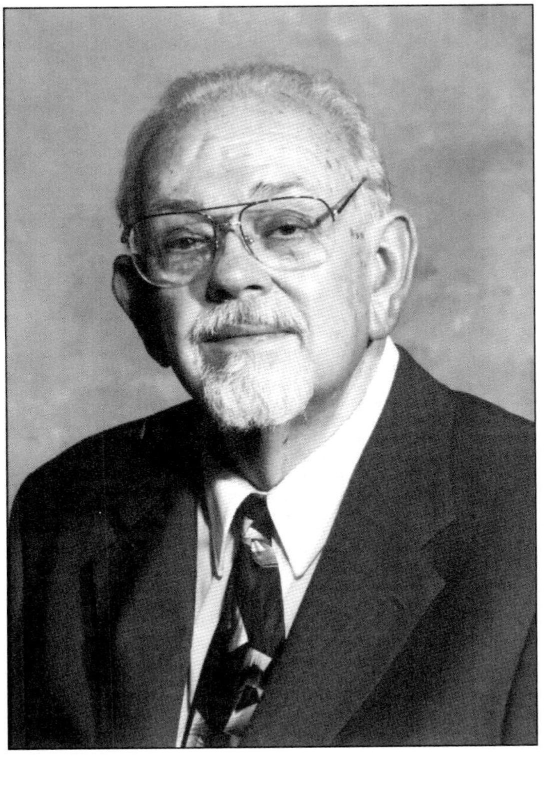

Ronald R. Rogers; 1999 (Montgomery Lodge, No. 94). Starting with the Order of DeMolay as a teenager, Rogers (1935–2000) was devoted to Freemasonry. Serving in numerous leadership roles in many bodies of the fraternity, he ultimately was elected Grand Master in October 1999. Tragically, he passed away with less than two months of his term remaining. He was only the second Grand Master of Ohio to die while in office. (GLofOH.)

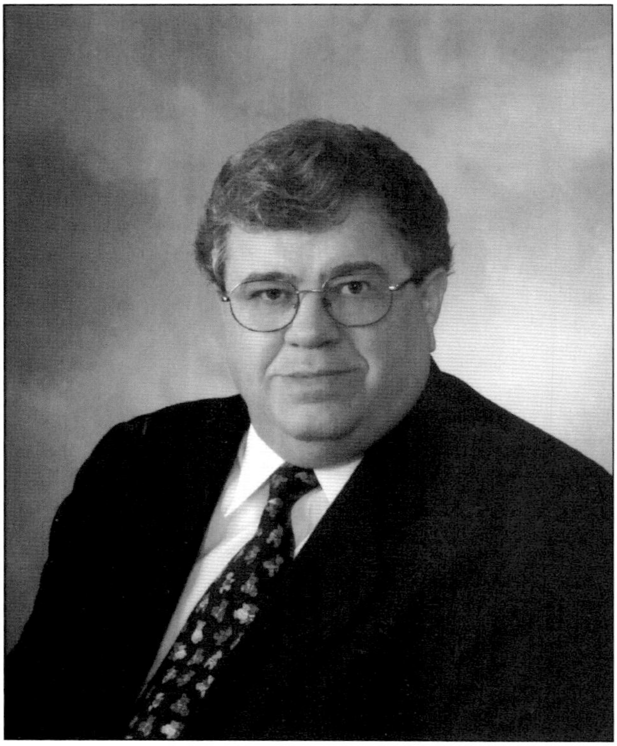

MICHAEL A. HIMES; 2006 (NORTH BEND 346). Himes (b. 1953) has served Cincinnati Masonry in almost every organization. With his election to the Grand East, he capped off years of fraternal devotion beginning in his teen years in DeMolay. During his term, Ohio Masons donated over $200,000 in support of the Special Olympics. Himes continues to be a presence in the fraternity in southwest Ohio, presently serving the Valley of Cincinnati, AASR, as Fraternal Secretary. (GLofOH.)

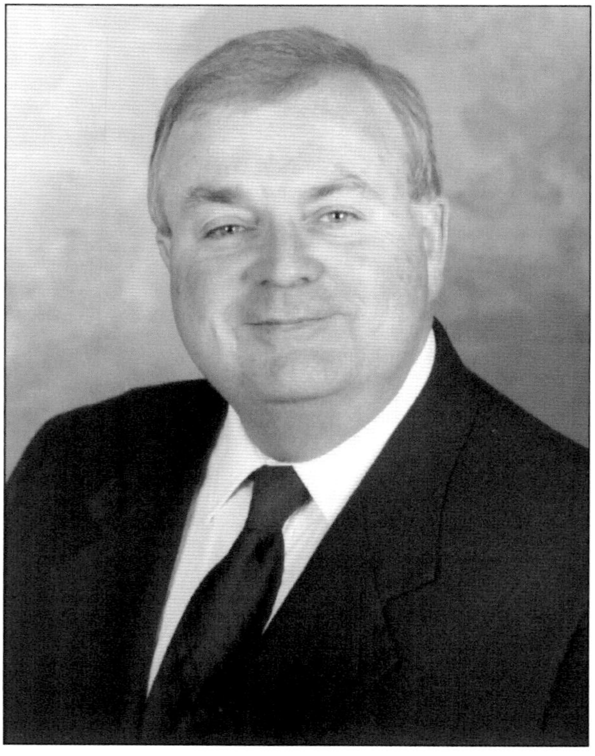

NORMAN J. MICK; 2013 (HOFFNER NO. 253 AND CINCINNATI-LAFAYETTE NO. 483). Elected Grand Master in October 2013, Most Worshipful Brother Mick (b. 1945) is serving in that capacity at the time of this writing. A very active member of the fraternity, he has been honored with the Knight York Cross of Honor and the 33rd Degree of the Scottish Rite. His year's theme has been "Freemasonry–A Timeless Treasure." (AASR.)

Three

Freemasonry in the Heart of Cincinnati

On December 28, 1788, a group of settlers landed on the north bank of the Ohio River between the Little and Great Miami Rivers. Original settlers to the new community received a half-acre lot in town and a four-acre outer lot. William McMillan received in-town lot 135, the northeast corner of Third and Walnut Streets. This would have a major effect on his Masonic lodge.

In less than three years, a number of Masons who had come to the outpost wanted to form a Masonic lodge. Many of the early settlers were from New Jersey, including John Cleves Symmes, the head of the land company promoting settlement in the area. New Jersey therefore seemed the logical place from which to request a charter. Dr. William Burnet, one of Cincinnati's first physicians, returned home and received a charter from the Grand Lodge of New Jersey on September 8, 1791. His father passed away during his stay and, due to family responsibilities, he realized he would not be able to return to Cincinnati.

Burnet most likely made arrangements for delivery of the charter at the October 23, 1794, meeting of St. John's Lodge No. 1 in Newark, New Jersey. Symmes, a member of Trenton Lodge No. 5, was at that meeting and was about to return to the Northwest Territory. He delivered the charter when he arrived at Cincinnati in late 1794.

Nova Caesarea Lodge No. 10 was unable to participate in any activities of the Grand Lodge of New Jersey. Surrendering its charter, it joined the Grand Lodge of Kentucky as Cincinnati Lodge No. 13 in 1805. This created a rift in its membership, which was not healed until the lodge joined with five other Ohio lodges and formed the Grand Lodge of Ohio in 1808. "Harmony" was added to the name Nova Caesarea to celebrate the old lodge making peace with itself.

This would be the only Masonic lodge in the area for a number of years. It built and operated three Masonic temples downtown. As the population grew, additional lodges were formed, many of which became tenants in these Masonic buildings.

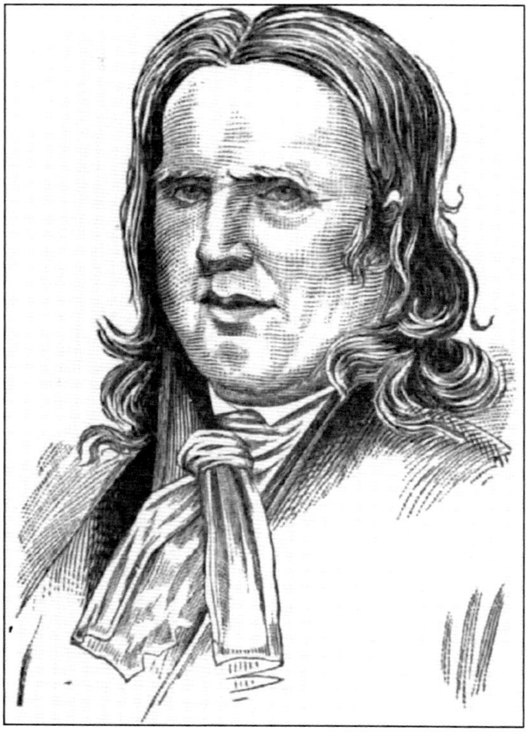

JOHN CLEVES SYMMES, FOUNDER OF THE MIAMI OR SYMMES PURCHASE. Symmes delivered Nova Caesarea Lodge's charter and moved on to North Bend, Ohio, which he hoped would become the region's main city. It did not. Symmes (1742–1814) occasionally attended meetings of the lodge, but never sought membership. His nephew, Daniel Symmes, was Master of the lodge while also serving as President of the Cincinnati Council. This image is from *Historical Collections of Ohio.*

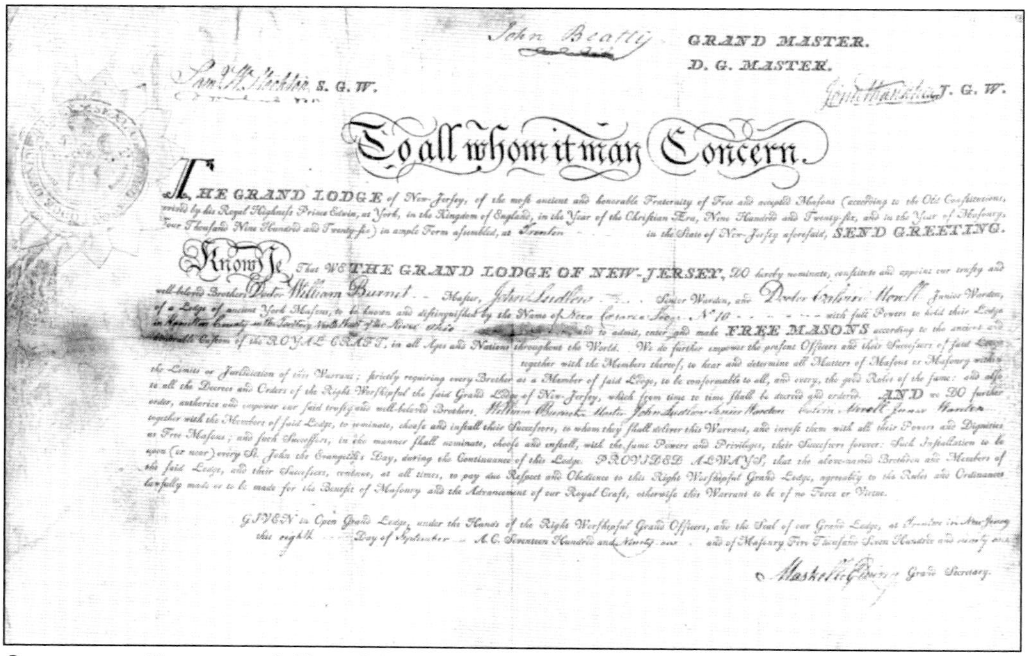

John Beatty GRAND MASTER.

D. G. MASTER.

[illegible] S. G. W. [illegible] J. G. W.

To all whom it may Concern.

THE GRAND LODGE of New-Jersey, of the most ancient and honorable Fraternity of Free and accepted Masons (according to the Old Constitutions, revised by his Royal Highness Prince Edwin, at York, in the Kingdom of England, in the Year of the Christian Æra, Nine Hundred and Twenty-six, and in the Year of Masonry, Four Thousand Nine Hundred and Twenty-six) in ample Form assembled, at Trenton in the State of New-Jersey aforesaid, SEND GREETING.

Know Ye That We THE GRAND LODGE OF NEW-JERSEY, DO hereby nominate, constitute and appoint our trusty and well-beloved Brothers Doctor William Burnet Master, John Ludlow Senior Warden, and Doctor Calvin Morell Junior Warden, of a Lodge of ancient York Masons, to be known and distinguished by the Name of Nova Caesarea Lodge No 10 with full Powers to hold their Lodge in [illegible] and to admit, enter and make FREE MASONS according to the ancient and honorable Custom of the ROYAL CRAFT, in all Ages and Nations throughout the World. We do further empower the present Officers and their Successors of said Lodge together with the Members thereof, to hear and determine all Matters of Masons or Masonry within the Limits or Jurisdiction of this Warrant; strictly requiring every Brother as a Member of said Lodge, to be conformable to all, and every, the good Rules of the same: and also to all the Decrees and Orders of the Right Worshipful the said Grand Lodge of New-Jersey, which from time to time shall be decreed and ordered. AND we DO further order, authorize and empower our said trusty and well-beloved Brothers, William Burnet Master John Ludlow Senior Warden Calvin Morell Junior Warden together with the Members of said Lodge, to nominate, choose and install their Successors, to whom they shall deliver this Warrant, and invest them with all their Powers and Dignities as Free Masons; and such Successors, in the manner shall nominate, choose and install, with the same Powers and Privileges, their Successors forever: Such Installation to be upon (or near) every St. John the Evangelist's Day, during the Continuance of this Lodge. PROVIDED ALWAYS, that the above-named Brethren and Members of the said Lodge, and their Successors, continue, at all times, to pay due Respect and Obedience to this Right Worshipful Grand Lodge, agreeably to the Rules and Ordinances lawfully made or to be made for the Benefit of Masonry and the Advancement of our Royal Craft, otherwise this Warrant to be of no Force or Virtue.

GIVEN in Open Grand Lodge, under the Hands of the Right Worshipful Grand Officers, and the Seal of our Grand Lodge, at Trenton in New Jersey this eighth Day of September A.C. Seventeen Hundred and Ninety one and of Masonry Five Thousand Seven Hundred and ninety one.

[illegible] Grand Secretary.

CHARTER OF CINCINNATI'S FIRST MASONIC LODGE. Nova Caesarea Lodge No. 10 was chartered on September 8, 1791, at a special session of the Grand Lodge of New Jersey. Nova Caesarea is the Latin name for New Jersey. The charter did not arrive in Cincinnati until 1794. Seven members met on December 27, 1794, St. John's Day, to organize the lodge. (NCH2.)

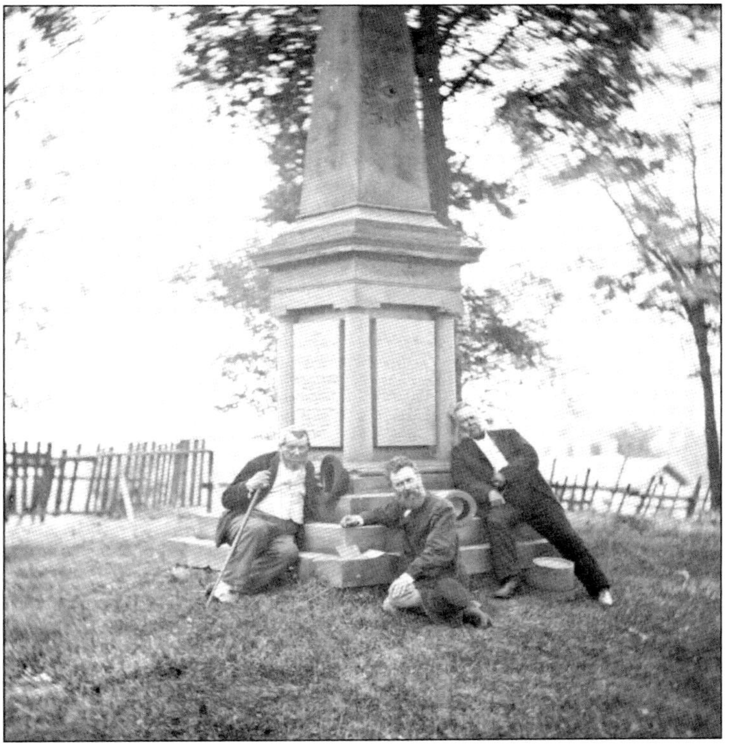

GRAVE OF WILLIAM MCMILLAN. McMillan died in 1804, bequeathing his in-town lot to Nova Caesarea Lodge No. 10 for the purpose of building a Masonic temple. Taxes and issues with purported heirs placed ownership in jeopardy, but they were overcome. In 1838, as a memorial to the generosity of Brother McMillan, the lodge erected this monument over his remains in Avondale. Here, from left to right, John Evans, John D. Caldwell, and J.B. Covert visit McMillan's grave in November 1868. (NCH2.)

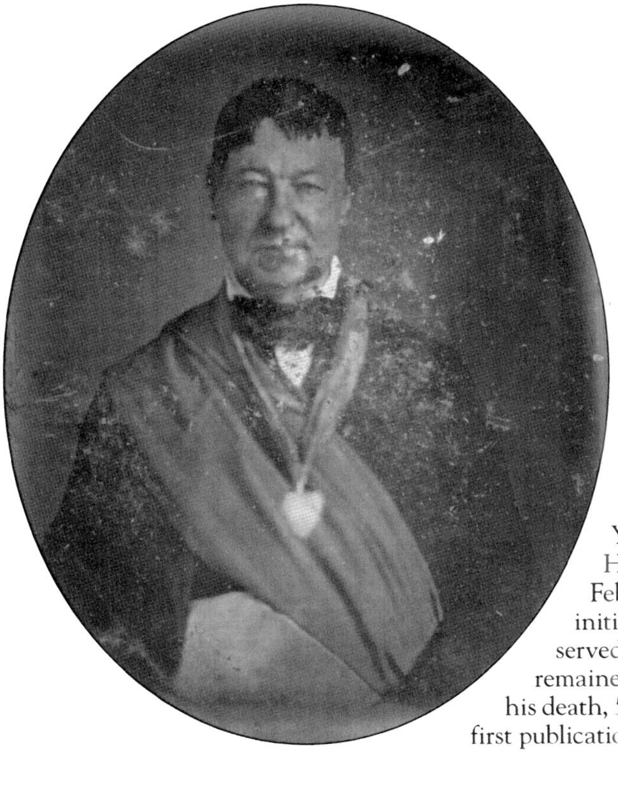

GRIFFIN YEATMAN, FIRST MAN INITIATED A FREEMASON IN CINCINNATI. Yeatman came to Cincinnati in 1793. He petitioned Nova Caesarea Lodge in February 1795 and, being approved, was initiated on March 4. Yeatman (1769–1849) served for many years as lodge treasurer and remained an active member of the lodge until his death, 54 years after his initiation. This is the first publication of this image. (NCH2.)

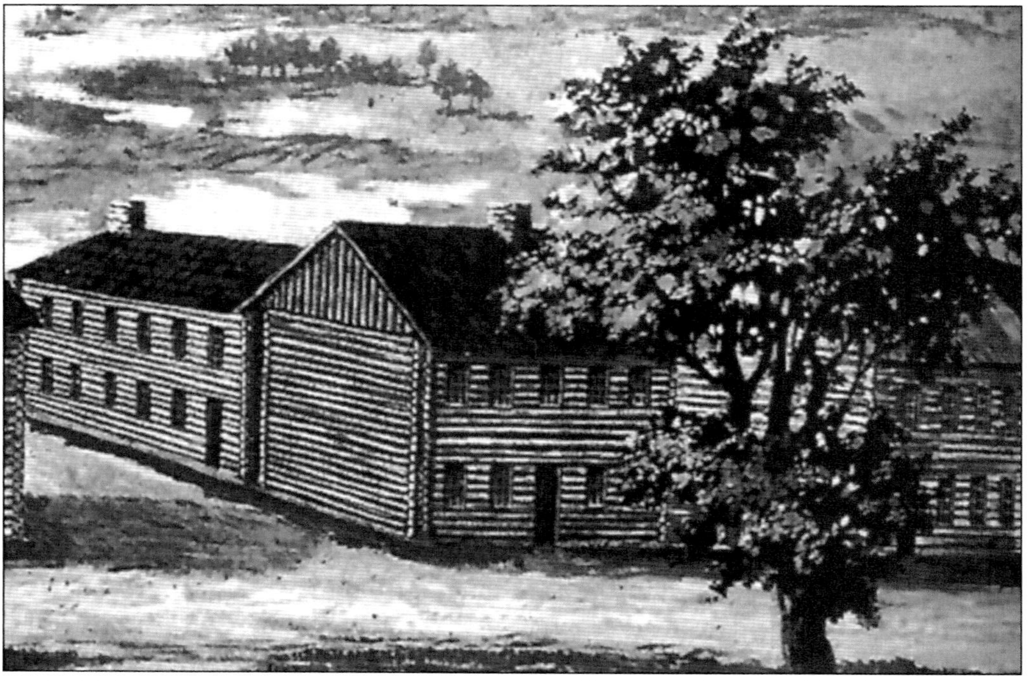

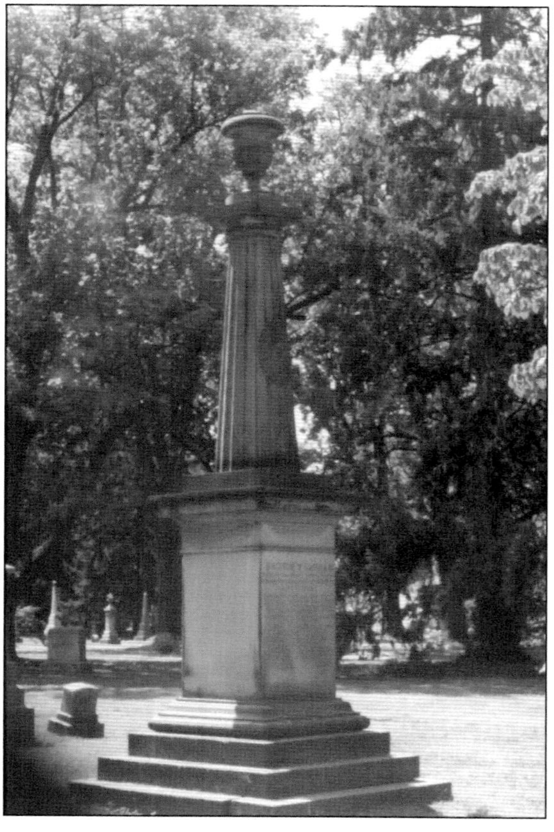

YEATMAN'S TAVERN, THE SQUARE AND COMPASSES. The name of the tavern, located on the riverfront at Front and Sycamore Streets, was an allusion to its owner's Masonic affiliation. An inn situated along Sycamore Street was added later. The tavern was a hub for the community, serving at various times as the first post office, a hospital, and site of the first territorial legislature, first territorial supreme court, and town council chamber. Many Masonic banquets were held here. (UC.)

YEATMAN GRAVE, SPRING GROVE CEMETERY. Yeatman was originally interred at the Episcopal Burial Grounds, now part of Washington Park in front of Music Hall. His remains were later moved to Spring Grove. The monument incorporates the "all-seeing eye," a Masonic and cultural allusion to God observing all of man's actions. (NCH2.)

JACOB BURNET, MASON. Burnet (1770–1853) was the brother of Nova Caesarea Lodge's charter Master, Dr. William Burnet. Jacob Burnet became a Mason in St. John's Lodge No. 2 in New Jersey in 1791. He came to Cincinnati in 1796, affiliating with Nova Caesarea No. 10, serving as Master from 1799 to 1801. He was elected Deputy Grand Master of the Grand Lodge three times (1810–1812). After the second temple was built, he maintained a law office in the decommissioned first temple building. (CHS.)

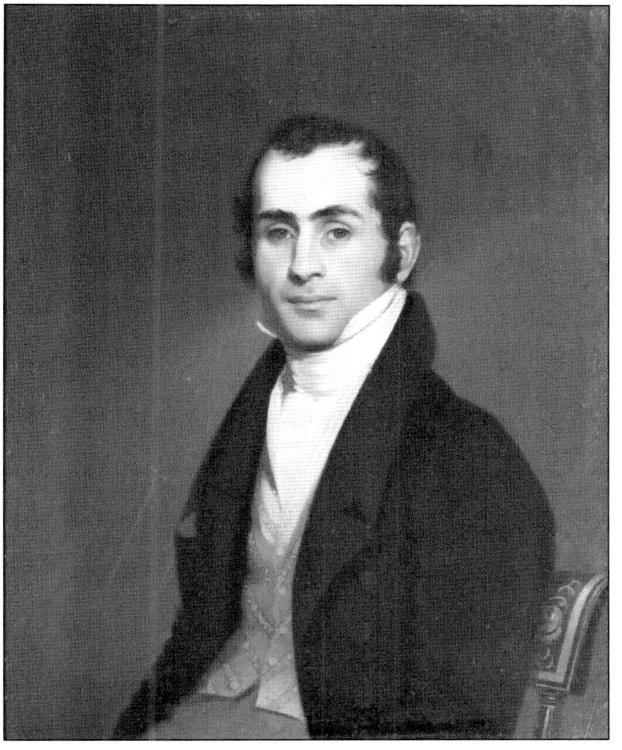

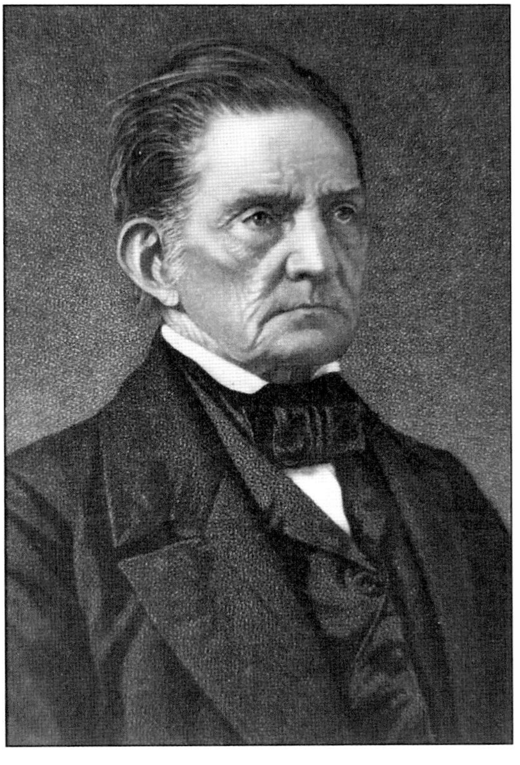

JACOB BURNET, CITIZEN. Burnet was selected to serve on the Territorial Council by Pres. John Adams. He represented Cincinnati in the Ohio House of Representatives in 1814. He served seven years on the Ohio Supreme Court starting in 1821 and was a US senator from 1828 to 1831. Returning to Cincinnati, Burnet founded an insurance company and, in 1847, published *Notes on the Northwest Territory*. (ohiohistorycentral.org.)

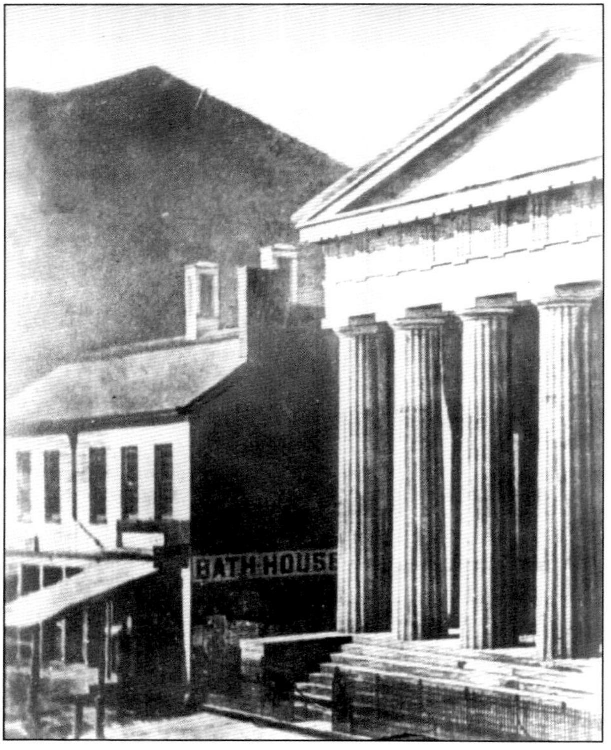

CINCINNATI'S FIRST MASONIC TEMPLE. Efforts to build a permanent home for Nova Caesarea Harmony Lodge No. 2 had been attempted several times beginning in 1817. The temple, the smaller building at left, was dedicated for Masonic purposes on December 27, 1824 (St. John's Day). This building was made financially viable through the combination of lodge monies; contributions of cash, supplies, and labor; and the renting of the first floor to the post office and the federal district attorney. (NCH2.)

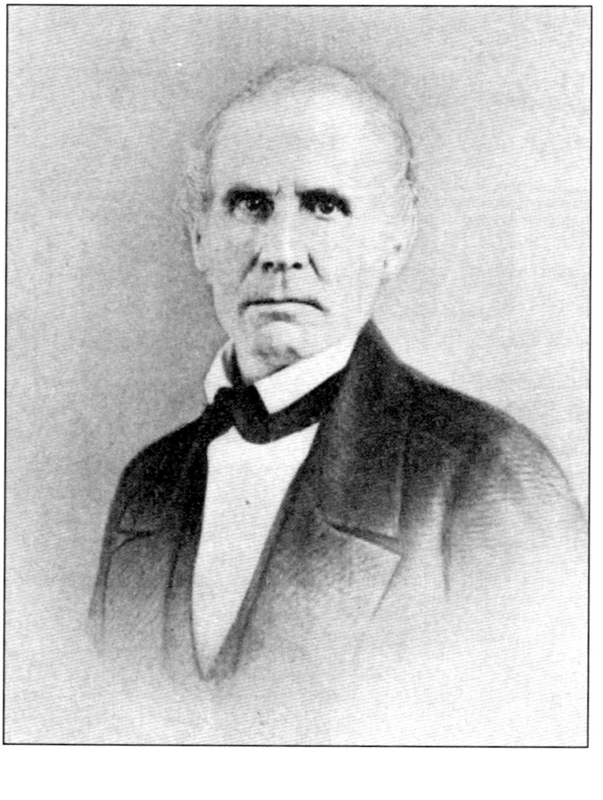

ELAM P. LANGDON, "THE TEMPLE BUILDER." Langdon's financial skills were indispensable in the creation of Nova Caesarea Harmony Lodge's three temples. Initiated on March 6, 1816, he served as Master in 1818, 1819, 1820, 1822, and 1837. Langdon (1791–1864), a banker, served a number of years on the board of trustees of the Common Schools of Cincinnati and in 1842 was a charter member of the Cincinnati Astronomical Society. (NCH2.)

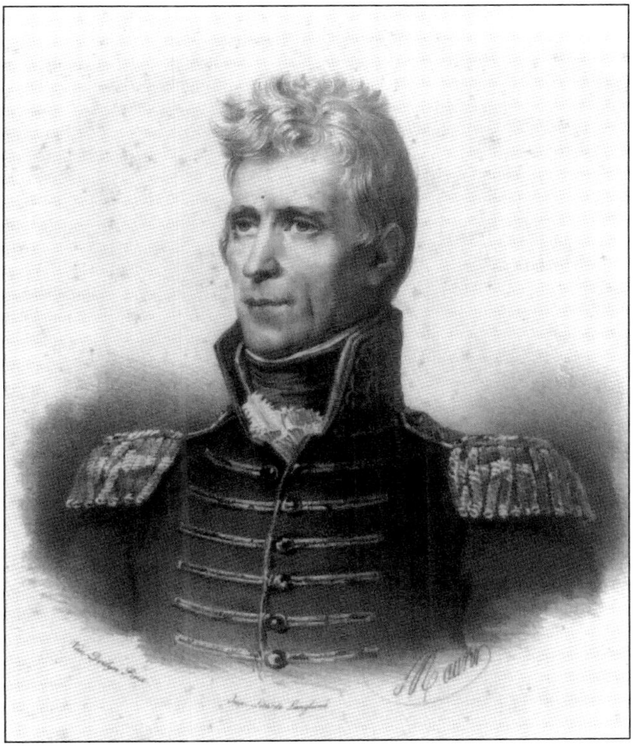

Andrew Jackson. Hero of the War of 1812, the Past Grand Master of Masons of Tennessee was the first of three Freemasons of national stature to visit the temple in its first year of existence. He visited Cincinnati in March 1825. Jackson was elected to the presidency in 1828. DeWitt Clinton, backer of the Erie Canal, Past Grand Master, and governor of New York, also visited the new temple in 1825 while touring Ohio to promote canal building. (Library of Congress.)

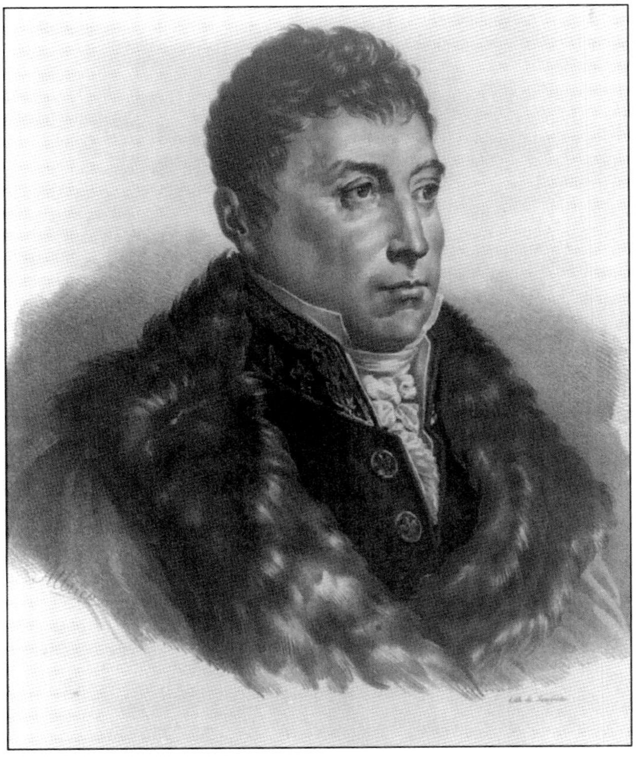

Marquis de Lafayette. The hero of the American Revolution visited Cincinnati on May 19, 1825, during his 1824–1825 grand tour of the United States. He was the guest of honor at a meeting in the new temple where lodges Nova Caesarea Harmony No. 2, Miami No. 46, and Lafayette No. 81 each in succession opened lodge and presented Grand Honors to their notable French brother. After the meeting, Lafayette was escorted to his hotel by more than 500 Masons. (Library of Congress.)

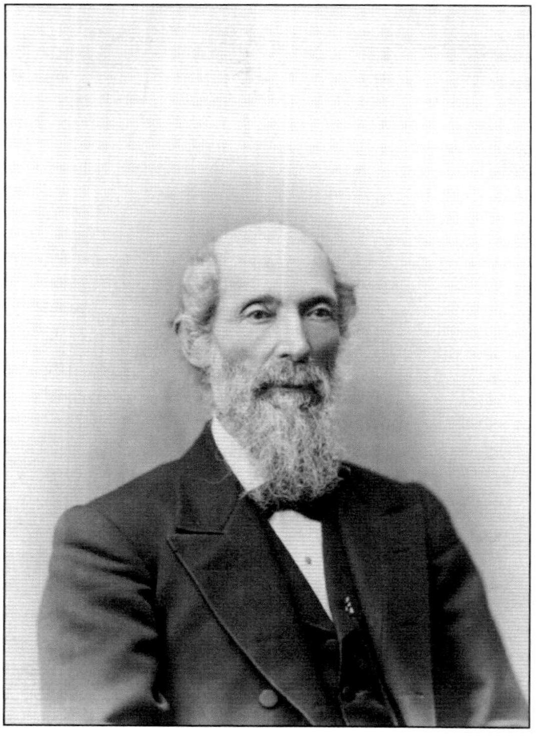

Theodore Sutton Parvin, Founder of Freemasonry in Iowa. After graduating from Cincinnati Law School in 1838, Parvin accompanied Iowa's territorial governor west to serve as his secretary. Parvin (1817–1901) received the Masonic degrees in Nova Caesarea Harmony Lodge before leaving Cincinnati. He founded several lodges in Iowa, helped form the Grand Lodge, and served continuously as Iowa's Grand Secretary from 1845 to 1901, except in 1852, when he was Grand Master. (UC.)

Founder of World-Class Masonic Library. In 1845, Parvin recommended that money be appropriated for an Iowa Grand Lodge library. The library had several locations before finding a permanent home in this building in 1885. A new library, constructed in 1955, still houses this premier Masonic collection. Parvin was instrumental in organizing every Grand Masonic body in Iowa in both the York and Scottish Rites.

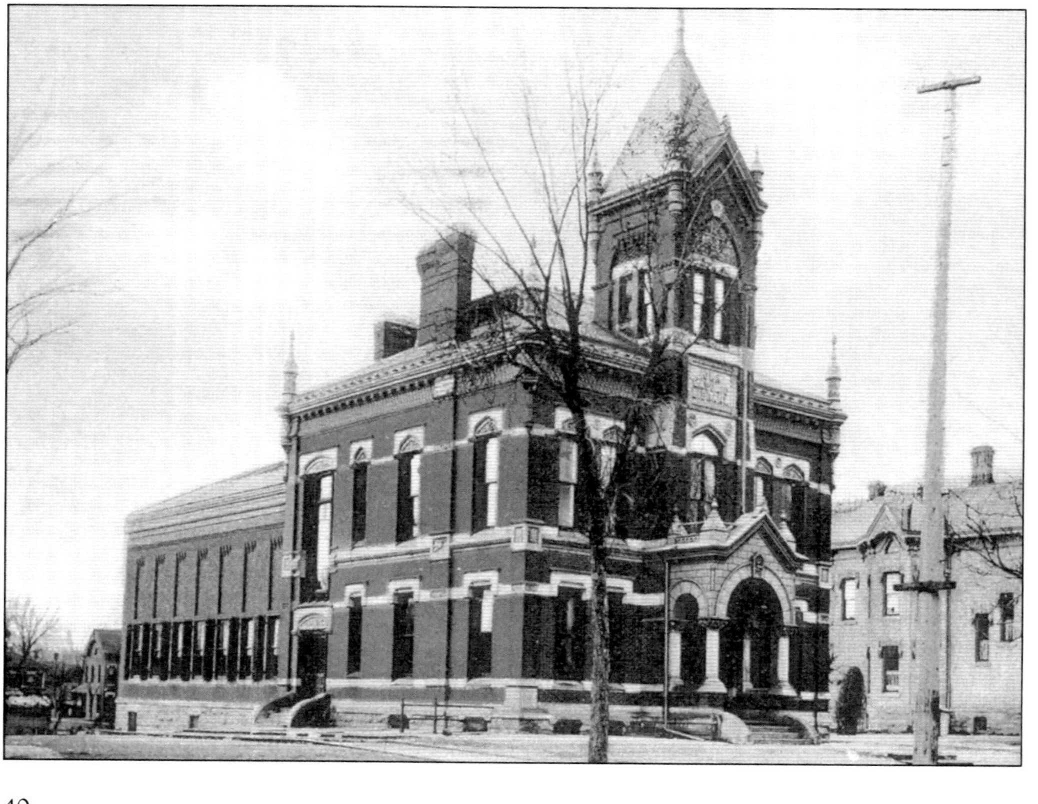

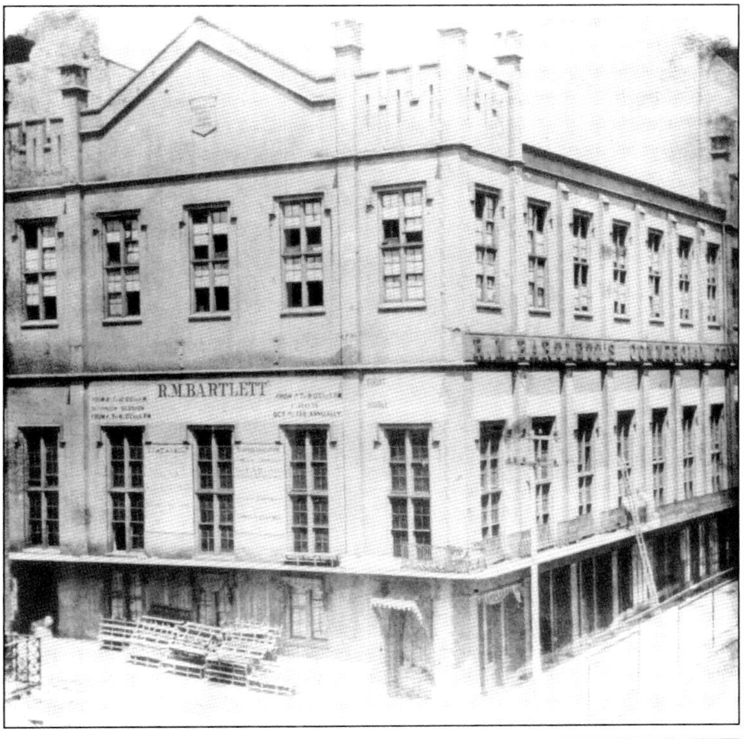

SECOND CINCINNATI TEMPLE. The second temple opened in December 1845. The third floor was for lodge functions. The second floor was a public hall, and the first floor was rented out for income to companies such as R.M. Bartlett's school of "business education and commercial knowledge." (NCH2.)

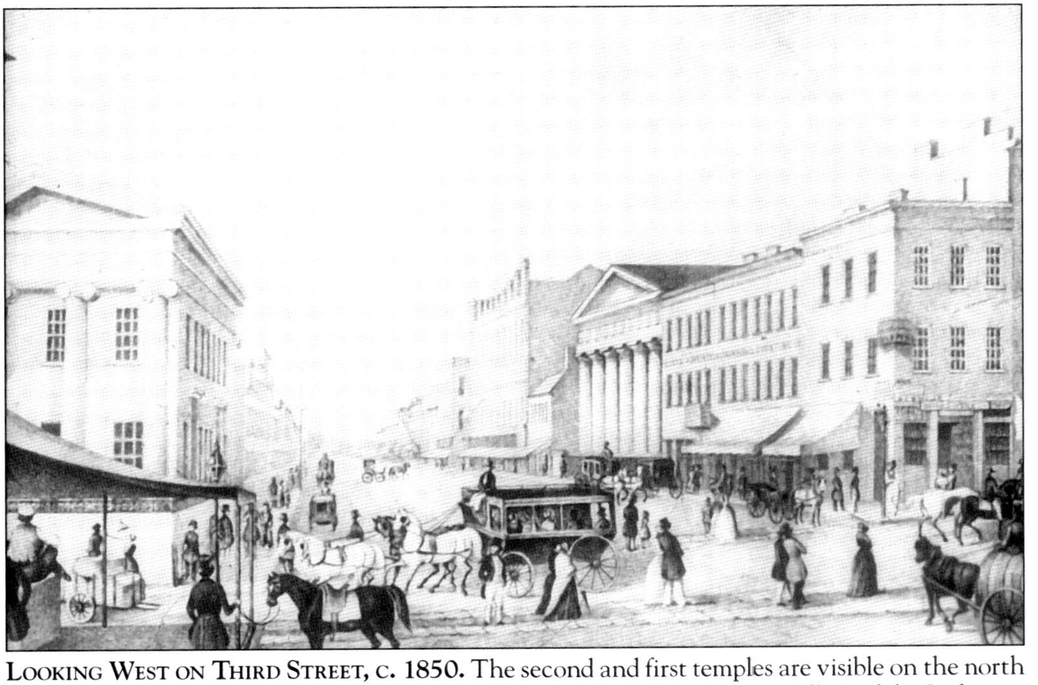

LOOKING WEST ON THIRD STREET, C. 1850. The second and first temples are visible on the north (right) side of the street. The first temple stands to the left of the massive pillars of the Lafayette Bank. At this point, it was rented out for income. The second temple is the building to the left of the first temple. (Public Library of Cincinnati and Hamilton County.)

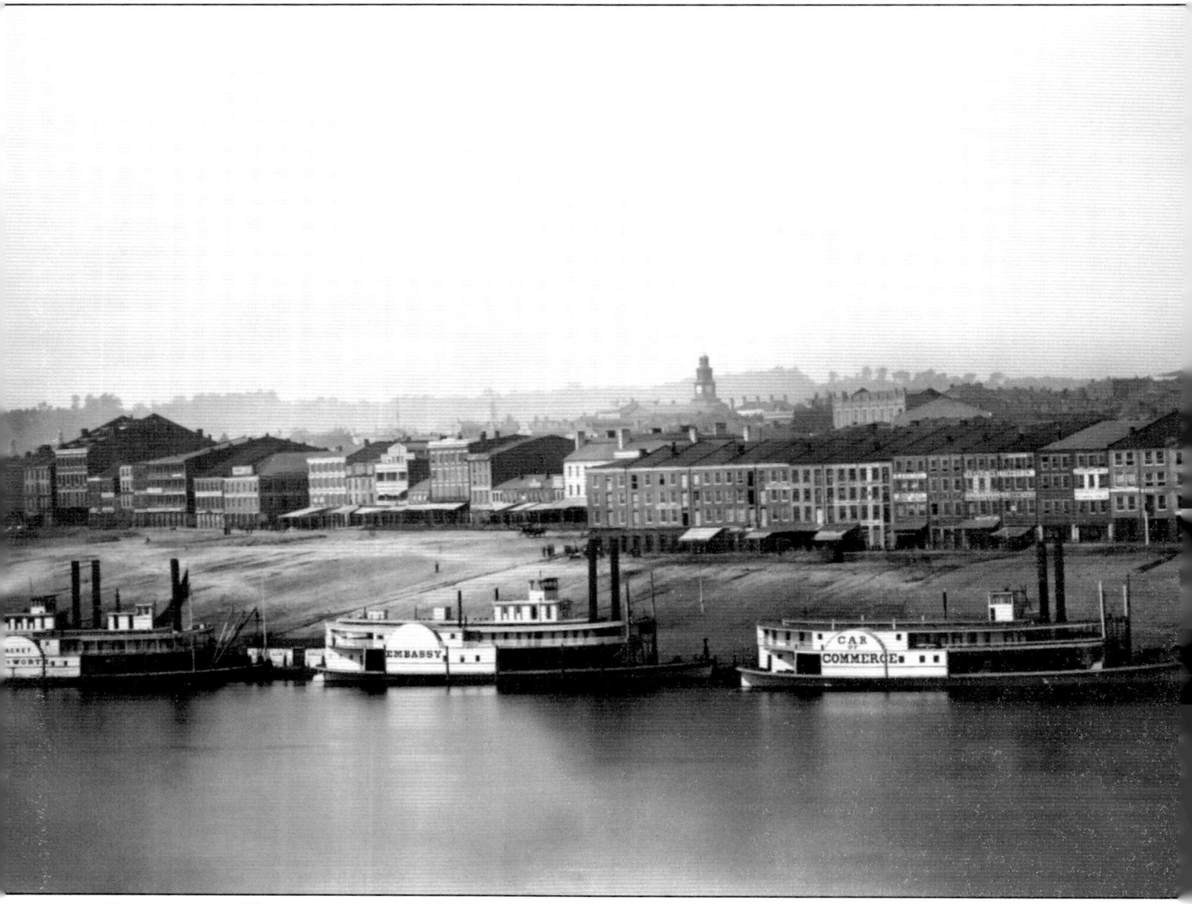

CINCINNATI WATERFRONT, 1848. On Sunday, September 24, 1848, Charles Fontayne and William Porter set up their camera on a rooftop in Newport, Kentucky, and took eight daguerreotype images, capturing Cincinnati's waterfront in a panorama. This is the second image from the left, or downriver end. The large light-colored building with the crenellated roofline to the right of the clock tower is the second temple. (Public Library of Cincinnati and Hamilton County.)

LAJOS (LOUIS) KOSSUTH. Hungary's leader during its short 1849 independence was an unusual occupation for a petitioner to a Cincinnati lodge. After escaping the reconquering Austrian army in his homeland, Kossuth ultimately came to the United States. While in Ohio seeking support for Hungarian autonomy, he and four compatriots petitioned for and were elected to receive the degrees of Masonry in Cincinnati Lodge No. 133. The three degrees occurred on February 19 and 20, 1852, after which demits and honorary memberships were granted. (Library of Congress.)

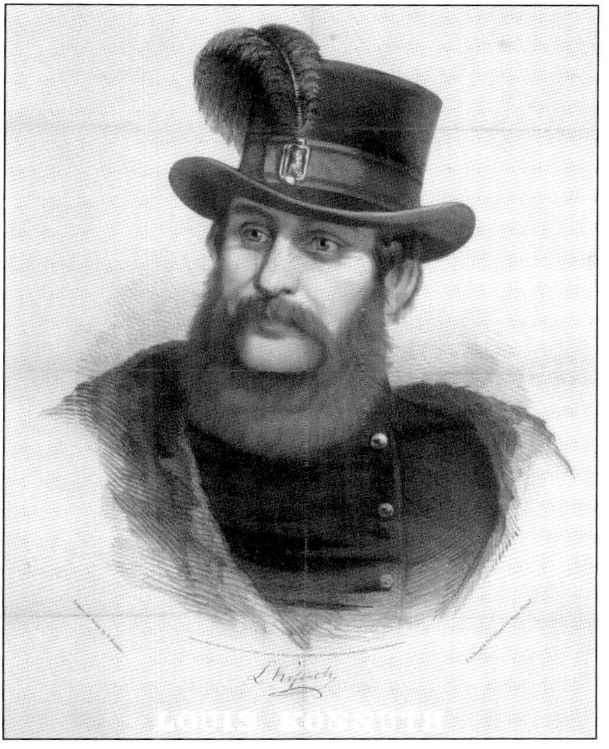

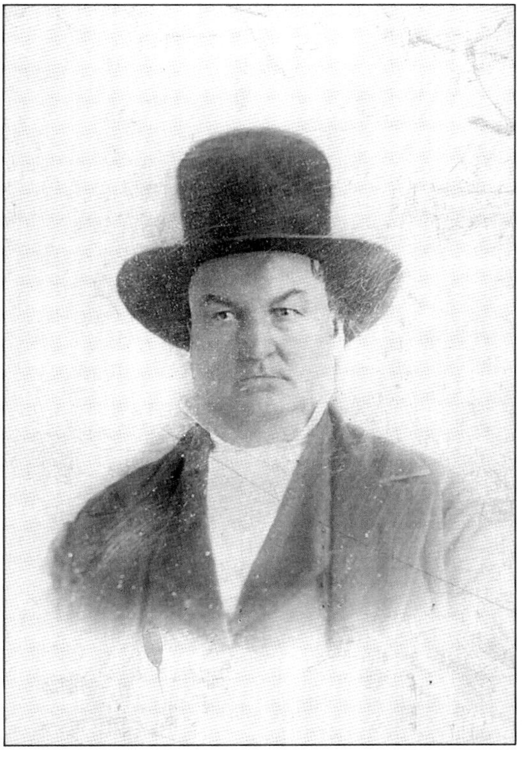

ABSALOM DEATH, ASSOCIATED WITH THREE CINCINNATI LODGES. Charter Master of Cynthia Lodge No. 155 in 1847, Death (1804–1856) was one of the seven founding members of the Scottish Rite in Cincinnati in 1852. He was Grand Master, Royal and Select Masters of Ohio from 1847 to 1849. His employment included superintendent of the Commercial Hospital and Insane Asylum. He was serving as Deputy Grand Master of the Grand Lodge at the time of his death. (AASR.)

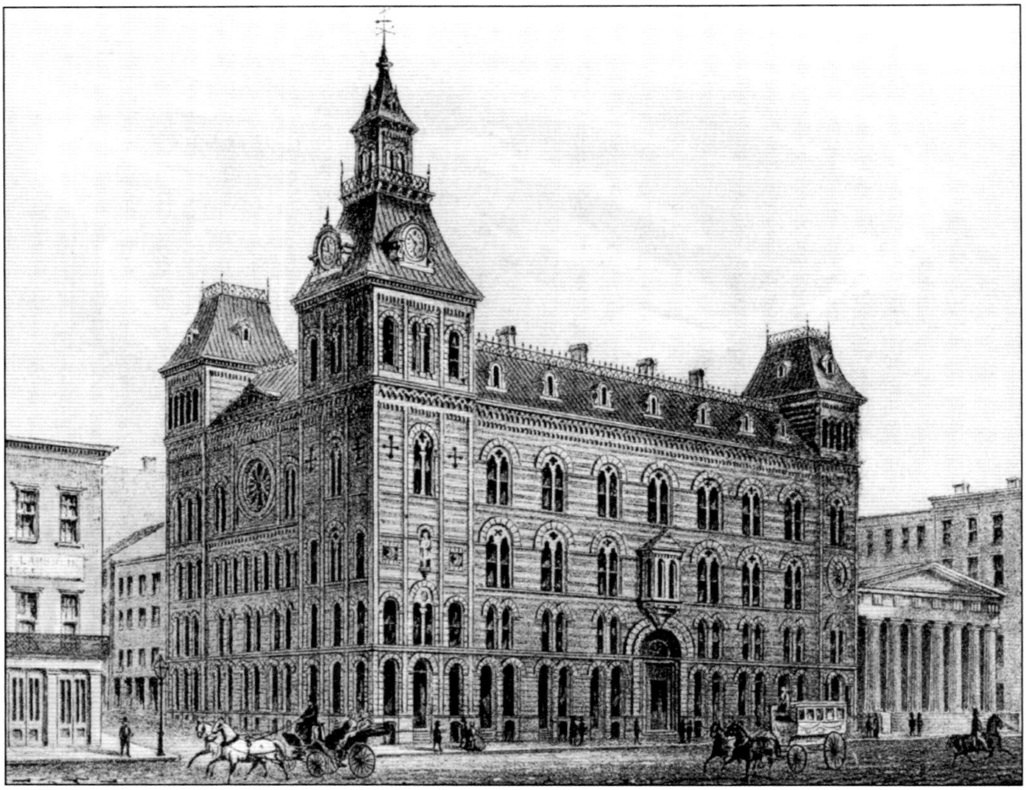

THIRD CINCINNATI MASONIC TEMPLE. This is the third temple as conceived by architects James W. McLaughlin and John R. Hamilton, who designed the building to fill the entire McMillan lot. The cornerstone was laid on July 22, 1858, with full Masonic honors. Grand Master of the Grand Lodge of Ohio Horace M. Stokes officiated. (NCH2.)

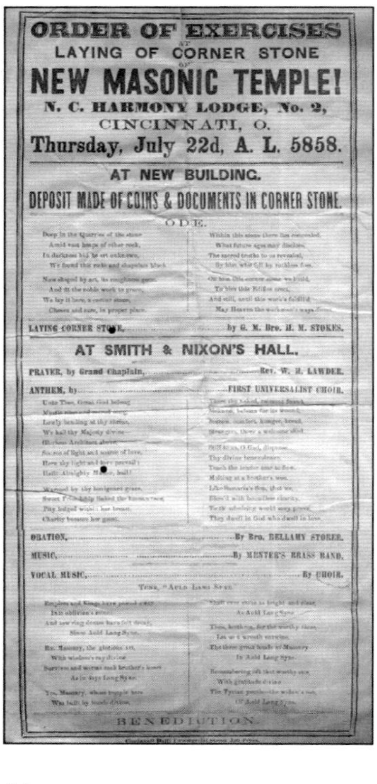

ORDER OF EXERCISES
AT
LAYING OF CORNER STONE
OF
NEW MASONIC TEMPLE!
N. C. HARMONY LODGE, No. 2,
CINCINNATI, O.
Thursday, July 22d, A. L. 5858.

AT NEW BUILDING.

DEPOSIT MADE OF COINS & DOCUMENTS IN CORNER STONE.

ODE.

LAYING CORNER STONE, ... by G. M. Bro. H. M. STOKES.

AT SMITH & NIXON'S HALL.

PRAYER, by Grand Chaplain, ... Rev. W. H. LAWDER.

ANTHEM, by .... FIRST UNIVERSALIST CHOIR.

ORATION, ... By Bro. BELLAMY STORER.

MUSIC, ... By MENTER'S BRASS BAND.

VOCAL MUSIC, ... By CHOIR.

TUNE, "AULD LANG SYNE."

BENEDICTION.

BROADSIDE, CORNERSTONE LAYING FOR THE THIRD MASONIC TEMPLE. The laying of the cornerstone of a building marks a significant point in its creation. This broadside was deposited in the cornerstone of the third temple. It was both an announcement and a program for the ceremony. (NCH2.)

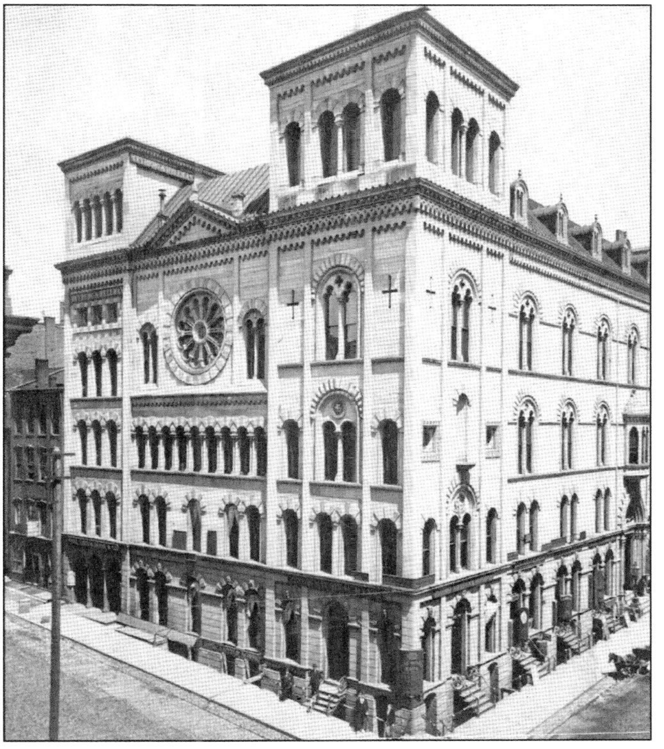

Third Masonic Temple, Completed. Among details never added to the temple were the peaked roofs on the towers and the clock in the tower at the corner of Third and Walnut Streets. The building came in very close to budget, but the onset of the Civil War drove up prices and reduced available manpower and supplies, making further work untenable. (NCH2.)

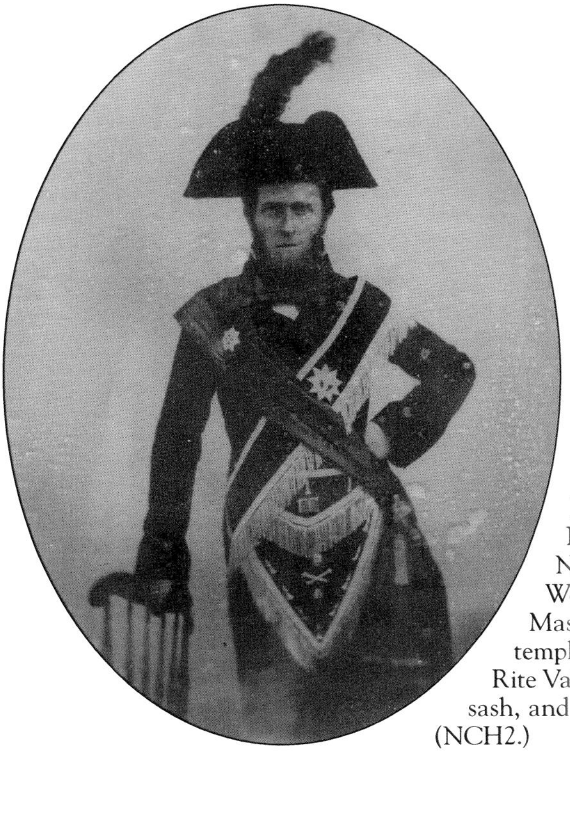

Daniel H. Mears in Commandery Regalia. Mears (1820–1875) presided over Nova Caesarea Harmony Lodge No. 2 as Worshipful Master from 1854 to 1862. He was Master during the construction of the third temple. He was an early member of the Scottish Rite Valley of Cincinnati, joining in 1857. His hat, sash, and apron are in the possession of his lodge. (NCH2.)

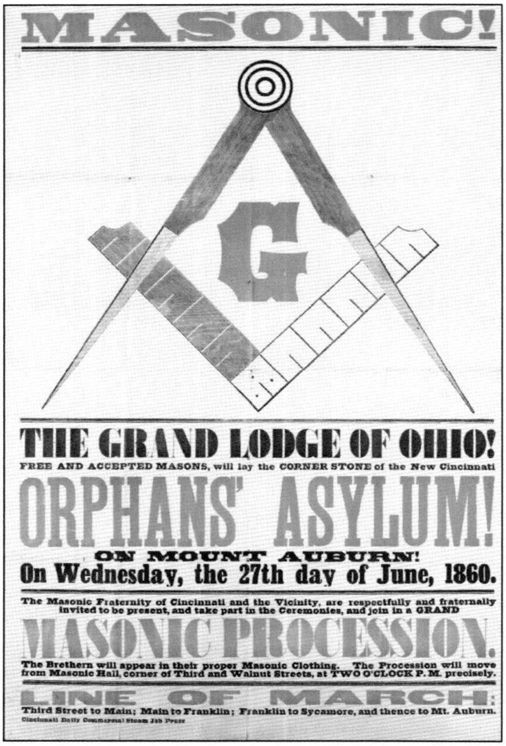

POSTER ANNOUNCING MASONIC PROCESSION. Masons are requested to lay cornerstones for Masonic and non-Masonic buildings, such as the Orphan's Asylum. The phrase "Brethren will appear in their proper Masonic Clothing" indicates that aprons, insignia of office, and other regalia were to be worn. This poster is in the collection of the Museum of the Grand Lodge of Ohio. (GLofOH.)

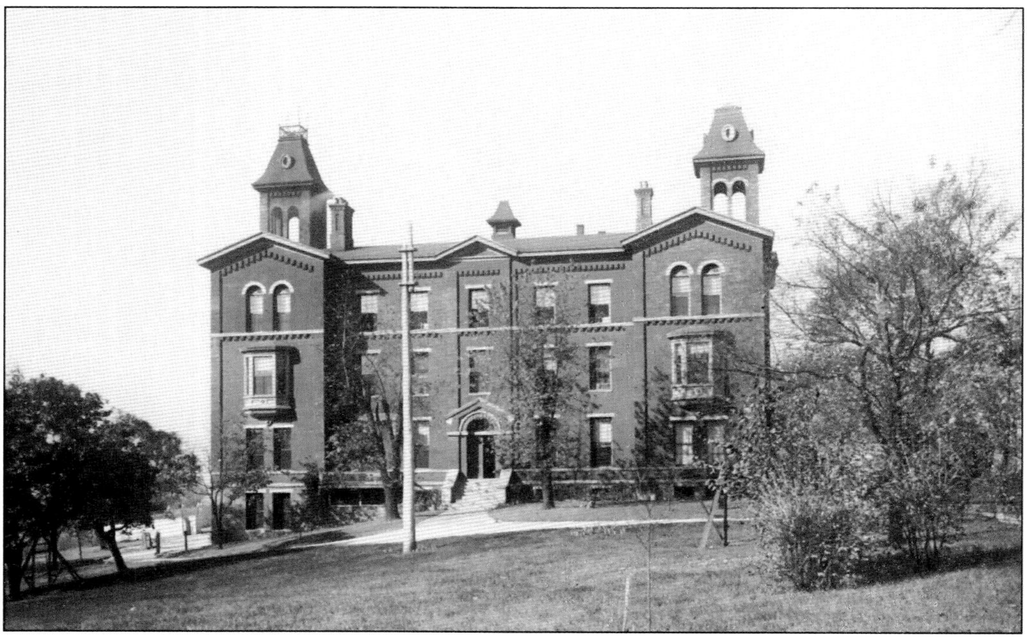

CINCINNATI ORPHANS' ASYLUM IN MOUNT AUBURN. This building, designed by James McLaughlin, architect of the third temple, was a substantial improvement over earlier facilities for parentless children, including one referred to as "The Pest House." The Masonic fraternity's interest in this facility is indicative of its commitment to charity. (CHS.)

J.B. Covert. Covert (1798–1876) was Grand Tyler (or equivalent) of the Grand Lodge, Chapter, Council, and Commandery (Encampment) of Ohio from 1848 to 1864. This office was frequently called upon to form and lead processions for parades and ceremonies. Grand Lodge awarded him a "Sword of Honor" upon his retirement as Grand Tyler in 1869. He also served as Tyler, an office that is part greeter and part doorkeeper, of Nova Caesarea Harmony Lodge No. 2 for 25 years. (AASR.)

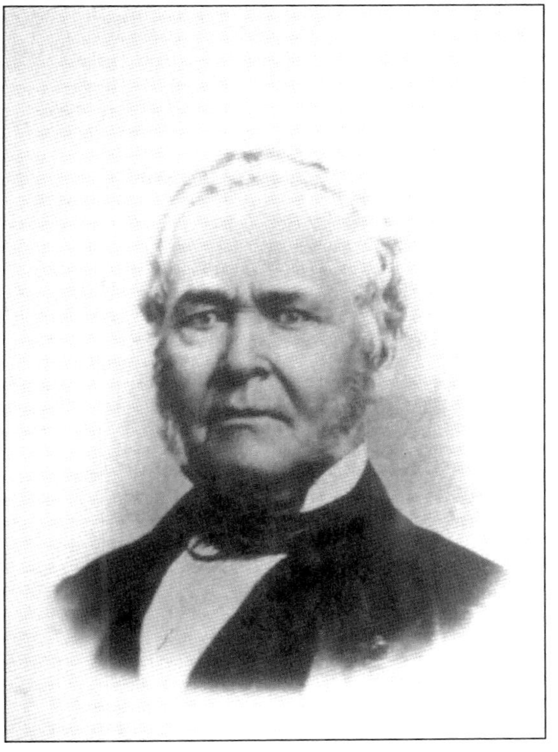

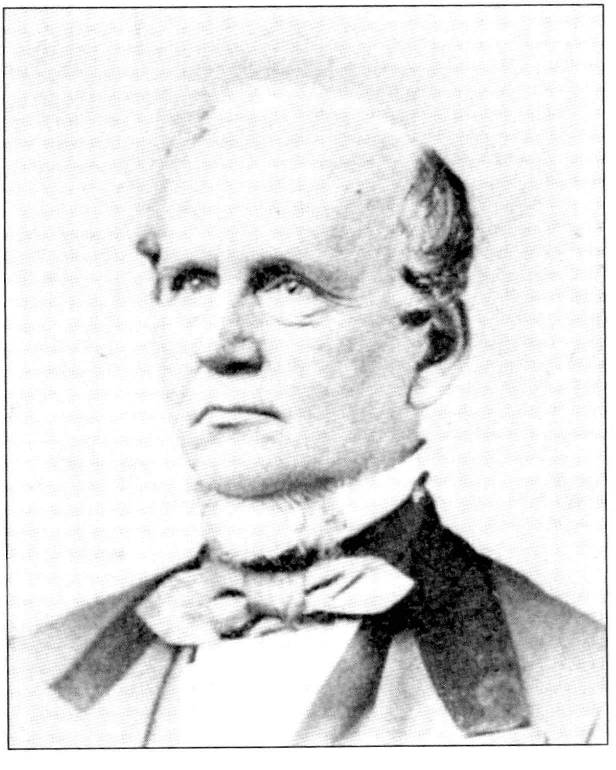

Dr. John L. Vattier, Charter Master of McMillan Lodge No. 141. Vattier (1809–1881) practiced medicine, ran a wholesale drug business, and was postmaster of Cincinnati from 1853 to 1859. He was one of the seven members of the Last Man Society, founded in Cincinnati in 1832. They purchased a bottle of wine and met annually, charging the final survivor with the duty of opening the wine and toasting his deceased fellows, which Vattier did in 1856.

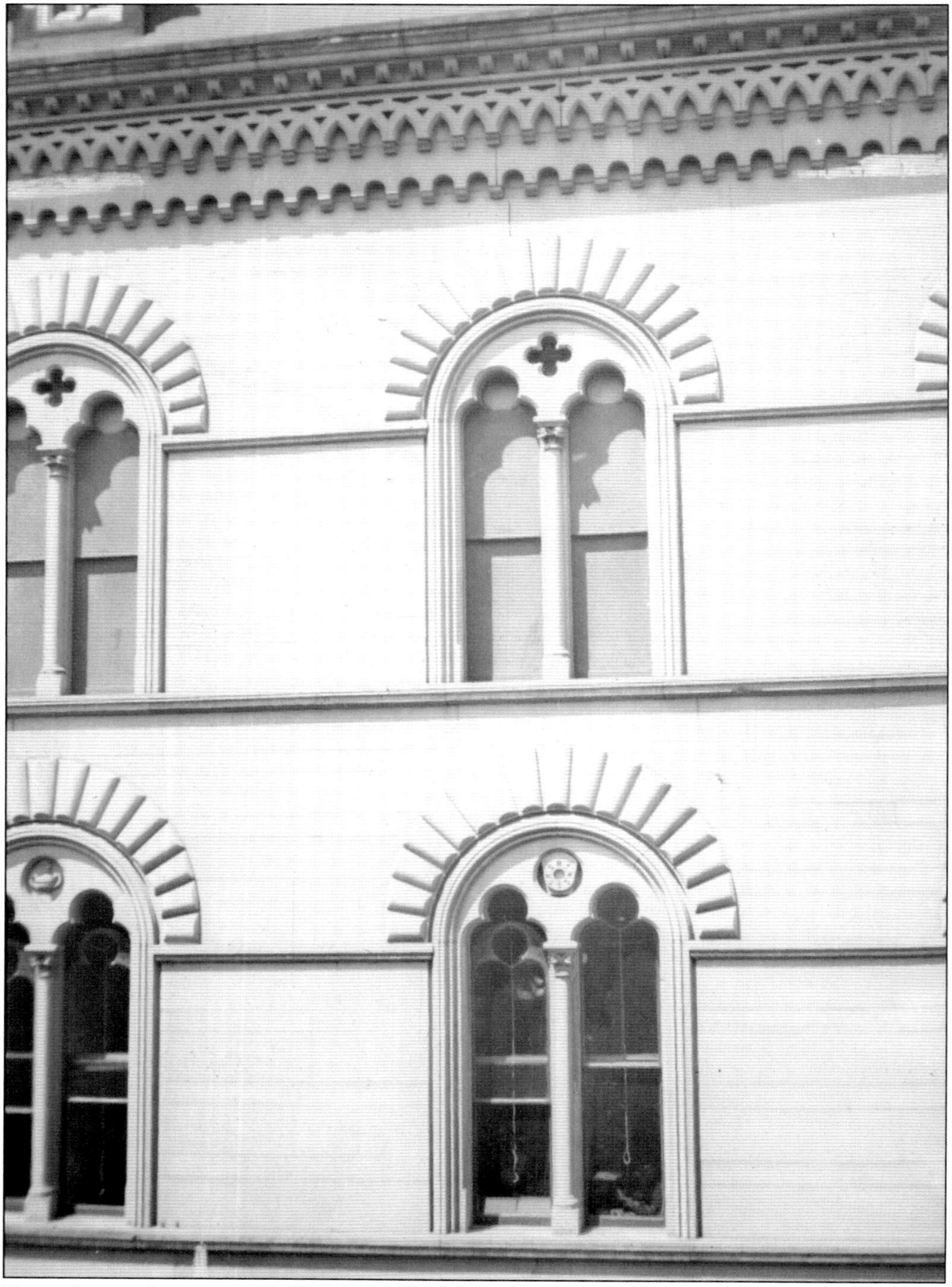

Third Street Side of the Third Temple. The architectural style of the third temple was described as Byzantine. Masonic symbols and emblems adorned the third-floor windows. The lower right window is decorated with the keystone emblem of the Royal Arch Masons. In the lower right pane of that window, a person is visible. (NCH2.)

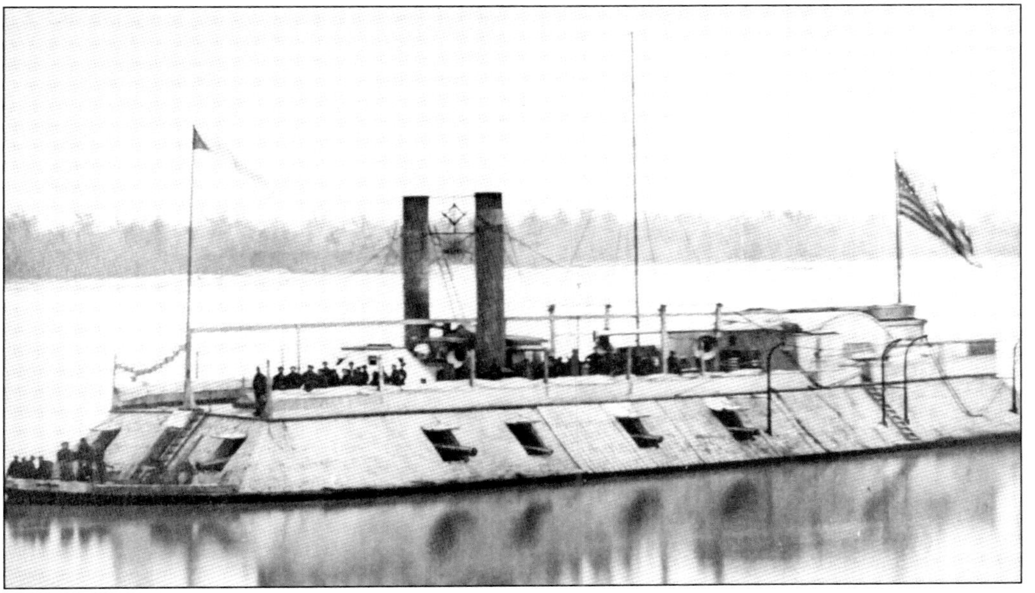

US Gunboat *St. Louis*. Later renamed USS *Baron DeKalb*, this vessel appears to sport a Masonic emblem between its stacks. This emblem has long been a Masonic mystery. No Masonic connection has previously been established for the vessel. Clues involving Cincinnati do, however, exist. The minutes of Nova Caesarea Harmony Lodge No. 2 include a transcription of a letter from the ship dated March 11, 1862, addressed to Past Grand Master William Dodds (see page 17), which accompanied a "cornerstone" from Columbus Lodge, Columbus, Kentucky. (Library of Congress.)

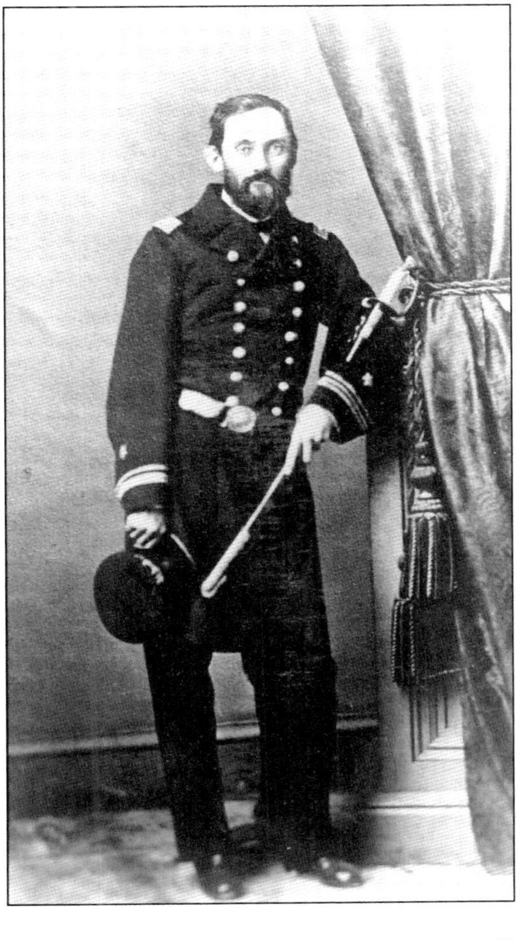

Lt. John V. Johnston, USN, Executive Officer of the *St. Louis*. Johnston sent the Columbus Lodge cornerstone to Cincinnati Masons for safekeeping. This was probably a metal box from inside the stone cornerstone. Columbus, Kentucky, part of the Confederate defense of the Mississippi River, was burned during the Confederate retreat from the town. Lieutenant Johnston is himself another clue to the mystery. He was a Mason, belonging to Cincinnati Lodge No. 133. (Missouri Historical Society.)

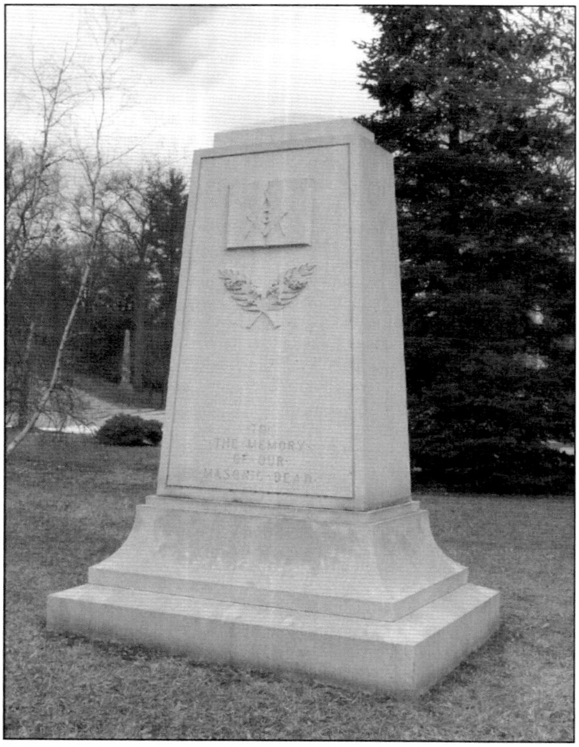

Monument Marking the Masonic Lot at Spring Grove Cemetery. The western end of section 23 continues to be maintained by a group of Masonic lodges. The remains of William McMillan, the benefactor of Nova Caesarea Harmony Lodge No. 2, were removed from Avondale and placed here. On the back side of the monument is a plaque honoring McMillan. (NCH2.)

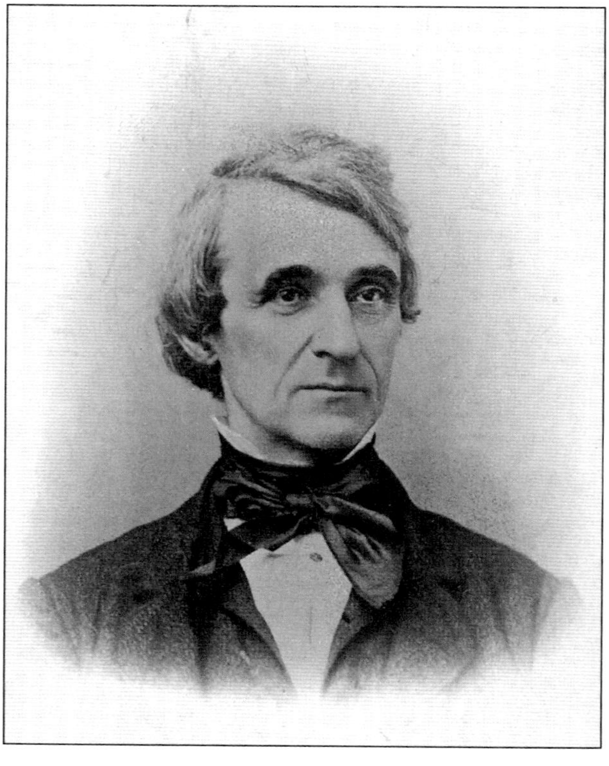

Cornelius Moore. Editor and publisher of the *Masonic Review*, Moore (1806–1883) moved to Cincinnati in 1845 after practicing law in Zanesville, Ohio. He published his Masonic digest in Cincinnati until 1876. Moore was a member of McMillan Lodge No. 141, serving as Worshipful Master from 1858 to 1863. (AASR.)

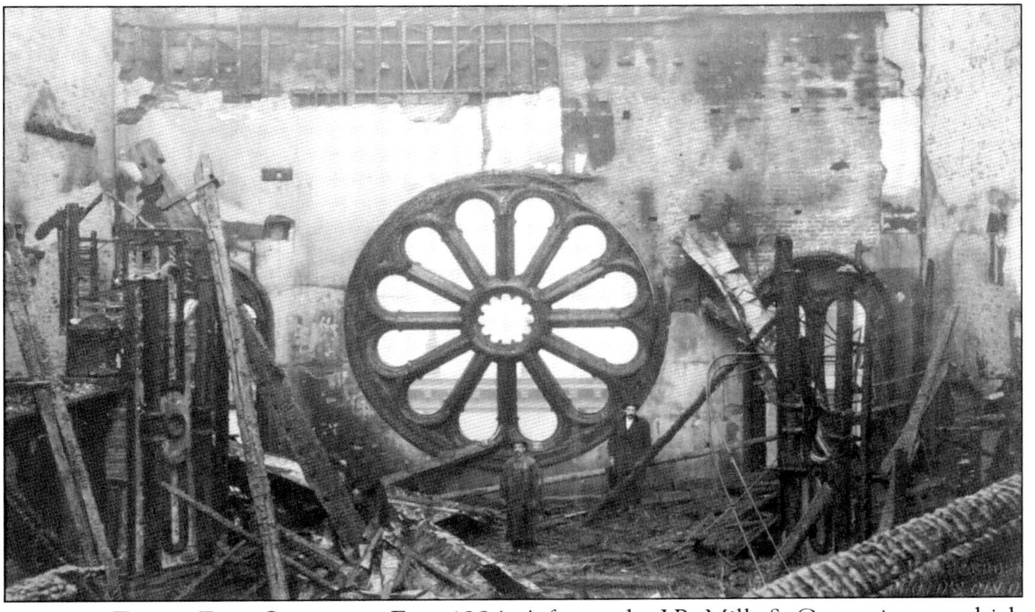

Masonic Temple Fire, Christmas Eve, 1884. A fire at the J.R. Mills & Co. stationers, which occupied the first floor and basement of the northwest corner of the temple, caused massive damage to the structure, especially the side facing Walnut Street. The northwest tower of the temple gave way. The Scottish Rite lost most of its property. E.T. Carson's Masonic library was saved only after Masons risked injury to rescue it. (AASR.)

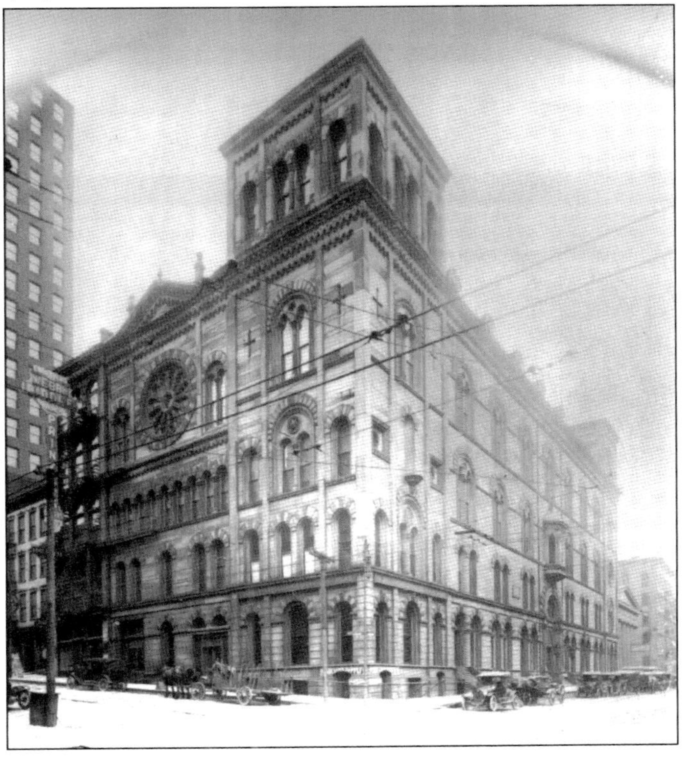

Restored Third Temple. Immediately after the fire, newspapers reported that the temple might be a total loss. Luckily, that was not the case. The building was repaired, and some substantial changes were made. The modification of the northwest tower, to the left of the rose window, is evident in this photograph. (See page 45). (NCH2.)

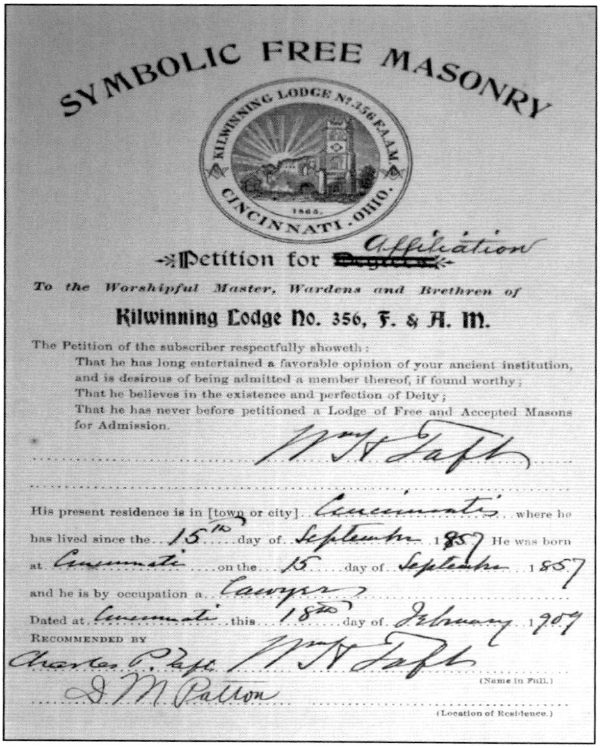

SYMBOLIC FREE MASONRY

KILWINNING LODGE No. 356 F.&A.M. 1865. CINCINNATI, OHIO.

Petition for ~~Degrees~~ Affiliation

To the Worshipful Master, Wardens and Brethren of

Kilwinning Lodge No. 356, F. & A. M.

The Petition of the subscriber respectfully showeth:

That he has long entertained a favorable opinion of your ancient institution, and is desirous of being admitted a member thereof, if found worthy;

That he believes in the existence and perfection of Deity;

That he has never before petitioned a Lodge of Free and Accepted Masons for Admission.

Wm H Taft

His present residence is in [town or city] Cincinnati where he has lived since the 15th day of September 1857 He was born at Cincinnati on the 15 day of September 1857 and he is by occupation a Lawyer

Dated at Cincinnati this 18th day of February 1909

RECOMMENDED BY

Charles P. Taft Wm H Taft (Name in Full.)

D. M. Patton (Location of Residence.)

William Howard Taft's Petition. Fourteen US presidents have been Freemasons. William Howard Taft, a Cincinnati native, is the only one to have been "made a Mason at sight." He was made a Mason in the old Scottish Rite Cathedral on Broadway (see page 107) on February 18, 1909. Over 800 Masons attended, while more than 2,000 others were turned away. (GLofOH.)

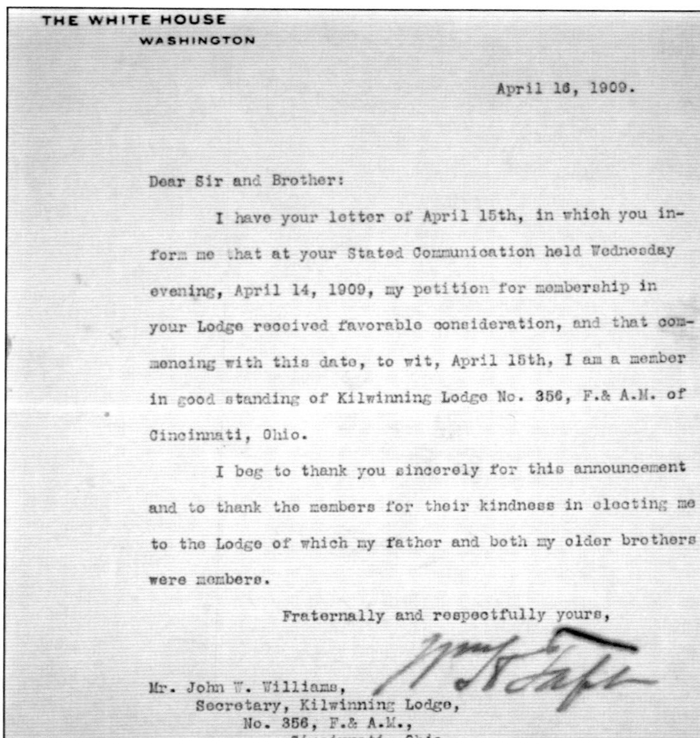

THE WHITE HOUSE
WASHINGTON

April 16, 1909.

Dear Sir and Brother:

I have your letter of April 15th, in which you inform me that at your Stated Communication held Wednesday evening, April 14, 1909, my petition for membership in your Lodge received favorable consideration, and that commencing with this date, to wit, April 15th, I am a member in good standing of Kilwinning Lodge No. 356, F.& A.M. of Cincinnati, Ohio.

I beg to thank you sincerely for this announcement and to thank the members for their kindness in electing me to the Lodge of which my father and both my older brothers were members.

Fraternally and respectfully yours,

Wm H Taft

Mr. John W. Williams,
Secretary, Kilwinning Lodge,
No. 356, F.& A.M.,
Cincinnati, Ohio.

Taft Acknowledged his Membership in Kilwinning Lodge No. 356. As a Mason at sight, Taft was required to petition a lodge for actual membership after receiving the secret work of the three Blue Lodge degrees in a single session. He affiliated with Kilwinning Lodge, to which his father and half-brother and primary backer for his presidential run, Charles P. Taft, belonged. (GLofOH.)

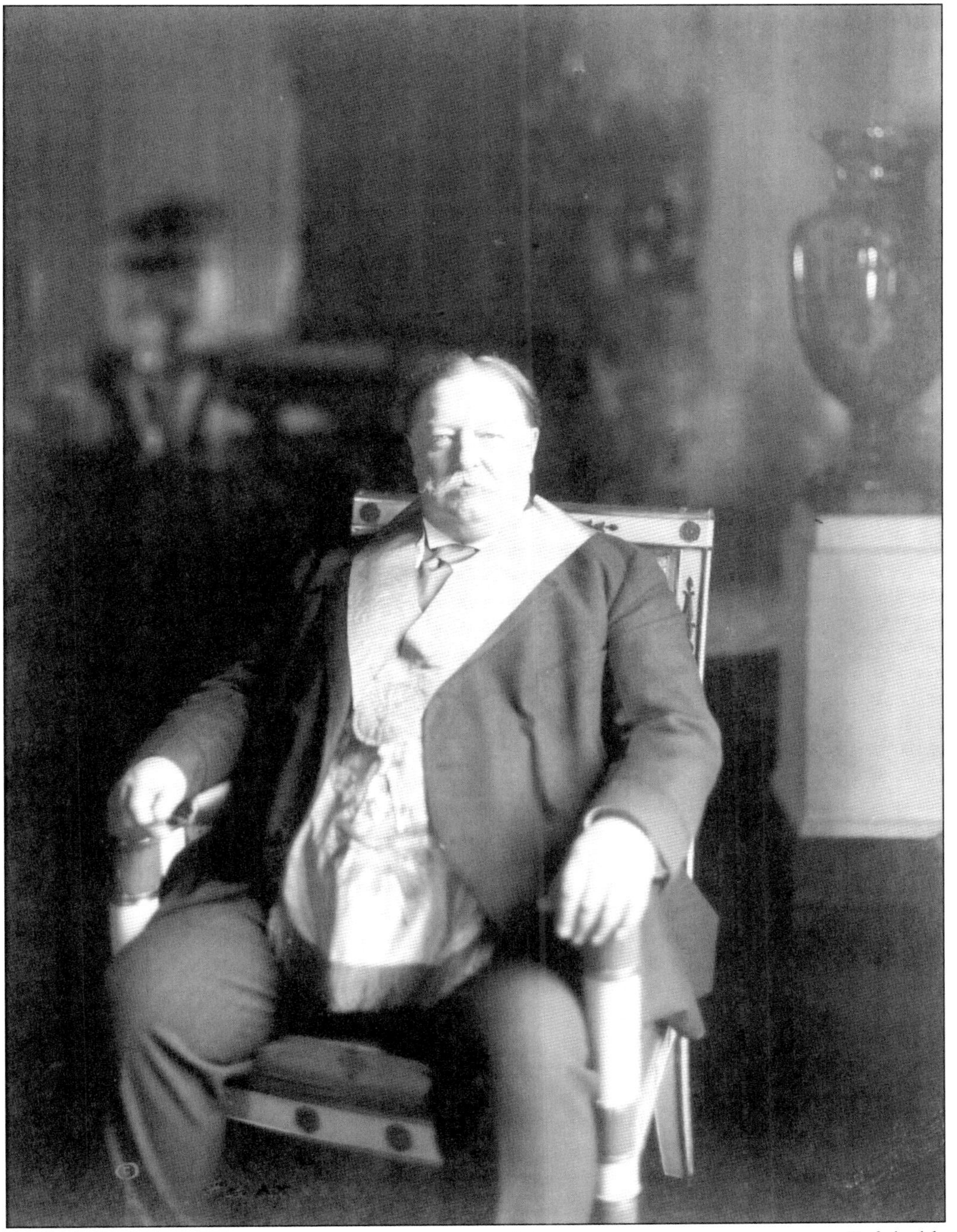

Pres. William Howard Taft Wearing George Washington's Masonic Apron. Taft holds the trowel used by Washington to lay the cornerstone of the US Capitol. Washington gave the trowel to his lodge after the Capitol's cornerstone ceremony. The Watson-Cassoul Apron was presented to Washington in 1782. It was later presented to Lodge No. 22 by Washington's nephew Lawrence Lewis. (Courtesy Alexandria-Washington Lodge No. 22.)

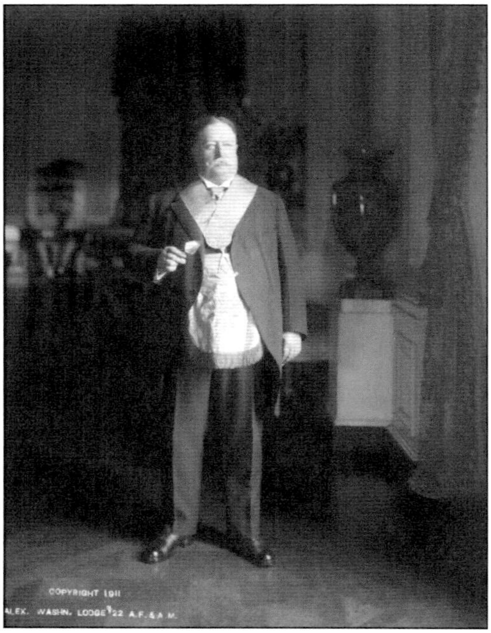

TAFT WEARING WASHINGTON'S APRON, MAY 9, 1911. At 2:30 p.m., in the Executive Mansion (the White House), a delegation from Alexandria-Washington Lodge No. 22, including Lawrence Washington, great-great-grandnephew of George Washington, met President Taft in the East Room, where this and several other photographs were taken. The images were used to solicit interest in the George Washington National Masonic Memorial. (Courtesy Alexandria-Washington Lodge No. 22.)

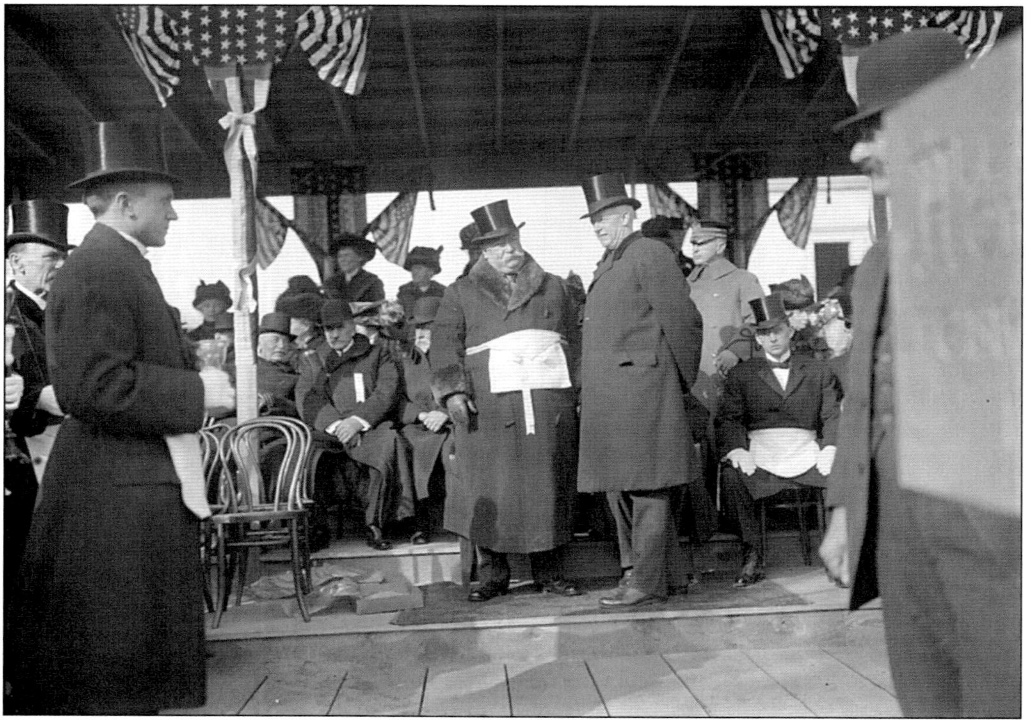

TAFT AT CORNERSTONE LAYING, 1913. President Taft took an interest in Masonry to the extent his executive and judicial duties permitted. On February 13, 1913, he participated in the cornerstone laying of the All Souls Unitarian Church at Sixteenth and R Streets, Washington, DC. The church was never constructed. The congregation ultimately built on a larger parcel of land elsewhere in the District. (Library of Congress.)

P. (PETER) R. FORTNEY. Past Master of Nova Caesarea Harmony Lodge No. 2, Fortney served as the Grand Lodge's First District Lecturer (now District Deputy) in the 1890s. Fortney (1843–1919) managed the third Masonic temple for almost 25 years while serving as an executive in the flour and seed business. A veteran of the Civil War, he enlisted at the age of 18 in the 83rd Ohio Volunteer Infantry. (NCH2.)

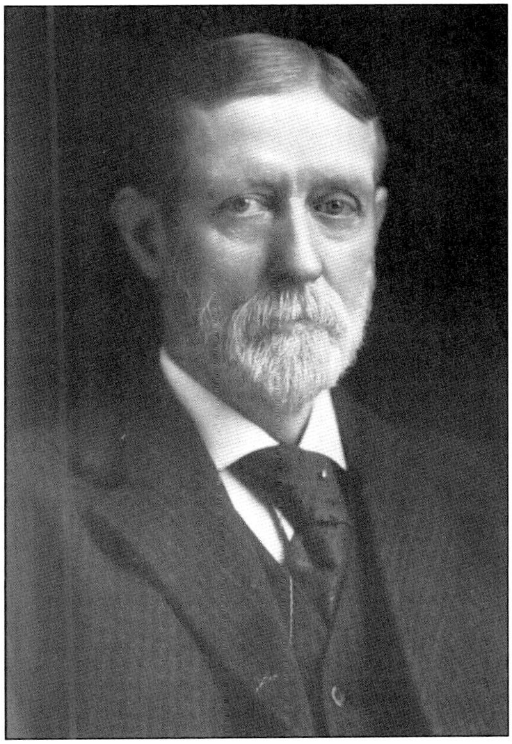

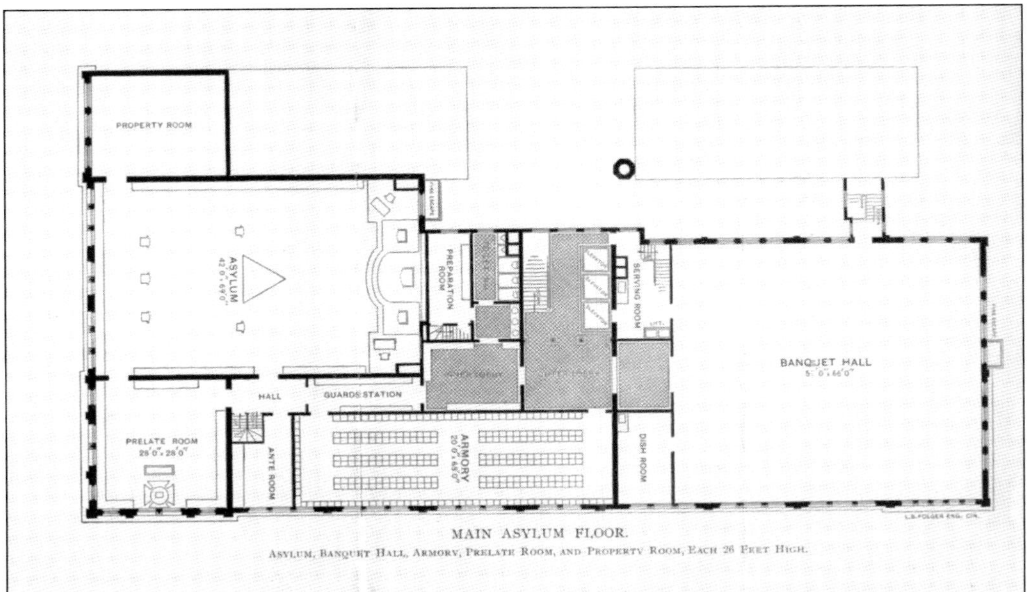

FLOOR PLAN OF THE THIRD TEMPLE. In 1898, Nova Caesarea Harmony Lodge No. 2 proposed modifying one floor of the temple to induce the three Commanderies of Knights Templar to return to the building. These plans show the space as it would have been modified. This is probably the third floor, the level below the rose window level. Negotiations began, but the work was never done. (NCH2.)

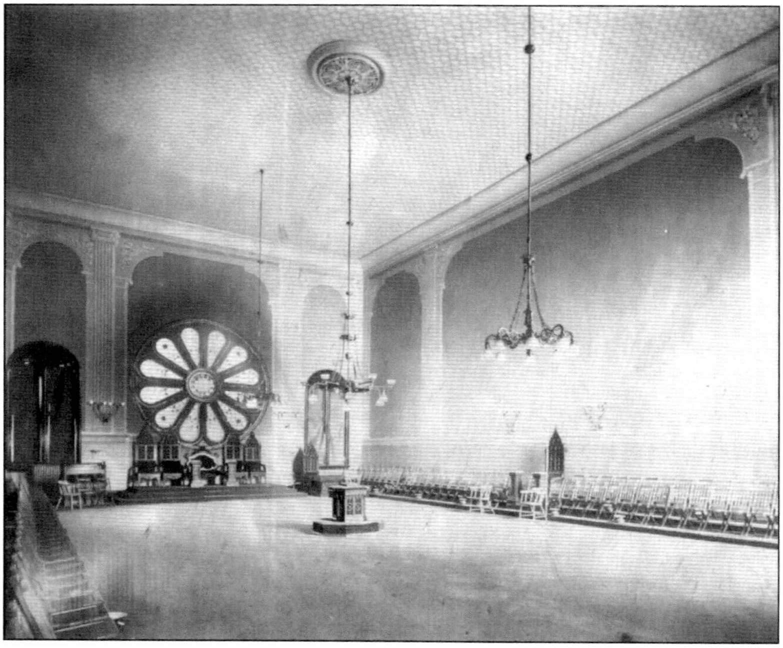

THIRD TEMPLE INTERIOR, "BLUE ROOM," 1915. The rose window, a prominent feature of the exterior facade, served as a backdrop for the presiding officer. This room was enlarged to 72 feet by 40 feet after the 1884 fire. The wall decorations were added in 1914. (NCH2.)

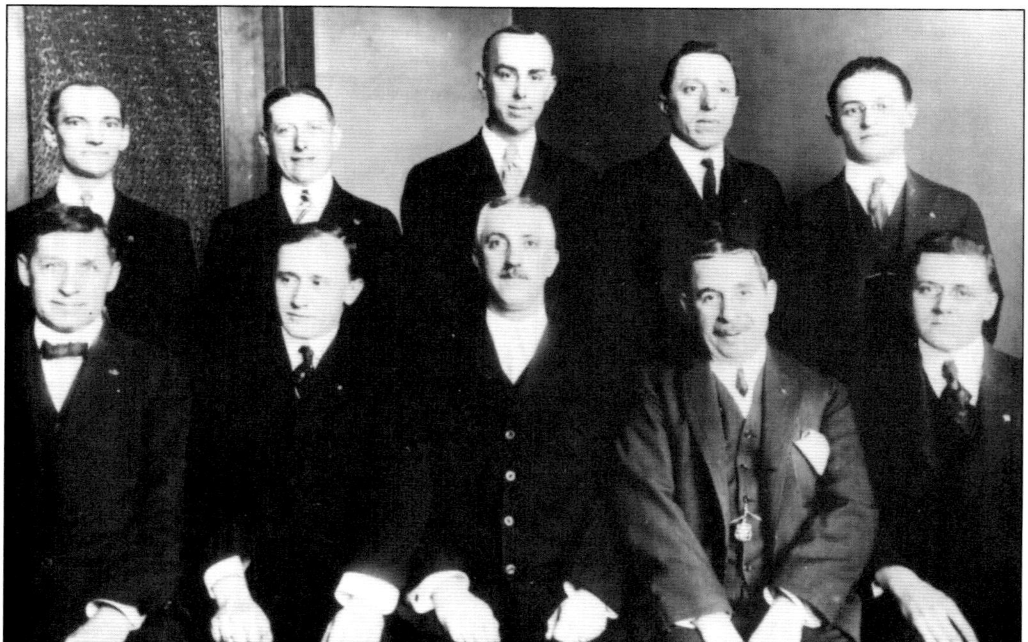

HIGH NOON LODGE NO. 635. Unable to attend meetings at night, musicians working in the theaters founded this lodge, which met on Saturday mornings. The first officers, in 1916, were, from left to right, (first row): John H. Louis, Treasurer; Theodore Hahn Jr., Senior Warden; Frank Zumstein, Worshipful Master; George Fish, Junior Warden; and August Schaefer, Secretary; (second row) Walter Ingram, Tyler; Charles Schweitzer, Junior Deacon; Walter Walker, Senior Deacon; Jacob Bruehl, Junior Steward; and Howard Dhonau, Senior Steward. (NCH No. 2.)

Four

THE CINCINNATI MASONIC TEMPLE

The Cincinnati Masonic Center (originally Temple) is seven stories in height, with two levels below ground. The major sections of the building are the Center, or Temple; the Taft Theatre; and the Scottish Rite Cathedral.

The effort to build a modern Masonic complex is usually dated to 1911, when a proposal was first contemplated by the Scottish Rite. However, articles in the *Cincinnati Enquirer* state that the matter was being discussed in 1897. As early as 1899, Nova Caesarea Harmony Lodge had received quotations to build a nine-story building as a replacement for the 1858 temple. The growth of the fraternity and needs for greater ceremonial, office, storage, and banquet space and the desire for modern conveniences made the late 1850s building less desirable.

The Cincinnati Masonic Temple Company was incorporated in 1914. The company, usually through either the Syrian Shrine or Scottish Rite, began to buy the properties on the south side of Fifth Street between Sycamore Street and Broadway. In 1924, a drive to garner funds to build a new temple supported by as many lodges and other bodies as possible was in full swing. At this stage, 18,144 donors contributed to the effort.

The Nevada Building, the old Guilford School, Liquid Carbonic, and other buildings and even the Scottish Rite's old cathedral, all needed to be removed. The Jon Van Range Company at Fifth Street and Broadway remained in place not only through the initial site clearance, but well into construction. Ground was broken on December 14, 1925, by Charles Phelps Taft, honorary chairman of the project. The cornerstone was laid by Grand Master Earle Stewart and the Grand Lodge officers on October 20, 1926. Dedication of the building took an entire week in January 1928. At that time, ten blue lodges, three Royal Arch Chapters, one Council of Royal and Select Masters, two Knights Templar Commanderies, three Eastern Star Chapters, one DeMolay Chapter, the Valley of Cincinnati of the Ancient Accepted Scottish Rite, and the Syrian Shrine moved in.

Today, the building is a monument to the hard work, vision, and devotion of the Freemasons who conceived and built it.

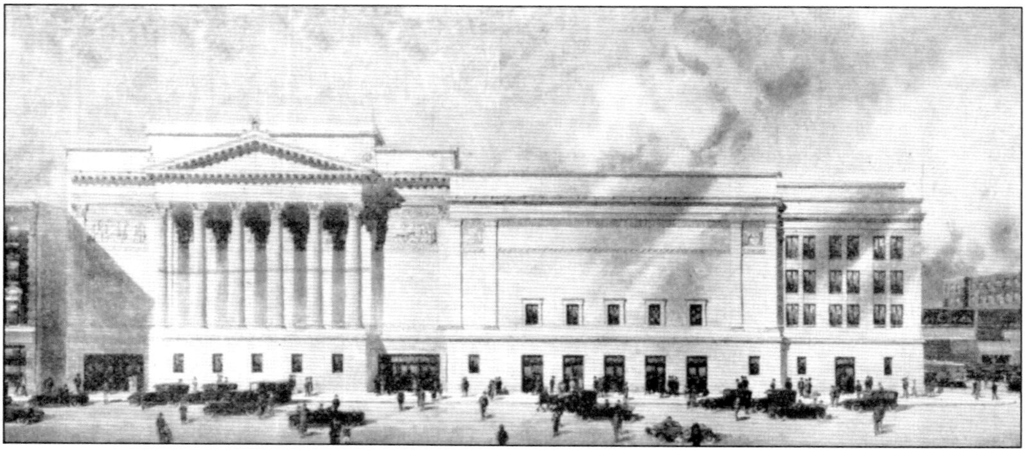

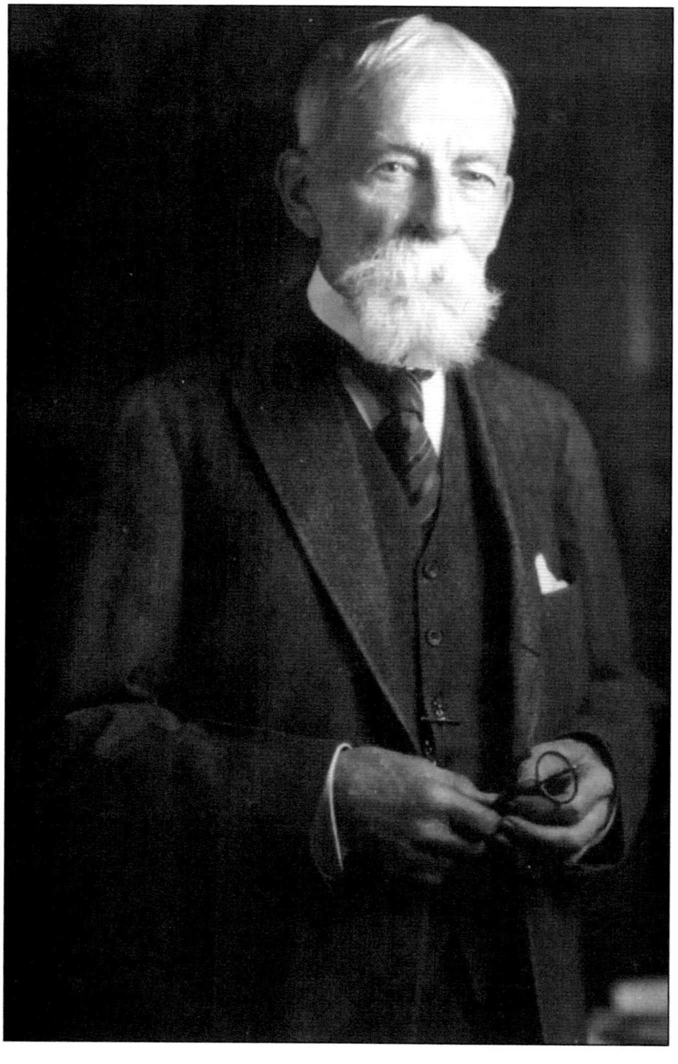

Proposed Cincinnati Masonic Temple. In the spring of 1924, a fund raising campaign for the new temple was underway. Images such as this were used to interest Masons and others in contributing. The asymmetry of the plan closely resembles the building as it was constructed. (AASR.)

Charles Phelps Taft, Temple Company's Honorary Chairman. A fundraising memo from Taft to the local membership, soliciting funds for the temple's construction, referred to the 1858 temple as "the old rookery at Third and Walnut Streets." Taft (1843–1929) was editor of the *Time Star* newspaper and a member of Killwinning Lodge No. 356. His home, now the Taft Museum, is two blocks from the temple site. (UC.)

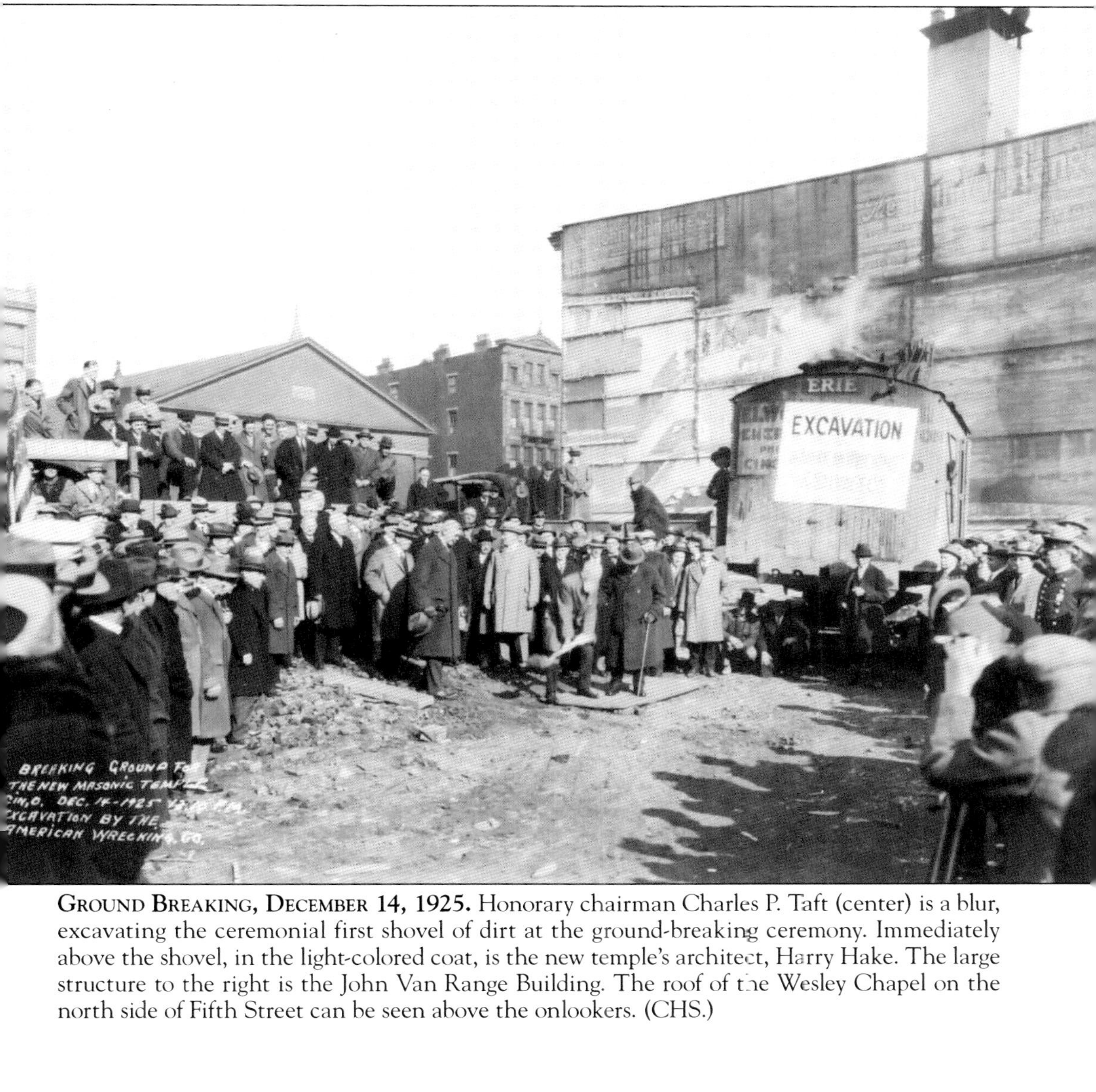

GROUND BREAKING, DECEMBER 14, 1925. Honorary chairman Charles P. Taft (center) is a blur, excavating the ceremonial first shovel of dirt at the ground-breaking ceremony. Immediately above the shovel, in the light-colored coat, is the new temple's architect, Harry Hake. The large structure to the right is the John Van Range Building. The roof of the Wesley Chapel on the north side of Fifth Street can be seen above the onlookers. (CHS.)

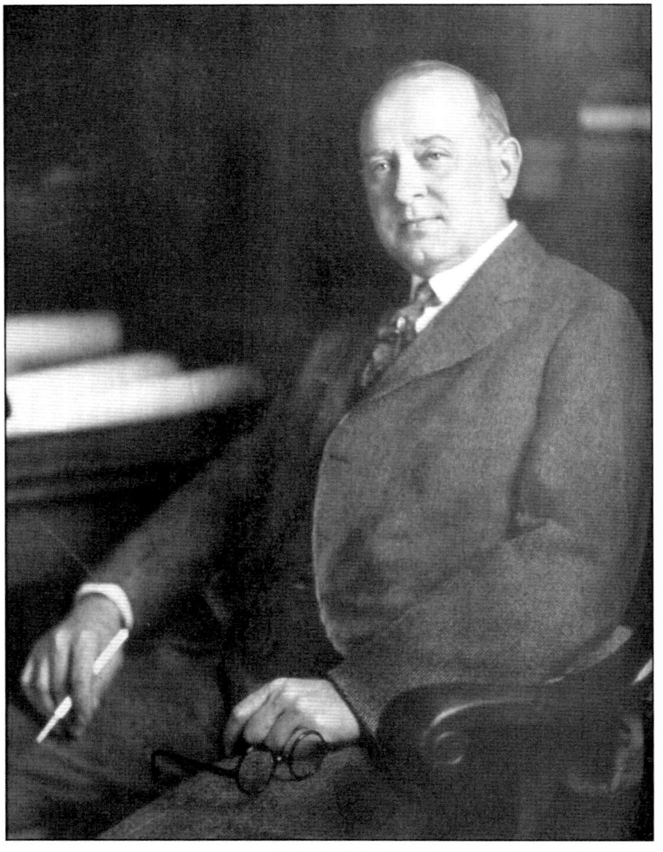

HARRY HAKE, ARCHITECT OF THE CINCINNATI MASONIC TEMPLE. Previously, Hake had designed Hanselmann Lodge's temple on Clifton Avenue and Enoch T. Carson Lodge's building on Ludlow Avenue. He also designed the Elks Temple on Ninth Street. Hake (1871–1955) was a member of Vattier Lodge No. 386. His other Cincinnati projects include the Western Southern Life Building across Broadway from the temple and the Cincinnati Bell Building at Seventh and Elm Streets. (UC.)

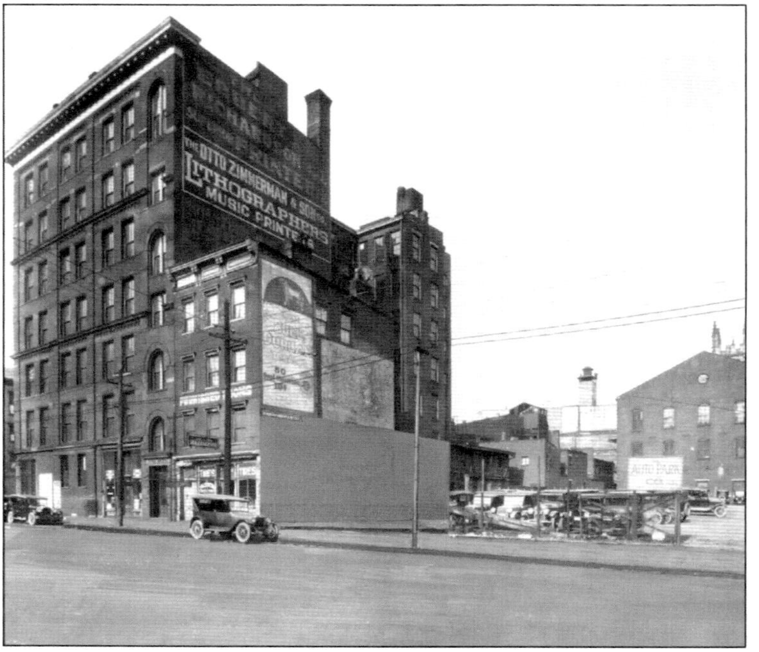

NEVADA BUILDING, SOUTHEAST CORNER, FIFTH AND SYCAMORE STREETS. Occupying the future site of the Taft Theatre, the Nevada Building was a general office building and the tallest structure on the future Cincinnati Masonic Temple site. A Kroger grocery store was located on its ground floor. (AASR.)

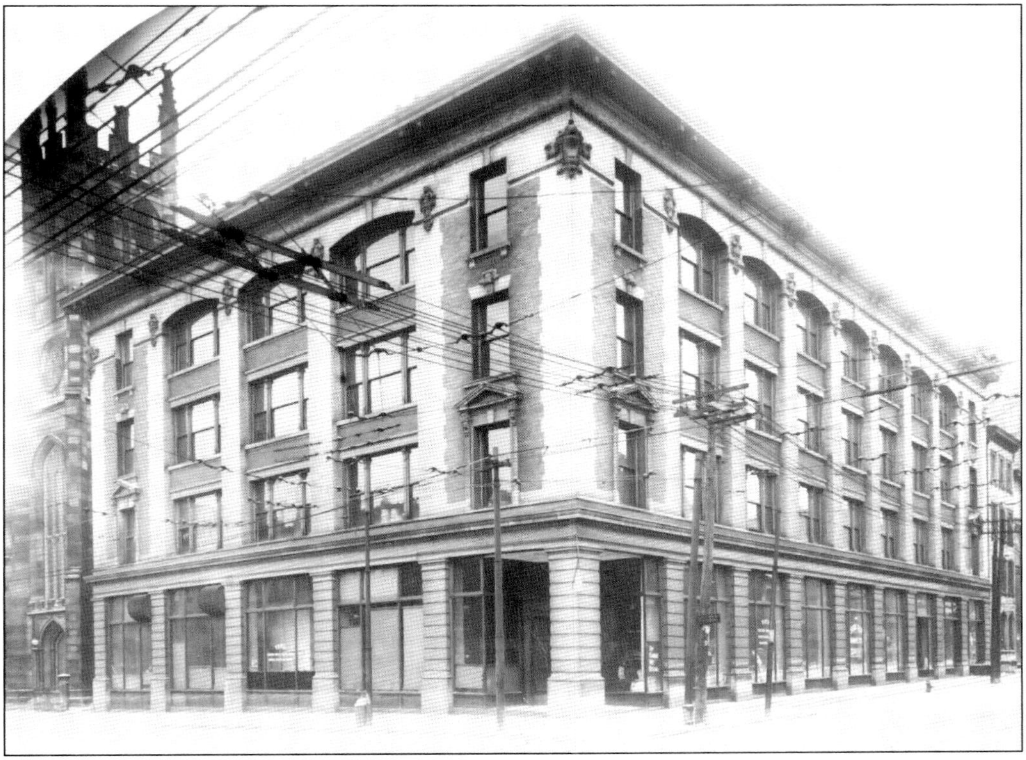

JOHN VAN RANGE COMPANY, SOUTHWEST CORNER, FIFTH STREET AND BROADWAY. This company was a manufacturer of stoves for restaurants and hotels. The last property removed from the temple site, it is visible in the ground-breaking and cornerstone construction photographs. It was located where the Fifth Street parking lot is today. The old Scottish Rite Cathedral is visible at left. (CHS.)

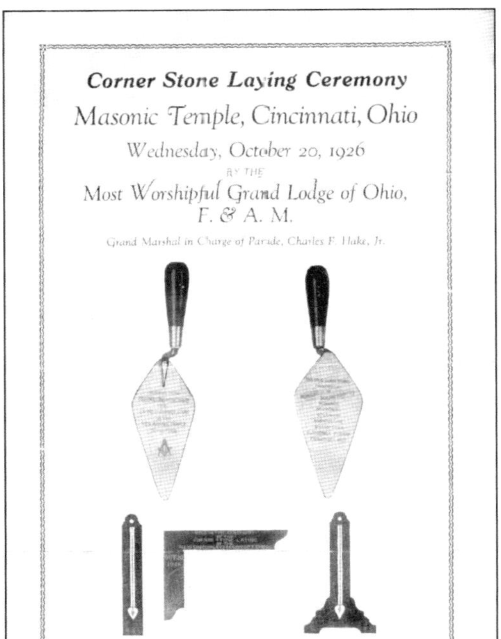

PROGRAM, CORNERSTONE CEREMONY FOR THE CINCINNATI MASONIC TEMPLE, OCTOBER 20, 1926. The Grand Lodge session recessed business at the Gibson Hotel. After lunch, the members marched to the site of the Masonic Temple. Thousands of Masons attended. The tools shown on the program and the shovel used at the ground breaking are in the museum of the Cincinnati Masonic Center. (E.T. Carson Lodge No. 598.)

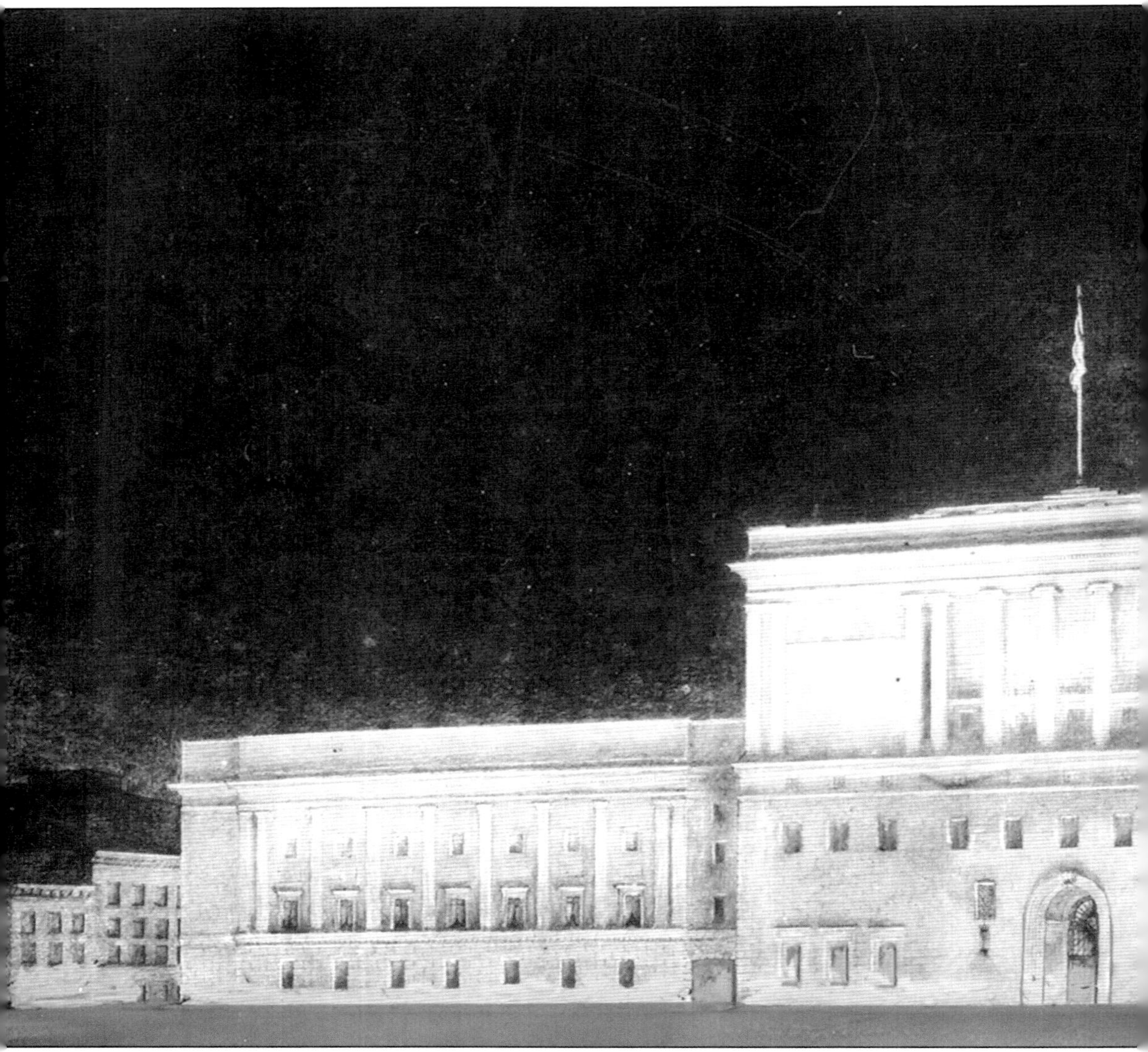

FINAL DESIGN, CINCINNATI MASONIC TEMPLE. The symmetry and mass of the building sweeping from Broadway to Sycamore Street was never realized. Upon completion of the Taft Theatre, Scottish Rite Cathedral, and the temple building, the Temple Company was in debt to the amount

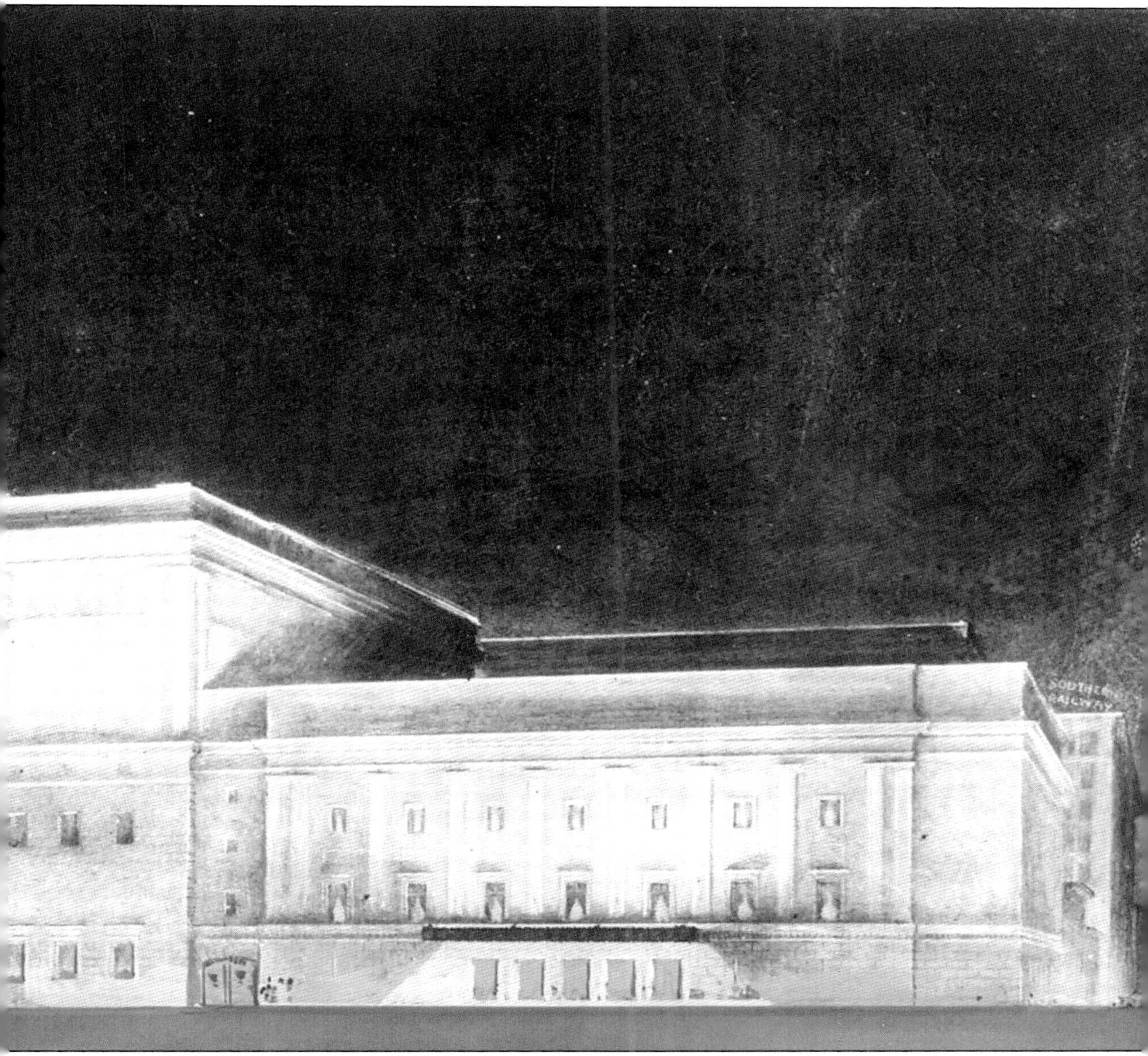

of $400,000. Efforts to cover this deficit, while ultimately successful, combined with the onset of the Great Depression to make the continuation of construction a fiscal impossibility. (AASR.)

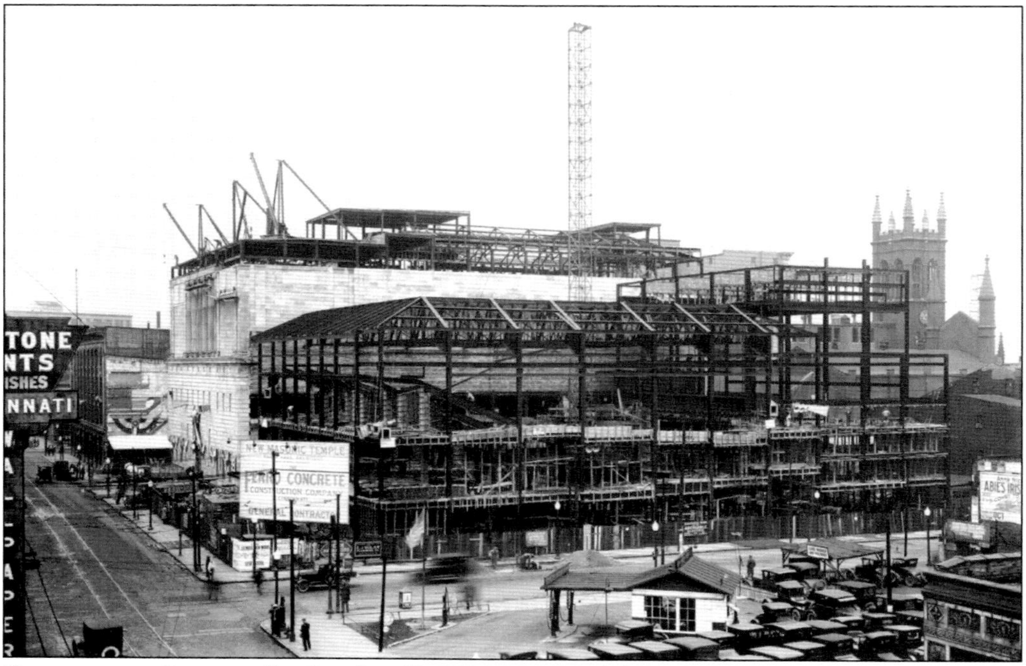

Cornerstone Laying. On October 20, 1926, as part of the 1926 Grand Lodge session, Grand Master Earle Stewart laid the cornerstone of the downtown temple. This photograph was taken at 11:30 a.m., prior to the event. The bunting, visible to the left of the central temple building's northeast corner, indicates the podium and cornerstone's location. The John Van Range Building, to the left of the podium, had yet to be demolished. (AASR.)

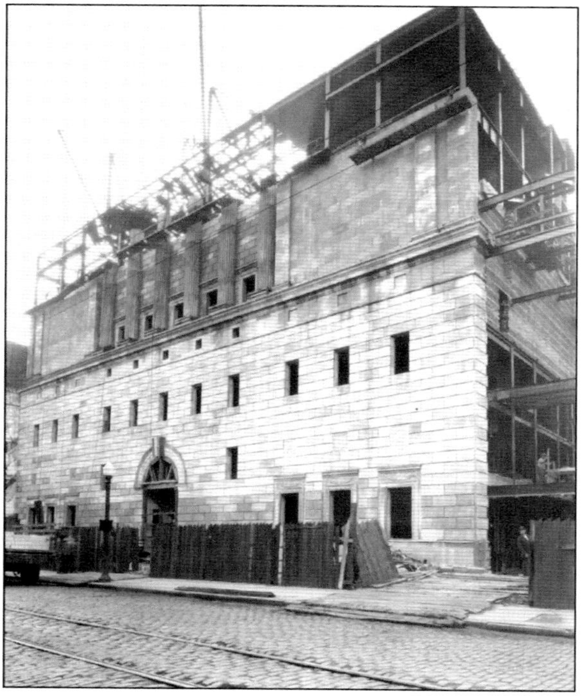

Front of Temple Begins to Take Shape, 1927. The front facade of the temple, seen here during construction, begins to take on the appearance it has today. The row of windows stretching across the entire front of the building indicates the third floor, where the dining rooms are located. (AASR.)

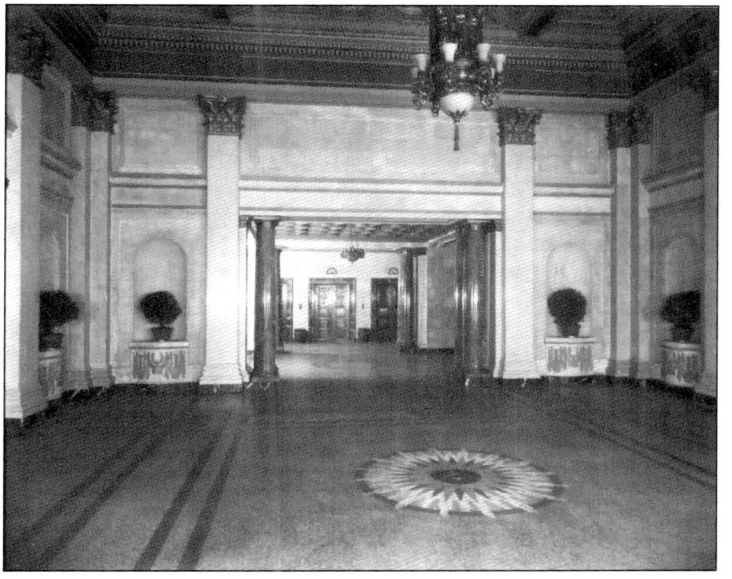

Foyer of the Cincinnati Masonic Temple. The square and compasses disk, which is now mounted above the doorway to the elevators and stairs, was originally imbedded in the floor, as seen here. The elevators, visible beyond the stairwell, were more decorative than the modern ones now installed. (CHS.)

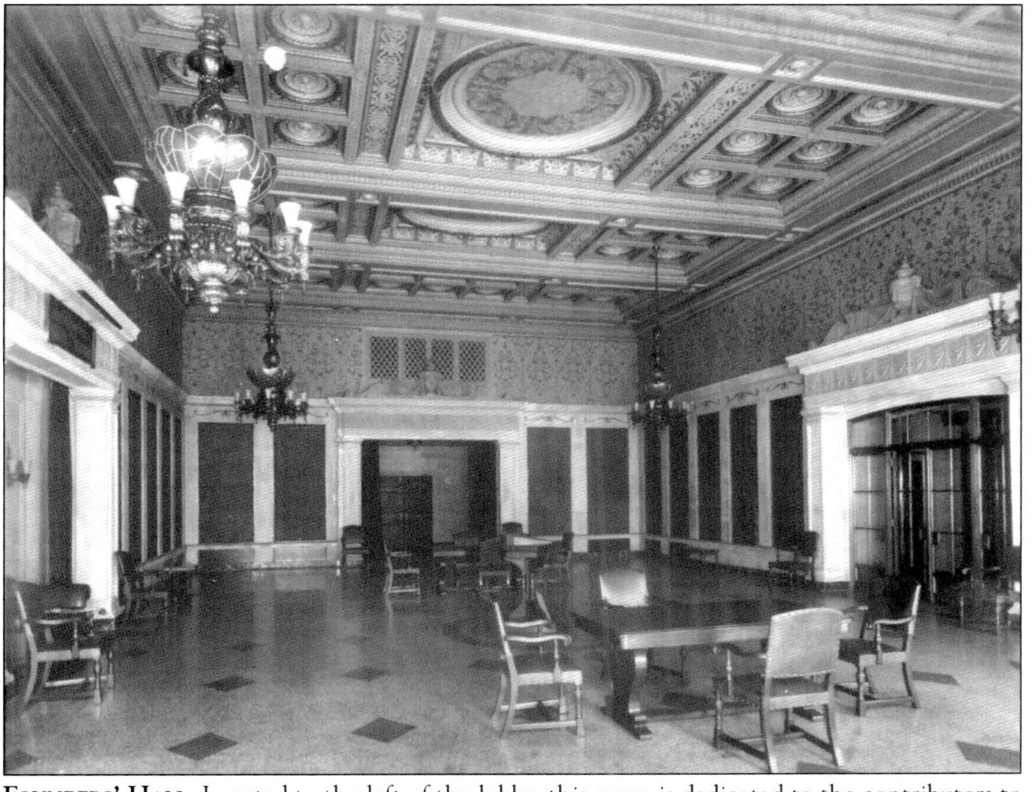

Founders' Hall. Located to the left of the lobby, this room is dedicated to the contributors to the temple's construction. Bronze wall plaques list contributors to the building's construction. Donations were made by members, nonmembers, businesses, and even other fraternal groups, such as the Odd Fellows. The alcove at the left was designed to accommodate a catafalque for funerals. (AASR.)

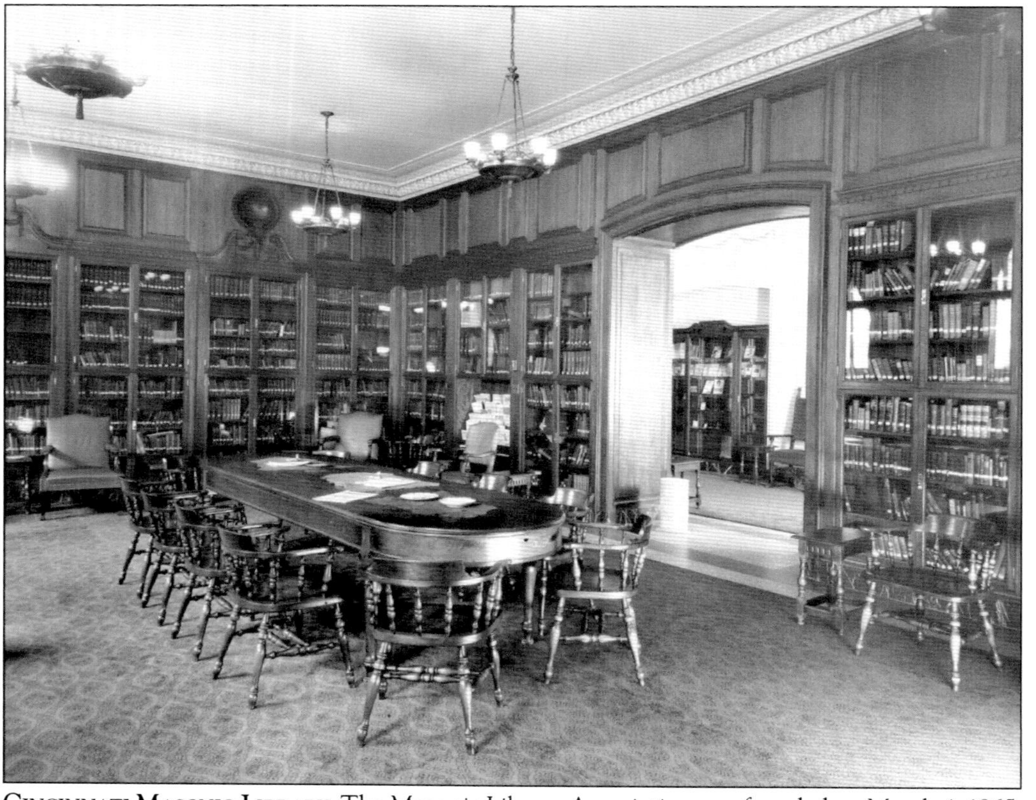

Cincinnati Masonic Library. The Masonic Library Association was founded on March 4, 1865. In 1876, the association purchased the personal Masonic library of Cornelius Moore (see page 50) for $982. Originally, it operated as a subscription library, but it reorganized, making itself the property of all Masons belonging to lodges in Hamilton County. The library is situated to the right of the foyer. (AASR.)

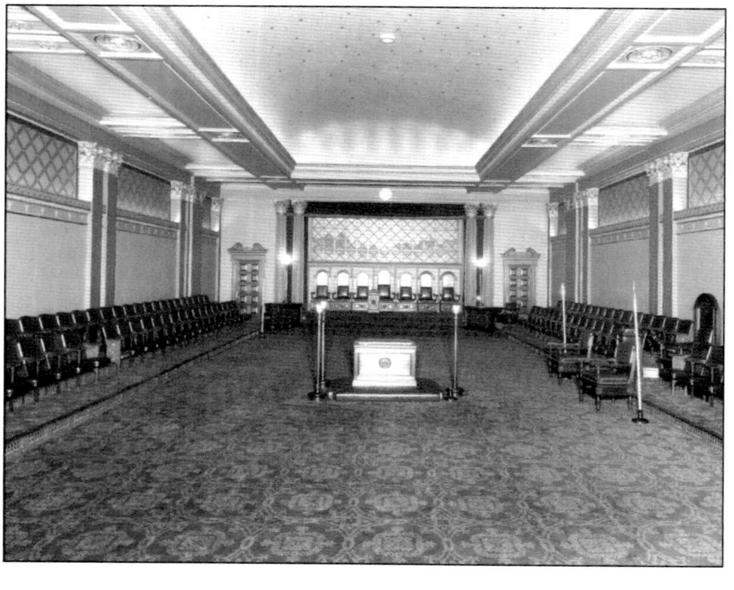

Lodge Room Number One, Looking Symbolically "East." This being the largest lodge room, it is frequently used for larger events. This room features a coved ceiling with stars depicting the "starry decked heavens." The Junior Warden's station is to the right. (AASR.)

FOURTH-FLOOR PLAN. This plan shows the arrangement of the four lodge rooms on the fourth floor. Each of these rooms had a choir loft and stairways leading to the building's fifth floor, where candidate waiting rooms were located. (AASR.)

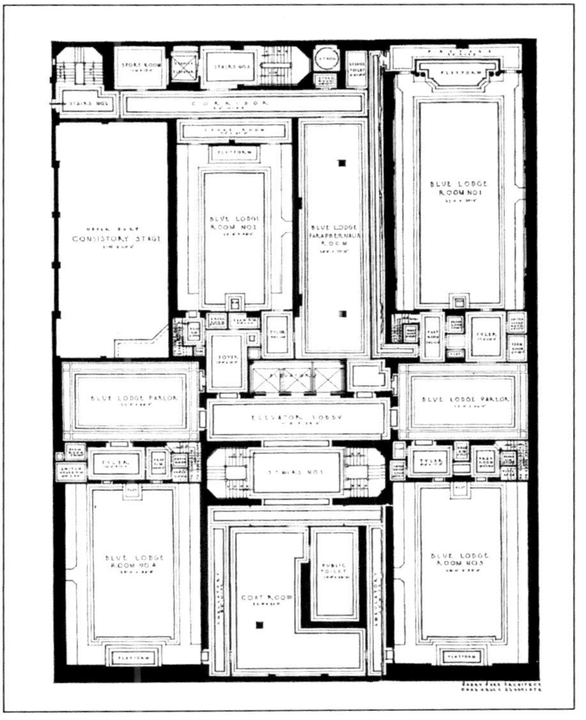

LODGE ROOM TWO. This lodge room, seating up to 158 people, is the only one that retains the original Belgian carpet installed when the building was constructed. (AASR.)

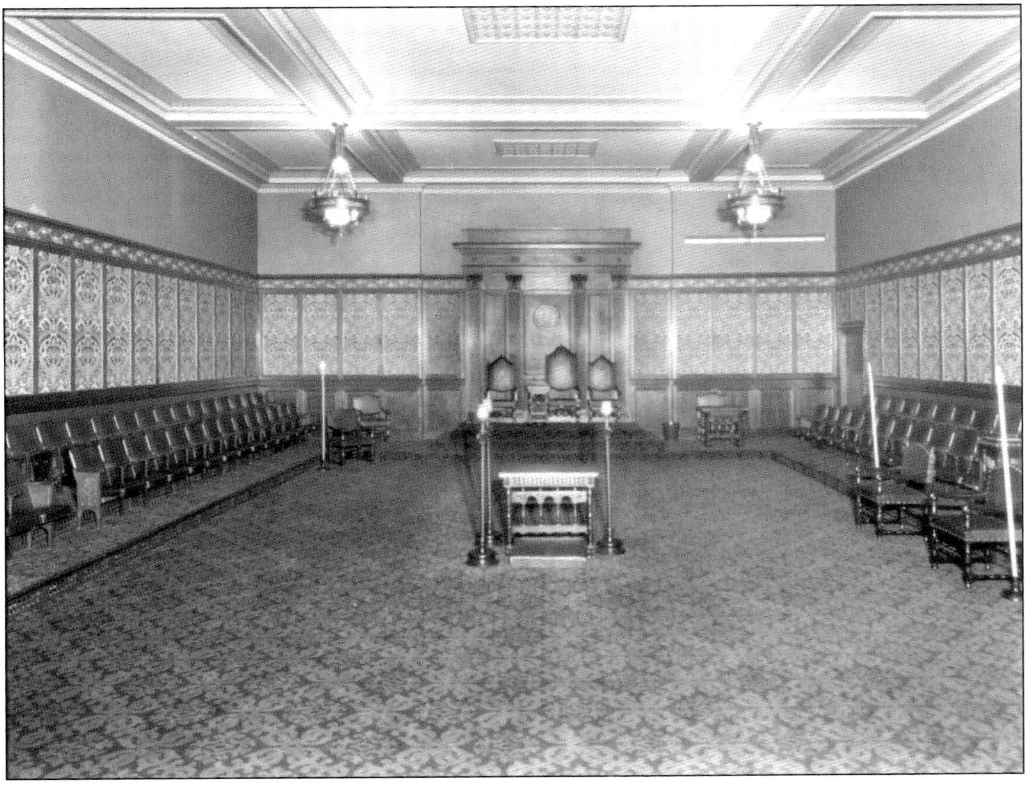

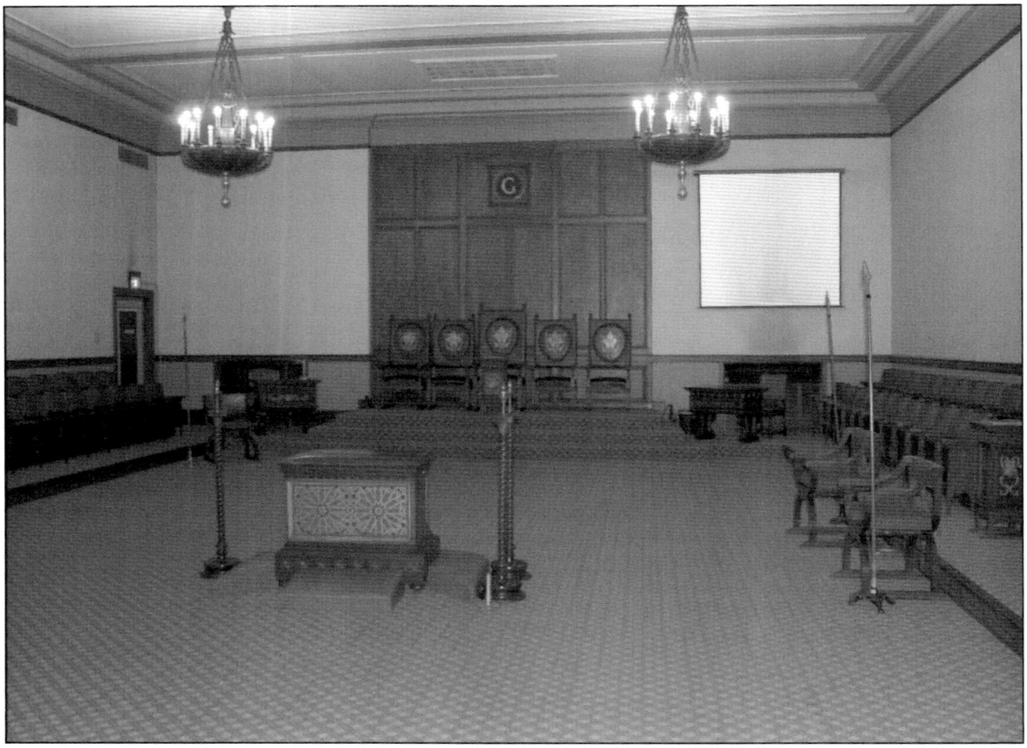

Lodge Room Three. This Blue Lodge room actually is predominantly blue, including the walls, modern carpet, and theater seats. Each ritualistic space in the Masonic Center has a particular character or motif, such as the stenciling seen here on the altar and the officers' chairs. In this manner, each space had a particular look and feel.

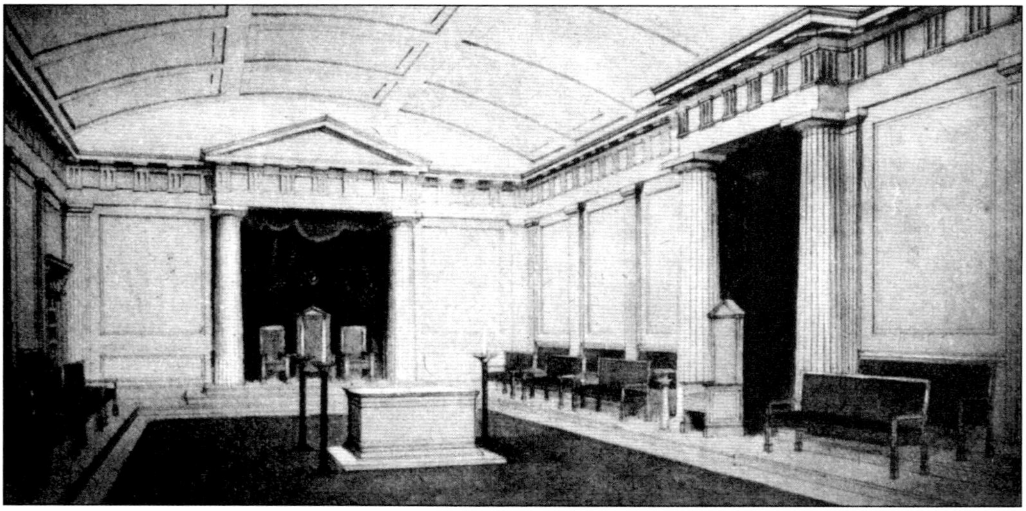

Proposed Lodge Room. This is Hake's proposed design for one of the lodge rooms. Images such as this promoted the 1924 public fundraising campaign for the temple. None of the lodge rooms were built with this design. (AASR.)

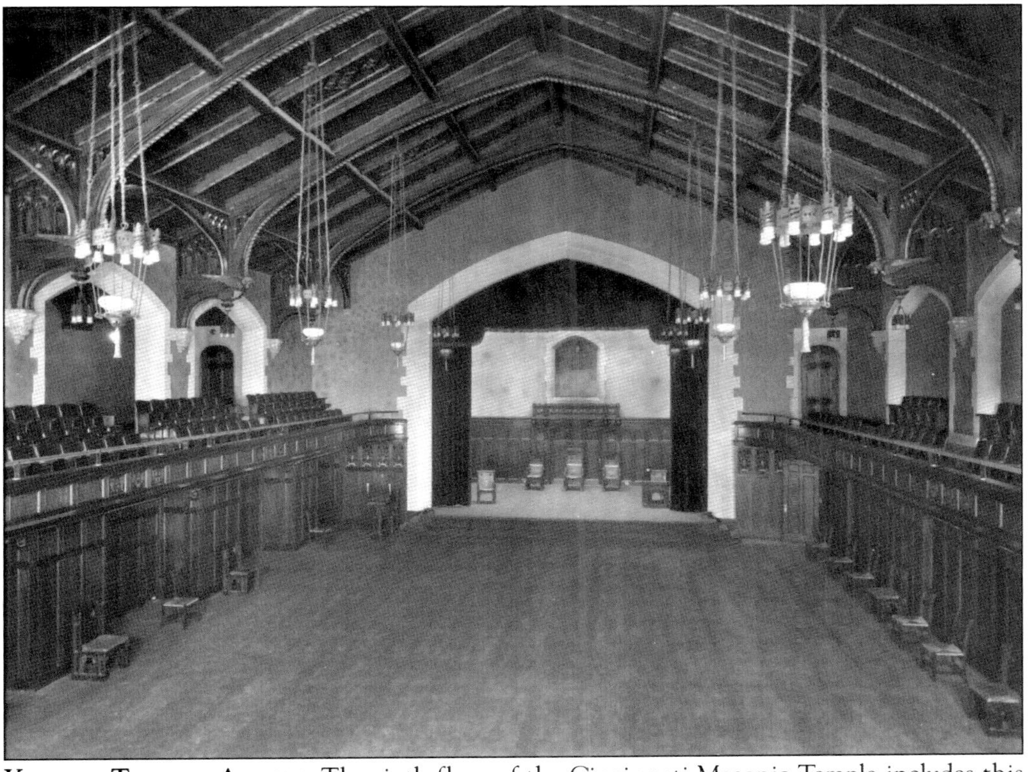

KNIGHTS TEMPLAR ASYLUM. The sixth floor of the Cincinnati Masonic Temple includes this room for the Commandery. The large open floor allows for the drill, which is part of the ritual work of the Knights Templar. The paneled walls and wood-beamed ceilings are visible in this photograph, which faces the presiding officer's dais. (CHS.)

CARSON ROOM. This room is located between the two entrance doors to the Scottish Rite Cathedral facing Broadway, to the right. The Cathedral lobby is to the left. The view seen here is from the wall where the massive portrait of E.T. Carson hangs (see page 108). (AASR.)

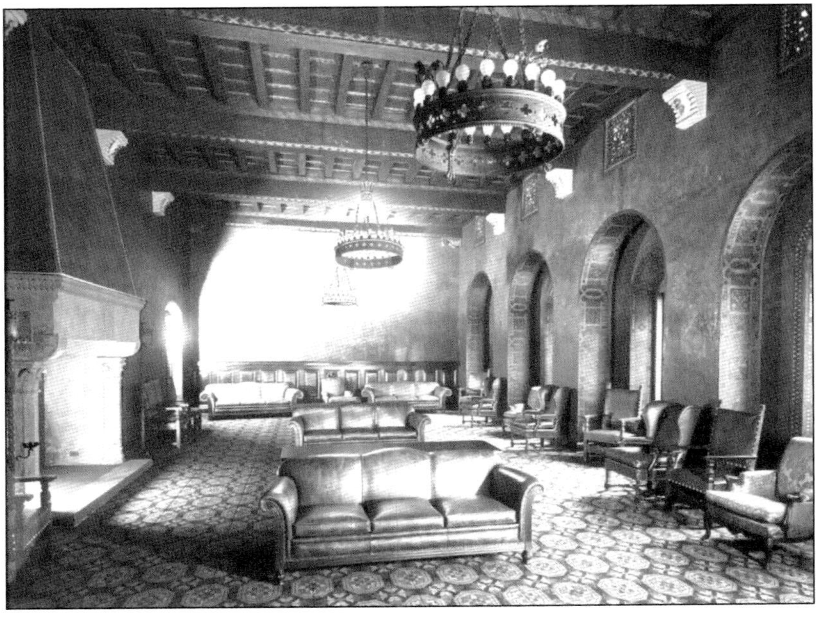

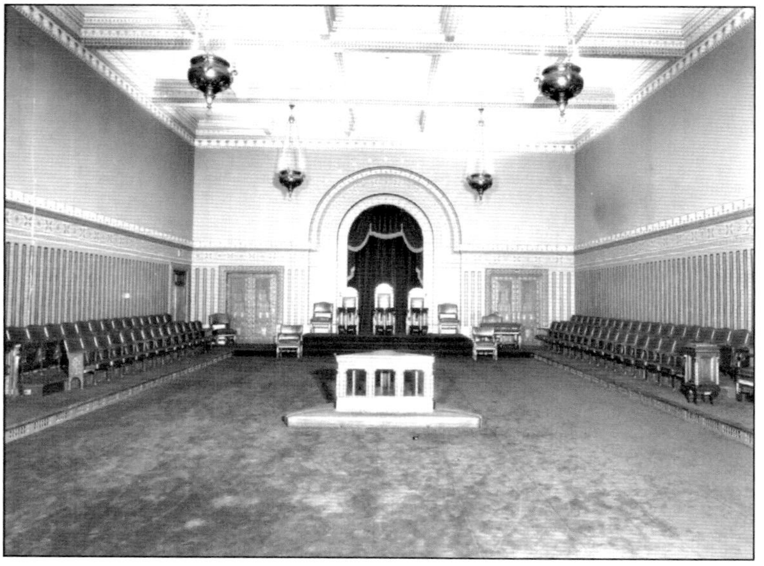

Chapter and Council Room. This large room on the sixth floor was designed as the home for three Royal Arch Chapters and one Council of Royal and Select Masters. The room's design was described as Assyrian. It is the only ritualistic space in the building that is situated east and west, though the symbolic "East" is actually in the geographic west. (AASR.)

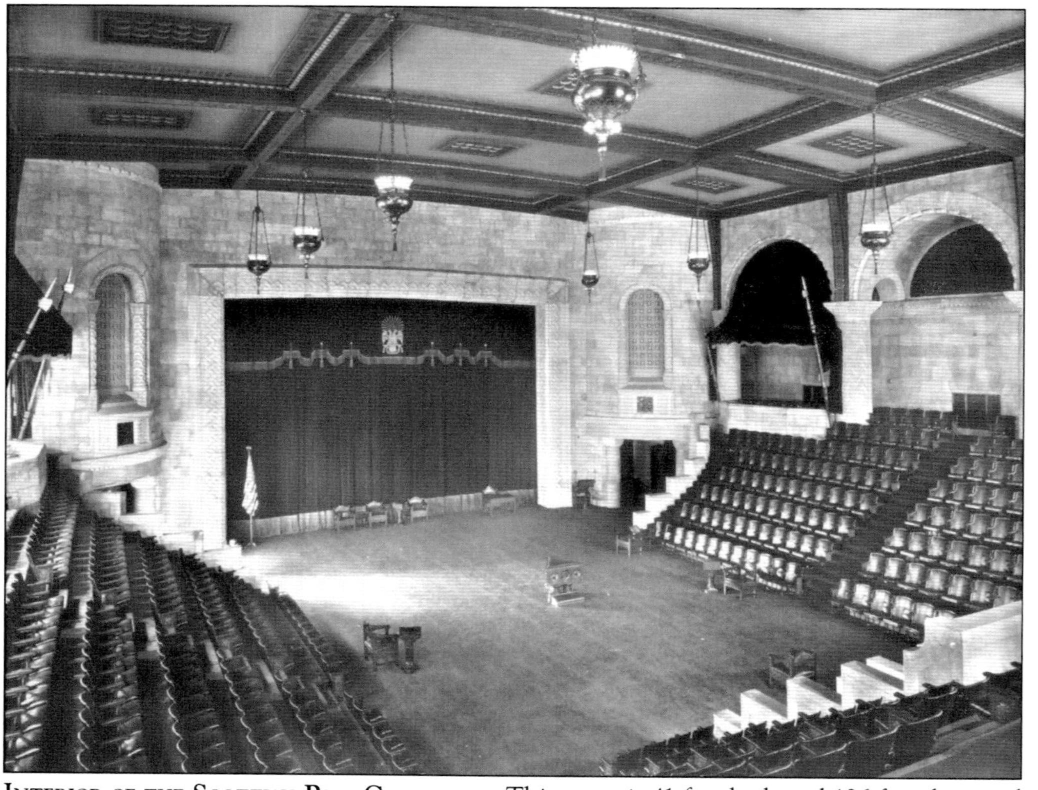

Interior of the Scottish Rite Cathedral. This space is 41 feet high and 106 feet deep and originally contained 872 theater seats. The floor-level stage was selected by the Scottish Rite during the construction phase. (AASR.)

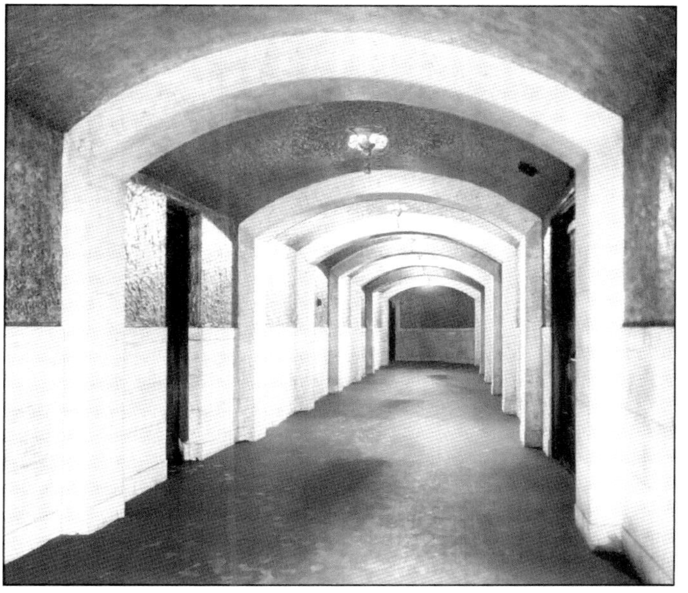

Hallway, Scottish Rite Cathedral. The depth of the auditorium of the cathedral is evident in this narrow passage, which runs along the side of the cathedral. This was designed in part to allow movement of cast members for the dramatic ritual work of the Scottish Rite. (AASR.)

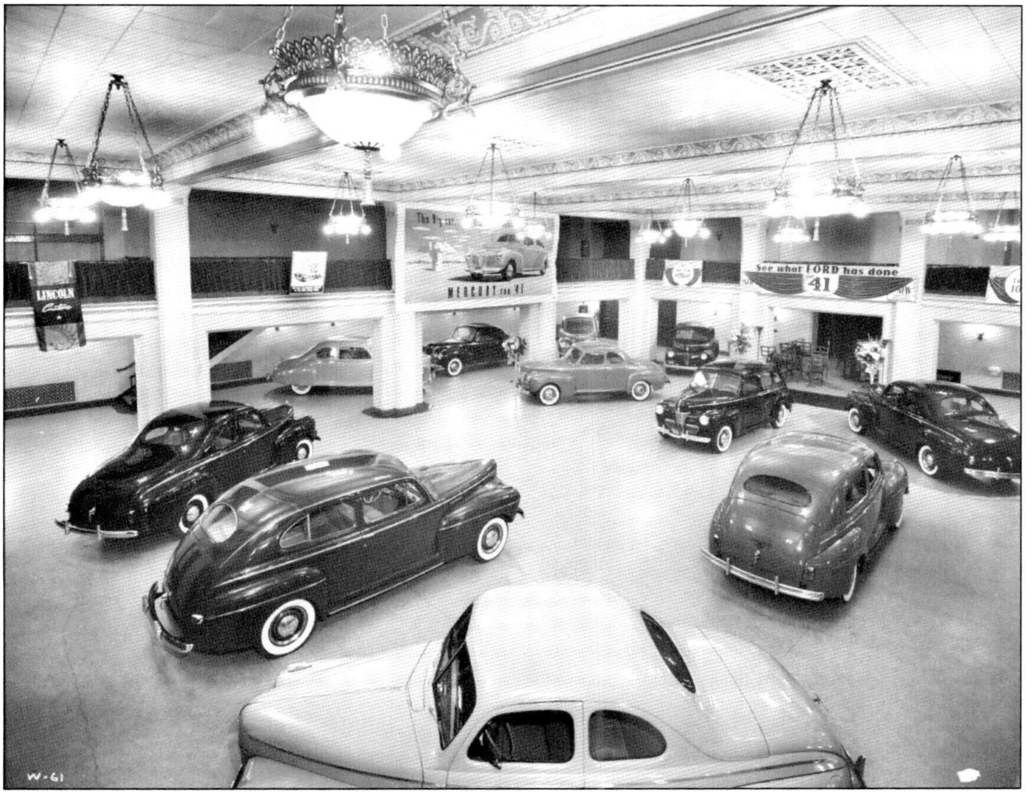

Ford Introduces New Cars in the Scottish Rite Ballroom. The basement of the temple was a frequent venue for both Ford and Chrysler to show off their latest vehicles. The relationship was so longstanding that the sideline seats in one of the lodge rooms were supposedly reupholstered with Chrysler vinyl. (AASR.)

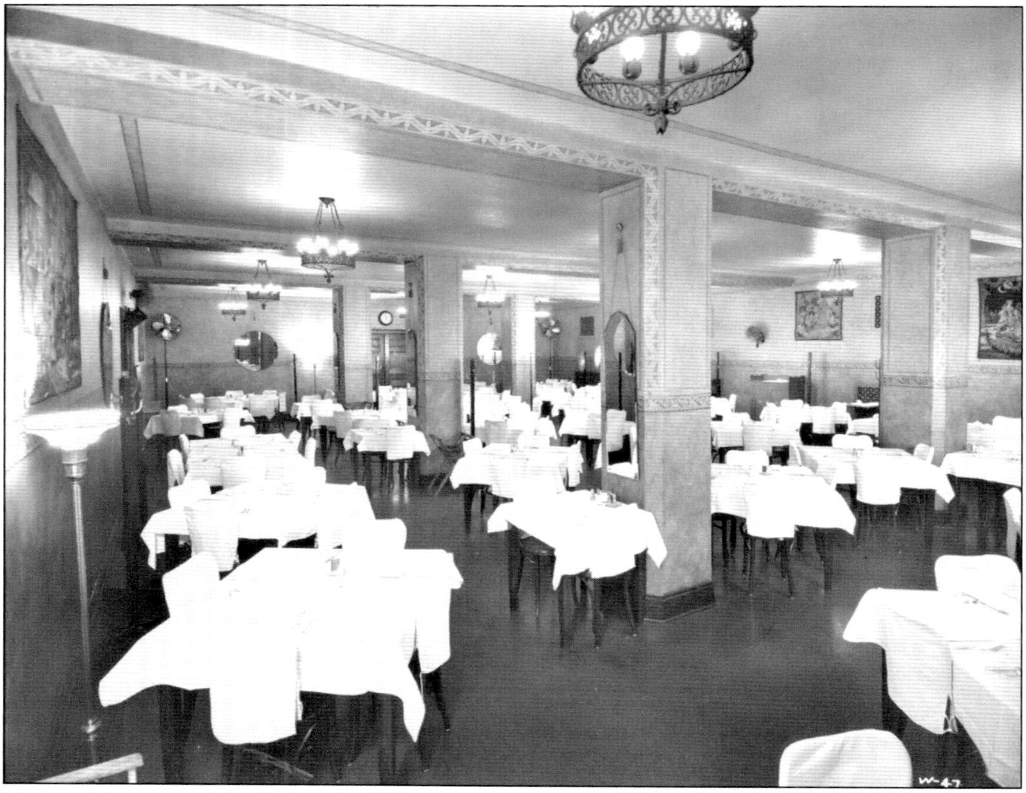

TEMPLE CATERERS. Until the mid-1970s, a restaurant was located on the mezzanine level of the temple, on the Taft Theatre side of the elevators. It was open to the public. Lodge minutes reference the restaurant with notes like, "Retired to mezzanine, after degree, for hamburger sandwiches." An executive dining room was located on the same level. (AASR.)

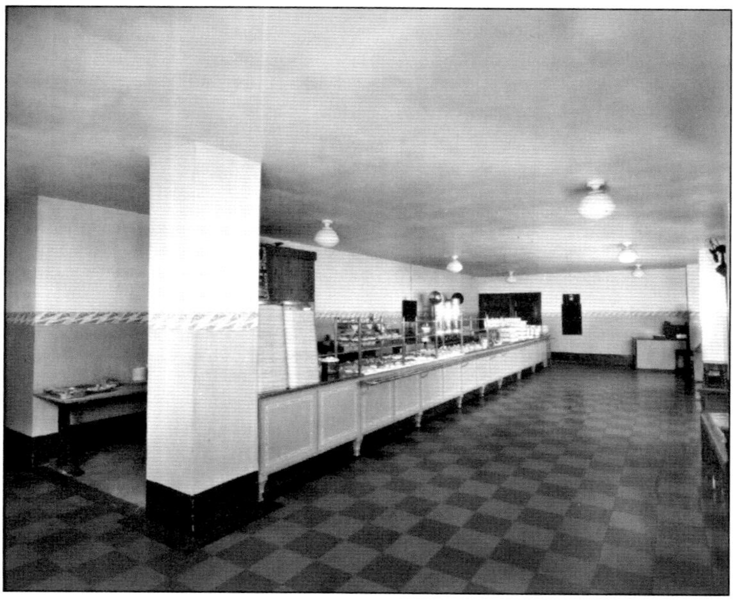

CAFETERIA, CINCINNATI MASONIC TEMPLE. Temple Caterers also ran the cafeteria on the same level. Advertisements indicate that, in the 1930s, the cafeteria served lunch from 11:00 a.m. to 2:00 p.m. Table service was available in the restaurant from 5:00 p.m. to 8:00 p.m. (AASR.)

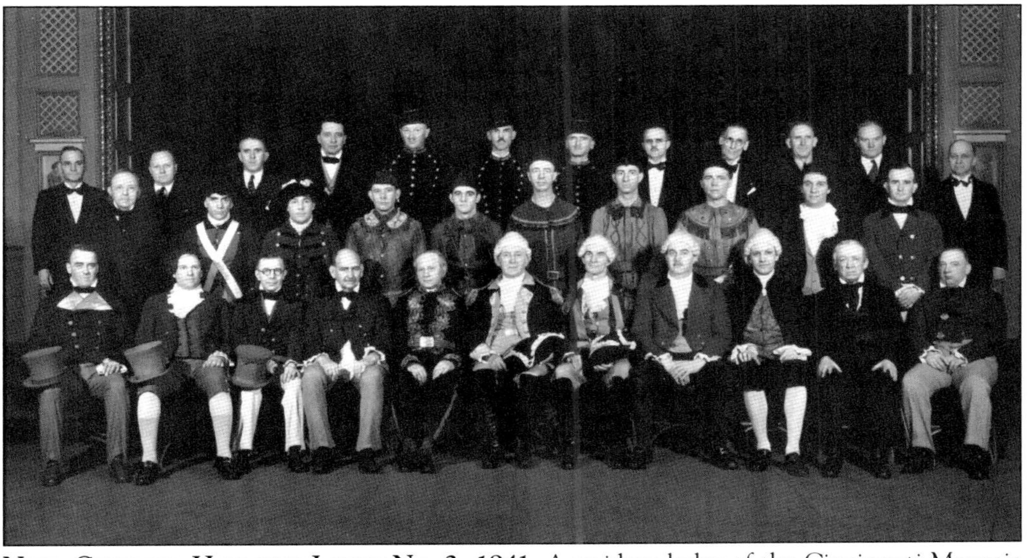

Nova Caesarea Harmony Lodge No. 2, 1941. A resident lodge of the Cincinnati Masonic Temple, the "Old Lodge" celebrated its sesquicentennial with a play consisting of scenes from the lodge's history. Only three members are identified, all of whom are seated in the first row: Walter J. Barker (fourth from left); George Kattenhorn, PM 1902 (sixth from left); and Dennison Duble, PM 1919 (fourth from right). (NCH2.)

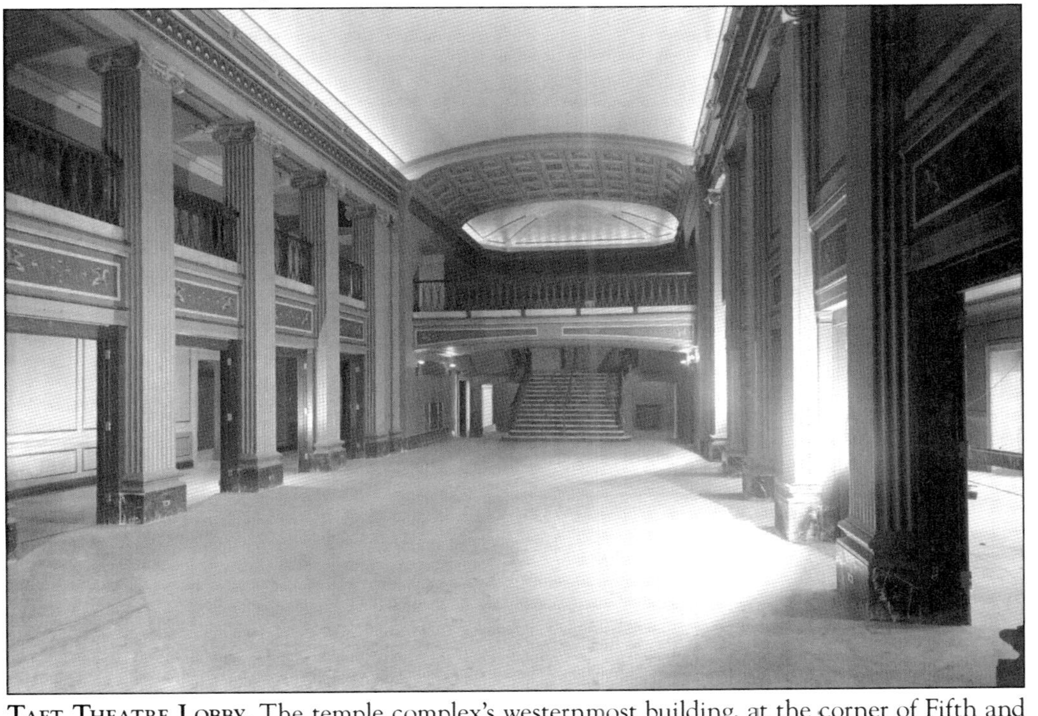

Taft Theatre Lobby. The temple complex's westernmost building, at the corner of Fifth and Sycamore Streets, is the Taft Theatre, named in honor of Charles Phelps Taft. This photograph of the lobby looks toward the Sycamore Street side of the building. The street entrance is to the right, and the auditorium is to the left. (AASR.)

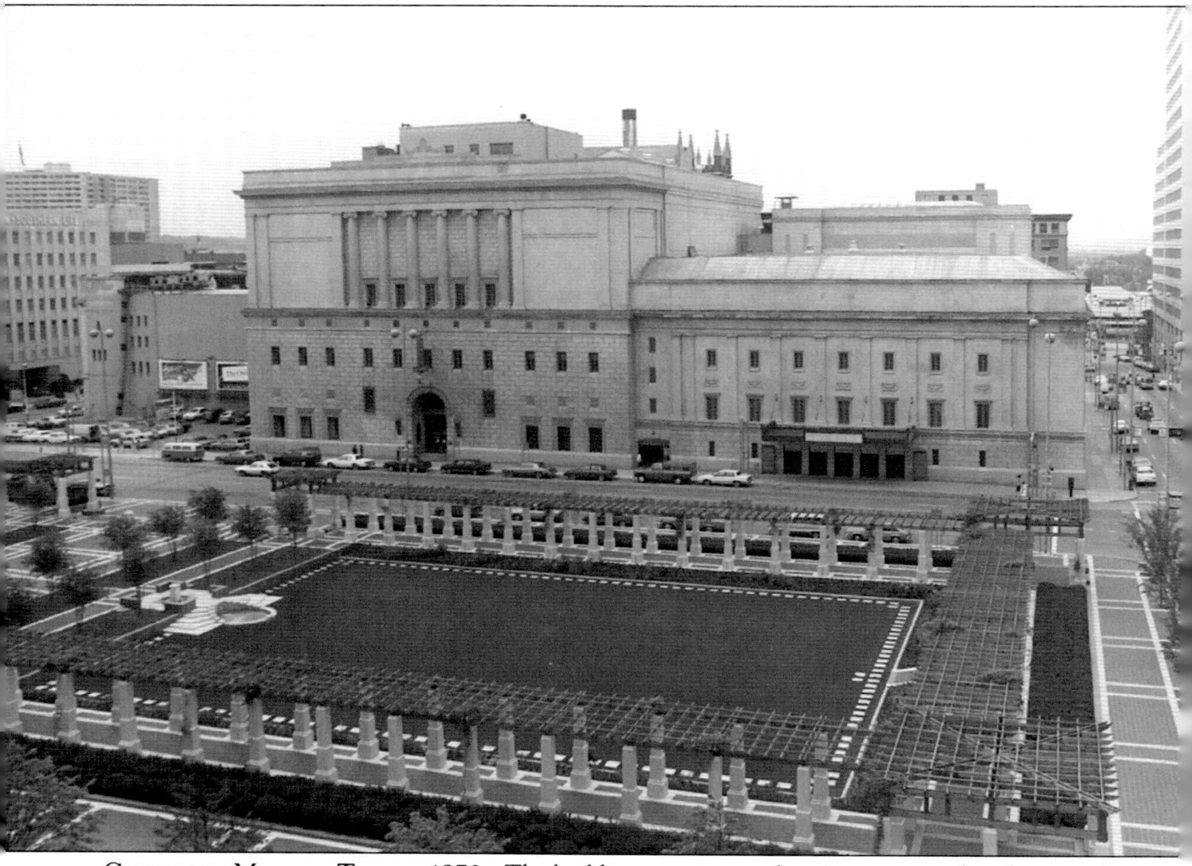

Cincinnati Masonic Temple, 1970s. The building remains much as it appears in this photograph. The Cincinnati Masonic Temple sign above the main entrance has been replaced with the Cincinnati Masonic Center lettering on the face of the building. (AASR.)

Five

Freemasonry around Town

Cincinnati was only one community founded on the Ohio River between the Great and Little Miami Rivers before 1790. Columbia, to the east, was settled a few months before Cincinnati. North Bend, to the west, was settled a few months after. Cincinnati became the most important of the three after the Army chose to build Fort Washington there. Even with the fort, settlement was slow until after the Treaty of Greenville, which ended the Northwest Indian War in 1795. After that, the population grew and moved farther out from the city center.

By 1800, Cincinnati's population was about 850. By 1840, it was 50 times that number. The city headed out of the basin, up the surrounding hills. With the city's growth in population and physical expansion, Cincinnatians created neighborhoods and suburbs and, within them, lodges. The second lodge in Hamilton County was Columbia Lodge No. 44, formed at Miamitown to the west of Cincinnati on the Great Miami River in 1817.

By 1900, seventeen lodges under the Grand Lodge existed in Cincinnati and its Ohio suburbs. That number increased to 30 by 1923. In the same year, 10 African American lodges were listed in the city directory. Many lodges built their own temples or rented space. A number of the temples built before 1930 were designed by Cincinnati architectural powerhouses Harry Hake and Samuel Hannaford & Sons.

Even into the 1960s, buildings with character, like the modernist Oakley Temple, were being erected. Late-20th-century fraternal buildings have tended to be more utilitarian. Single-story buildings more easily accommodate an aging membership, permit easier exterior maintenance, and tend to be less expensive to build.

Lodges have come and gone. Some Masonic temples have been converted to other purposes. As an example, at the time of this writing, negotiations were under way for the Price Hill Masonic Temple to be acquired by a neighborhood social service agency.

This chapter contains images of representative lodge buildings and people, telling part of the story of the Freemasonry around Cincinnati.

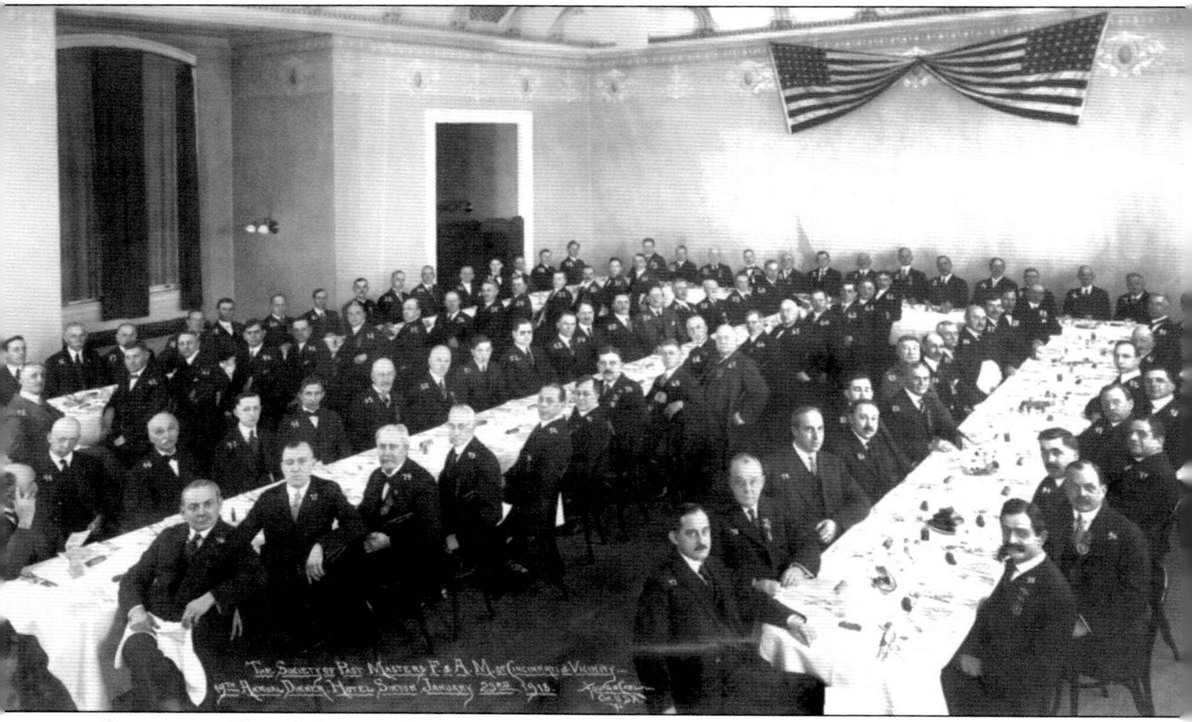

Society of Past Masters Dinner, 1918. The annual dinner meeting of the Society of Past Masters of Cincinnati & Vicinity was held on January 23, 1918, at the downtown Hotel Sinton. An accompanying legend identifies each man in the photograph by number. The head table is numbered, from left to right, 13, 12, 11, 10, 9, 8, 1, 2, 3, 4, 5, 6, 7. The men at the three parallel tables are numbered from left to right on the far side of the table and right to left on the near side. Numbering for 97–102 (far right), is treated as an additional row running from left to right, or front to back. No. 14 is out of frame to the far left and 101 (far right) is mostly obscured. (Yeatman–Mt. Washington Lodge No. 162.)

1 John Sauer, Pres. SPM, Linwood Lodge No. 567
2 James N. Ramsey, Secy. SPM Lafayette Lodge No. 81
3 Hon. Joel C. Clore, PGM, Lafayette Lodge No. 81
4 Hon. Jacob H. Bromwell, Grand Secy. Wyoming Lodge No. 186
5 Alfred E. Reinauer, Past Pres. SPM, Kilwinning Lodge No. 356
6 Henry B. Michie, Treas. SPM, Vattier Lodge No. 386
7 Dr. Thomas M. Stewart, Past Pres. SPM, Avon Lodge No. 542
8 Rev. Ernest C. Wareing, DD., Chaplain, E.T. Carson Lodge No. 598, "Guest Of Honor"
9 John Nicholas Soetje, Past Pres. SPM, Vattier Lodge No. 386
10 Arthur R. Morris, Past Pres. SPM, Cheviot Lodge No. 140
11 Joseph W. Kahler, Past Pres. SPM, Lafayette Lodge No. 81
12 John H. Dickerson, Vice Pres. SPM, Queen City Lodge No. 559
13 William J. Howard, Past Pres. SPM, Excelsior Lodge No. 369
14 Stephan J. Hauser, College Hill Lodge No. 641
15 Edw. B. Reemelin, Cheviot Lodge No. 140
16 Hon. John G. O'Connell, Yeatman Lodge No. 162
17 August Vos, Lafayette Lodge No. 81
18 Clarence L. Herzer, Parkland Lodge No. 638
19 John Venn, Samuel Reed Lodge No. 478
20 Herman A. Roehr, Enoch T. Carson Lodge No. 598
21 Howard L. Bevis, McMakin Lodge No. 120
22 Dan Williams, Linwood Lodge No. 567
23 Walter F. J. Walker, High Noon Lodge No. 635
24 Frederick W. Schaefer, Lafayette Lodge No. 81

25 John A. Meyer, Excelsior Lodge No. 369
26 Chas. F. Kleine, Excelsior Lodge No. 369
27 Ottis M. Miller, Excelsior Lodge No. 369
28 C.O. Rose, Excelsior Lodge No. 369
29 Edw. H. Beiderwelle, Excelsior Lodge No. 369
30 Wm. E. Teklenburg, Price Hill Lodge No. 524
31 Carl G. Buchanan, Price Hill Lodge No. 524
32 Frank J. Rewwer, Cynthia Lodge No. 155
33 William B. Hall, Amelia Lodge No. 590
34 Chas. L. Judd, Winton Lodge No. 614
35 Owen A. Witham, Winton Lodge No. 614
36 William R. Suhre, Cheviot Lodge No. 140
37 Lester Blair, NC Harmony Lodge No. 2
38 Harry J. Plogstedt, Norwood Lodge No. 576
39 Edward H.L. Haefner, Hanselmann Lodge No. 208
40 John W. Cowell, Columbia Lodge No. 44
41 Edward G. Schultz, North Bend Lodge No. 346
42 John H. Louis, Linwood Lodge No. 567
43 Frank J. Zumstein, High Noon Lodge No. 635
44 Pierce J. Cadwalader, McMillan Lodge No. 141
45 W.A. Sorin, Walnut Hills Lodge No. 483
46 Ernst Troy, Hanselmann Lodge No. 208
47 W.A. Schulenberg, *Commercial Tribune* Reporter, Robert Burns Lodge No. 163, Newport
48 Frank Krinn, Robert Burns Lodge No. 163
49 Wm. A. Gregg, Vattier Lodge No. 386
50 Chas. G. Brooks, McMillan Lodge No. 141
51 Henry J. Sachs, Cincinnati Lodge No. 133
52 John R. Lewis, Cincinnati Lodge No. 133
53 Fred Opelt, Miami Lodge No. 46
54 Frederick J. Brunner, Vattier Lodge No. 386
55 Geo. W. Piehl, Richmond Lodge No. 196
56 John Q. Martin, Aberdeen Lodge No. 149
57 Wm. H.W. Roberts, McMillan Lodge No. 141
58 Joseph Hart, McMillan Lodge No. 141
59 Harry S. Johnson, Vice Pres. SPM, Hoffner Lodge No. 253
60 Samuel W. Barnett, Golden Rule Lodge No. 345
61 John W. Chambers, Monitor Lodge No. 445
62 Charles W. Hauck, McMillan Lodge No. 141
63 Horace A. Chipman, Monitor Lodge No. 445
64 Edward Zind, Monitor Lodge No. 445
65 Dr. T.V. Fitzpatrick, Norwood Lodge No. 576
66 Rev. J.H. Locke, Hoffner Lodge No. 253
67 Chas. H. Dater, Hoffner Lodge No. 253
68 Prof. W.S. Cadman, Norwood Lodge No. 576
69 Dr. J.B. Kersey, Carthage Lodge No. 573
70 Harry A. Phillips, Carthage Lodge No. 573
71 Edward G. Anschutz, McMillan Lodge No. 141
72 Wm. F. Anschutz, McMillan Lodge No. 141
73 Thomas Bell, Norwood Lodge No. 576
74 Edward F. Witthoff, Vattier Lodge No. 386
75 Geo. R. Walter, Pleasant Ridge Lodge No. 282
76 Arthur J. Davies, Cheviot Lodge No. 140
77 Oscar Euphrat, Lafayette Lodge No. 81
78 Geo. W. Blum, Lafayette Lodge No. 81
79 Prof. Frank E. Elliott, Madisonville Lodge No. 419
80 George W. Tuxworth, Linwood Lodge No. 567
81 W.B. Kincaid, Martins Station Lodge No. 188
82 Albert J. Hauser, E.T. Carson Lodge No. 598
83 John W. Morgan, E.T. Carson Lodge No. 598
84 Robert L. Stokes Jr., E.T. Carson Lodge No. 598
85 J. Henry Denghausen, Cheviot Lodge No. 140
86 Paul Hi Koehne, Cheviot Lodge No. 140
87 Clinton D. Garrison, North Bend Lodge No. 346
88 Edward H. Morgan, Avon Lodge No. 542
89 Joseph T. Harrison Kilwinning Lodge No. 356
90 William A. Greaves, Hyde Park Lodge No. 589
91 Willie H. Dille, Thacher Lodge No. 439
92 Leonard Garver Jr , Linwood Lodge No. 567
93 Wm. V. Althaus, Columbia Lodge No. 44
94 Wm. B. Barr, Linwood Lodge No. 567
95 Charles J. Koelblin, Kilwinning Lodge No. 356
96 William Fred Landwehr, Kilwinning Lodge No. 356
97 Gustav R. Werner, Hanselmann Lodge No. 208
98 Banning Hopping, Columbia Lodge No. 44
99 Hon. Fred L. Hoffman, Linwood Lodge No. 567
100 David E. Griffith, Yeatman Lodge No. 162
101 Chas. A. Stevens, Hyde Park Lodge No. 589
102 Arthur L. Behymer, Yeatman Lodge No. 162

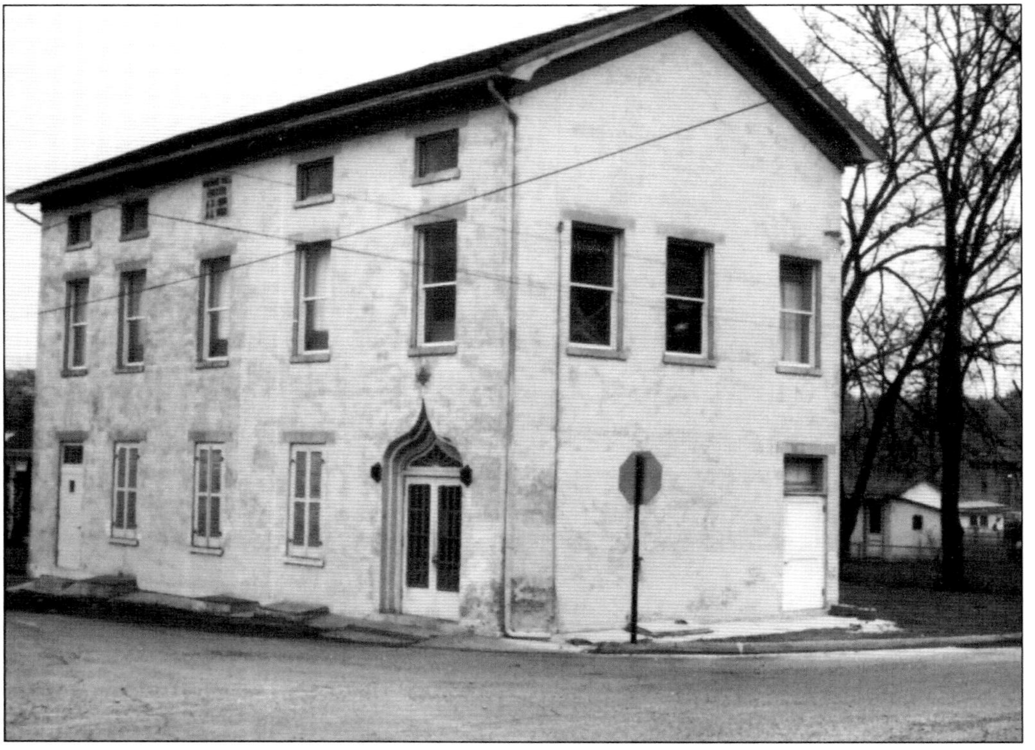

OLDEST MASONIC BUILDING IN USE IN HAMILTON COUNTY. The cornerstone of Columbia Lodge's building was laid on June 24, 1850, and the first meeting was held here on the same day in 1853. An addition, more than doubling the temple's size, was built in 1983–1984. (Columbia Lodge No. 44.)

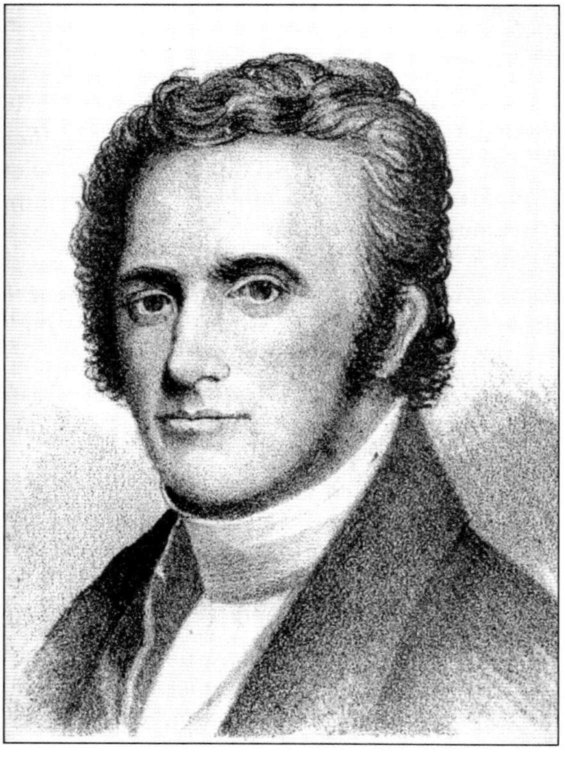

OTHNIEL LOOKER, COLUMBIA LODGE NO. 44'S FIRST MASTER. Looker (1757–1845), a New Jersey native, was awarded a land grant west of Cincinnati for his service in the American Revolution. He served as speaker of the Ohio General Assembly. When Gov. Return J. Meigs Jr. left office to become postmaster general of the United States, Looker became Ohio's fifth governor. This image from *The History of the State of Ohio: From the Discovery of the Great Valley, to the Present Time* resembles the portrait in the lodge's possession.

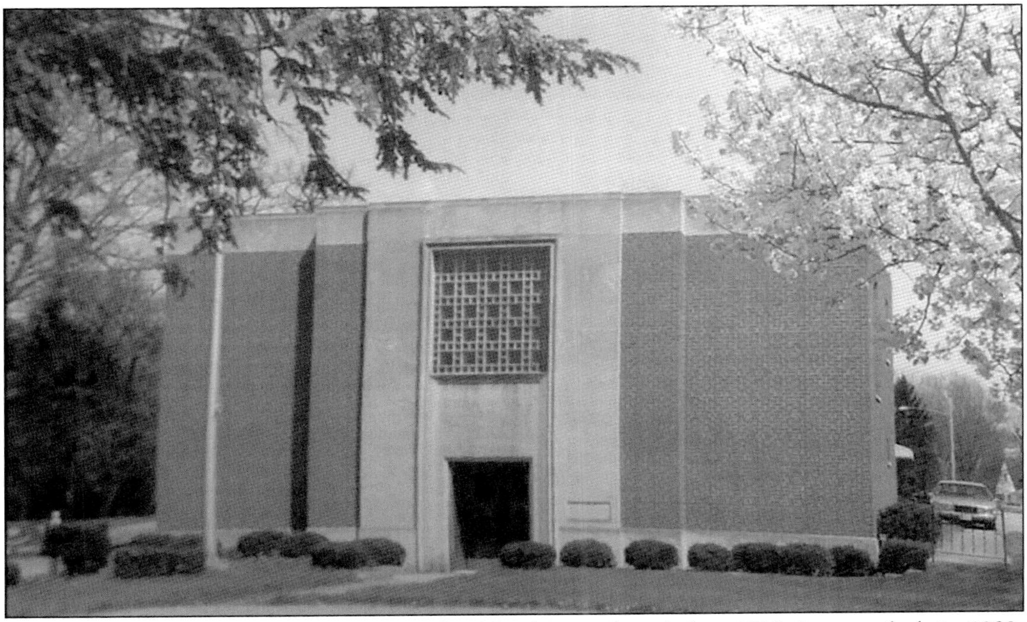

Montgomery Temple. Montgomery Lodge No. 94 was founded in 1827. It went dark in 1832, but was resurrected with its old number in 1846. Grand Lodge had sold the officers' jewels and reimbursed the lodge for them when it reopened. This building, designed as two stories, was initially finished as only one floor in 1937 due to limited funds. The second story was added in 1961. (Montgomery Lodge No. 94.)

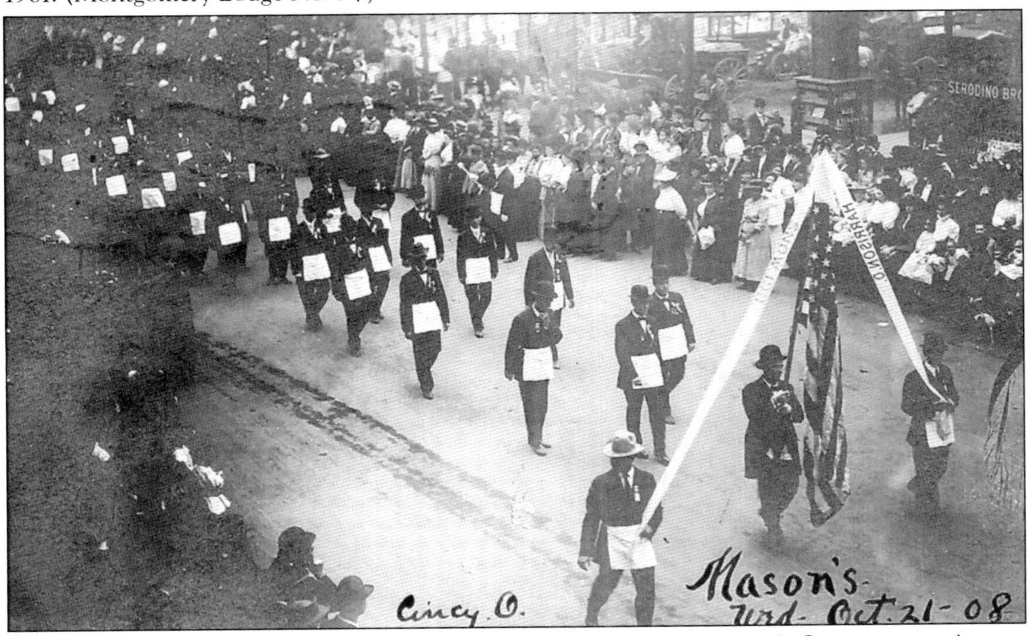

Snow Lodge No. 193 of Harrison, Ohio, Celebrates Ohio Masonry's Centennial. As part of the 100th anniversary session of the Grand Lodge of Ohio, thousands of Masons from all over Ohio marched through the streets of Cincinnati to Music Hall. This photograph was taken near Fountain Square on October 20, 1908. (cincinnativiews.net.)

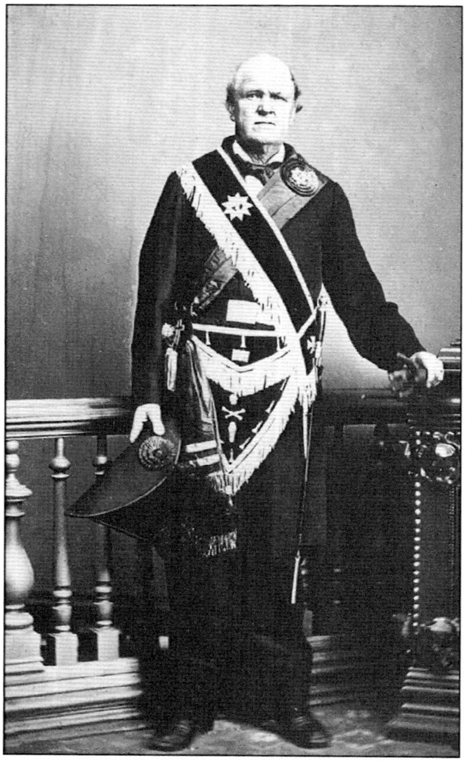

GEN. JOHN MCMAKIN. Born in England, McMakin (1804–1879) came to the United States as a child, arriving in Cincinnati in 1810. After unsuccessful attempts at farming, McMakin and his father opened a tavern in Camp Washington. He later opened a dry-goods store in Cumminsville (now Northside), in which Hoffner Lodge met at one time. In 1838, McMakin was chosen as brigadier general of the 1st Division of the Ohio Militia, an office he held for 20 years. (AASR.)

MCMAKIN TEMPLE. John McMakin was initiated into Marion Lodge No. 120 in 1849. He was held in such high esteem by its members that the lodge's name was changed to McMakin Lodge during his lifetime. An active brother, he was the first Mason admitted into the Scottish Rite after its establishment in Cincinnati in 1853. This temple is located on Hamilton Avenue in North College Hill.

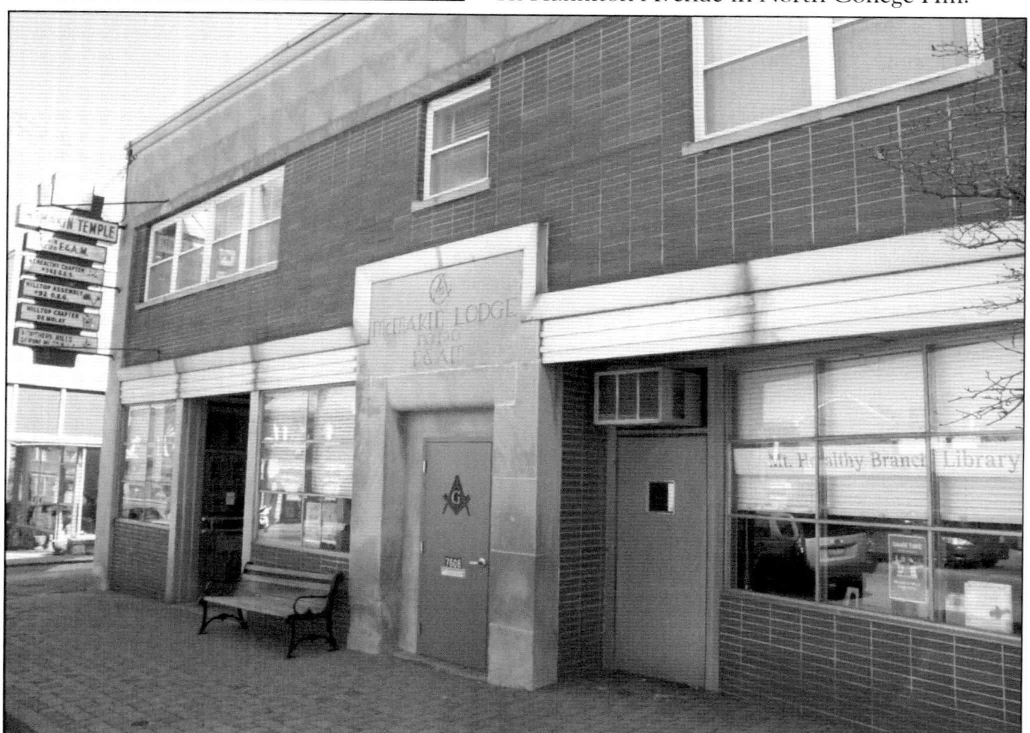

Masonic Temple, Westwood. This temple, completed in 1902, was the home of Cheviot Lodge No. 140, founded in 1846. In 1848, the lodge created a semipermanent home when it agreed to construct a third floor to a private residence at Cheviot and Gamble Streets. The building shown here, at Harrison and Montclair Avenues in Westwood, was designed by Samuel Hannaford & Sons. Cheviot Lodge and Western Hills Lodge consolidated in 2003. (Public Library of Cincinnati and Hamilton County.)

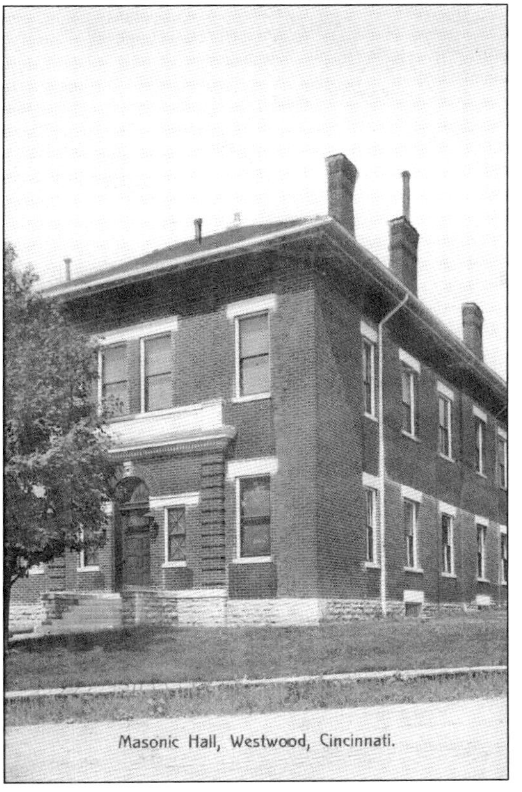

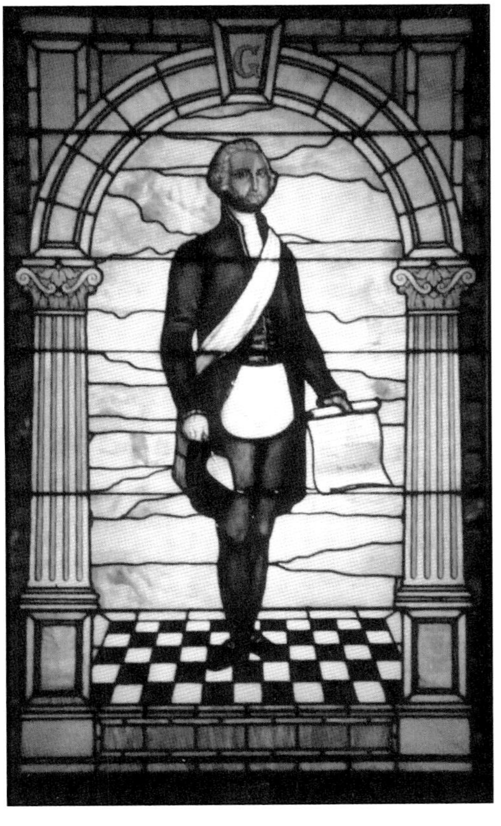

George Washington Window. The first Grand Lodge of Freemasons was formed by four London lodges wishing to celebrate together the feasts of Masonry's patron saints, St. John the Baptist and St. John the Evangelist. Images of the first US president, dressed in Masonic regalia, appear so frequently in American Masonic temples that Washington may appear to be the fraternity's patron saint. This stained-glass window was a feature of Yeatman Lodge's temple. (Yeatman–Mt. Washington Lodge No. 162.)

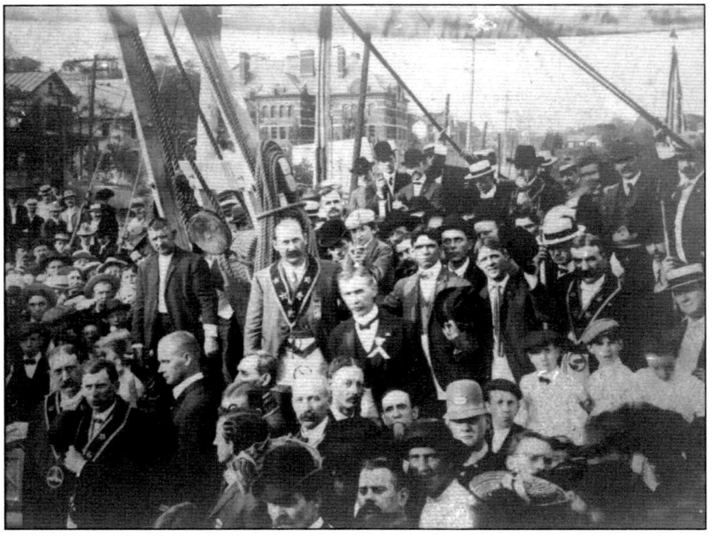

Cornerstone Laying of Yeatman Temple, September 4, 1904. The Grand Lodge and lodge officers are seen here preparing to lay the cornerstone. Worshipful Master John O'Connell is at center, wearing an inverted square on his lapel. Grand Lodge officers are wearing collars with stars. The Lincoln School on Delta Avenue can be seen in the background. (Yeatman–Mt. Washington Lodge No. 162.)

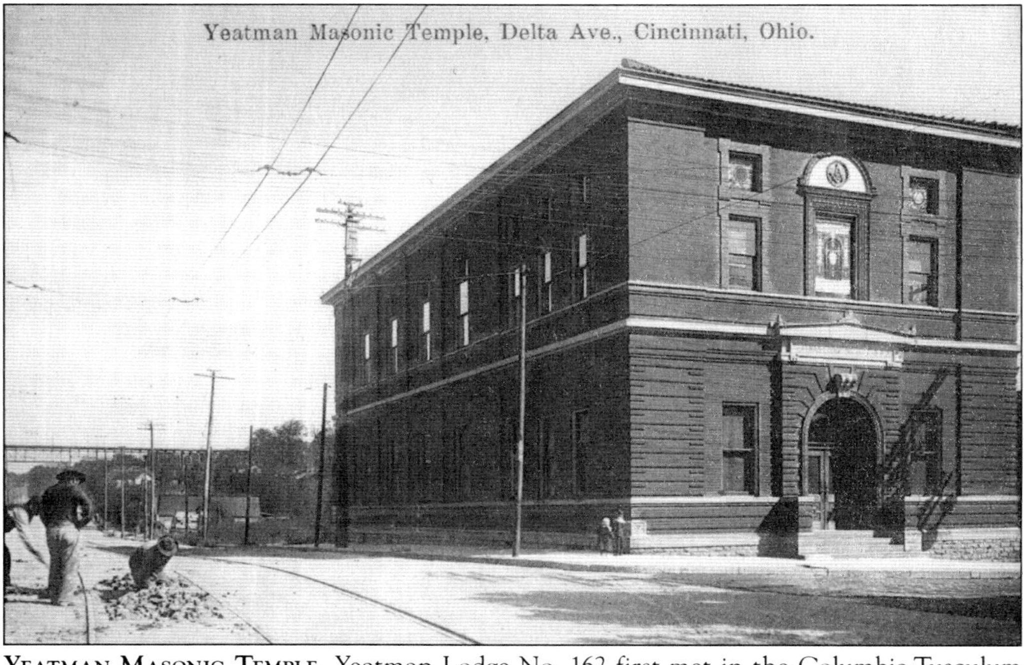

Yeatman Masonic Temple. Yeatman Lodge No. 162 first met in the Columbia-Tusculum Temperance Hall on Wooster Pike (now Eastern Avenue) in 1848. After meeting in at least two other locations, in the early 1900s, the lodge decided to build this temple, designed by Hannaford & Sons, at Delta Avenue and Columbia Parkway. The lodge left this building to consolidate with Mt. Washington Lodge No. 642 in 1994. (Public Library of Cincinnati and Hamilton County.)

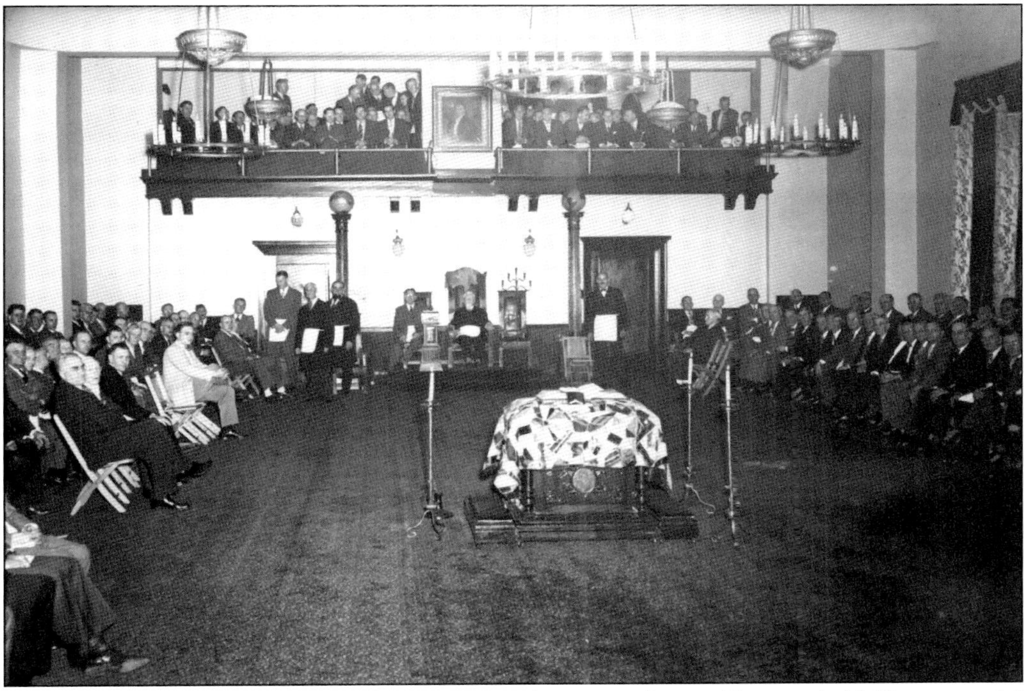

Old-Timers' Night, Yeatman Centennial. An event during Yeatman's 1948 centennial celebration was a costumed affair, with lodge members presenting their version of the world 100 years earlier. This photograph looks to the Senior Warden's station. The portrait of Griffin Yeatman, the lodge's namesake, is visible in the middle of the loft. Brothers in frock coats and long beards, atypical fashion in 1948 Cincinnati, prepare for the event. (Yeatman–Mt. Washington Lodge No. 162.)

Mt. Washington Masonic Temple. Mt. Washington Lodge, which merged with Yeatman in 1994, was the second body with that name in that eastside neighborhood. Mt. Washington Lodge No. 450 existed from 1870 to 1885. The second lodge by that name was founded in 1917 and was given the number 642. The lodge's old quarters at Frugal Electric Co. burned down in August 1928. Fortuitously, this building was almost complete at that time.

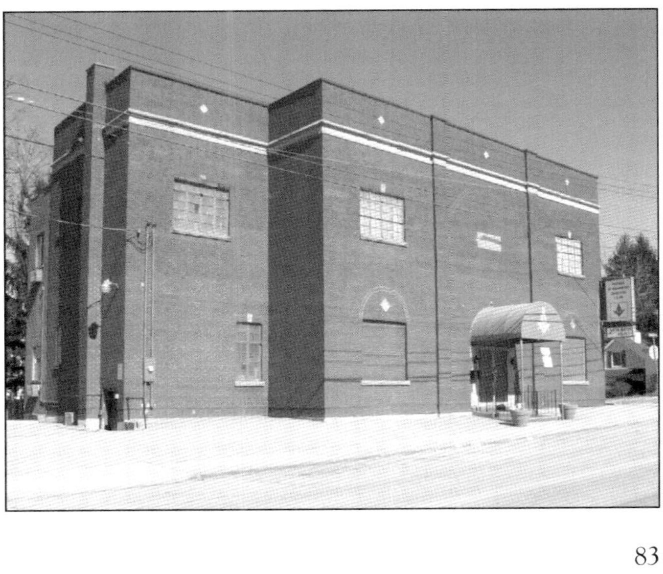

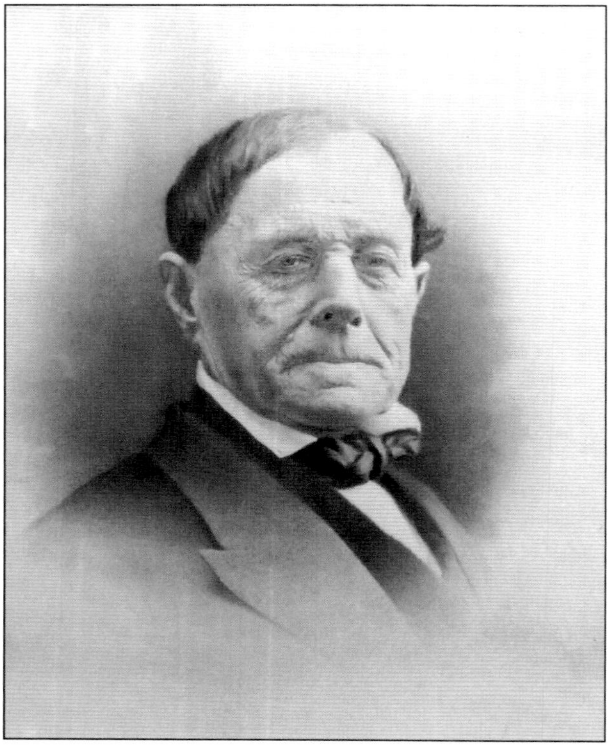

Christopher F. Hanselmann. The founder of Hanselmann Lodge No. 208, the "Squire" emigrated from Germany, arriving in Cincinnati in 1818. He founded a sausage-making business in 1825. He also owned a steamboat and traded coal. Hanselmann (1798–1874) joined Nova Caesarea Harmony Lodge No. 2 in 1825 and was elected Master in 1841 and 1843. He joined Cincinnati Commandery, Knights Templar, and ultimately served as Ohio's Grand Commander from 1851 to 1858. Hanselmann Commandery No. 16 bears his name. (Hanselmann Lodge No. 208.)

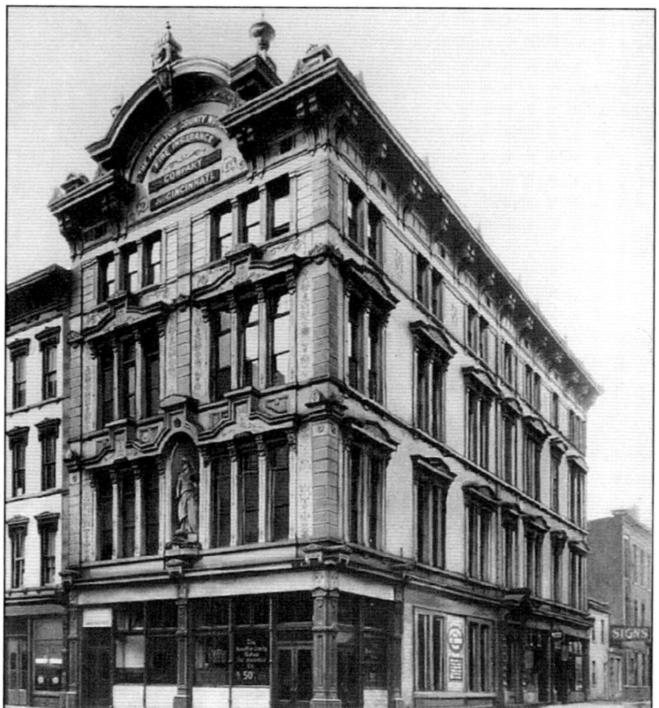

Germania Building. Hanselmann Lodge No. 208 occupied this building from 1884 to 1914. Prior to that, the lodge was a tenant in the third temple. The lodge drew members mostly from the German community, and this building's location in the heavily Germanic Over-the-Rhine neighborhood was probably convenient to its membership. After the 1884 fire in the third temple, the Scottish Rite met here. (AASR.)

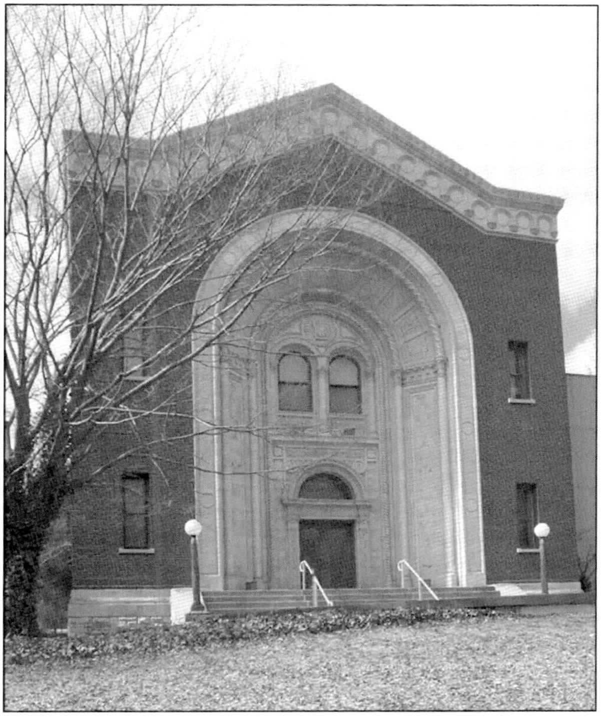

Hanselmann Masonic Temple. Hanselmann Lodge No. 208 was chartered in 1851. For many years, it presented the ritual work in German. This building, located on Clifton Avenue, is now part of Hebrew Union College. The lodge erected this Harry Hake–designed building in 1914.

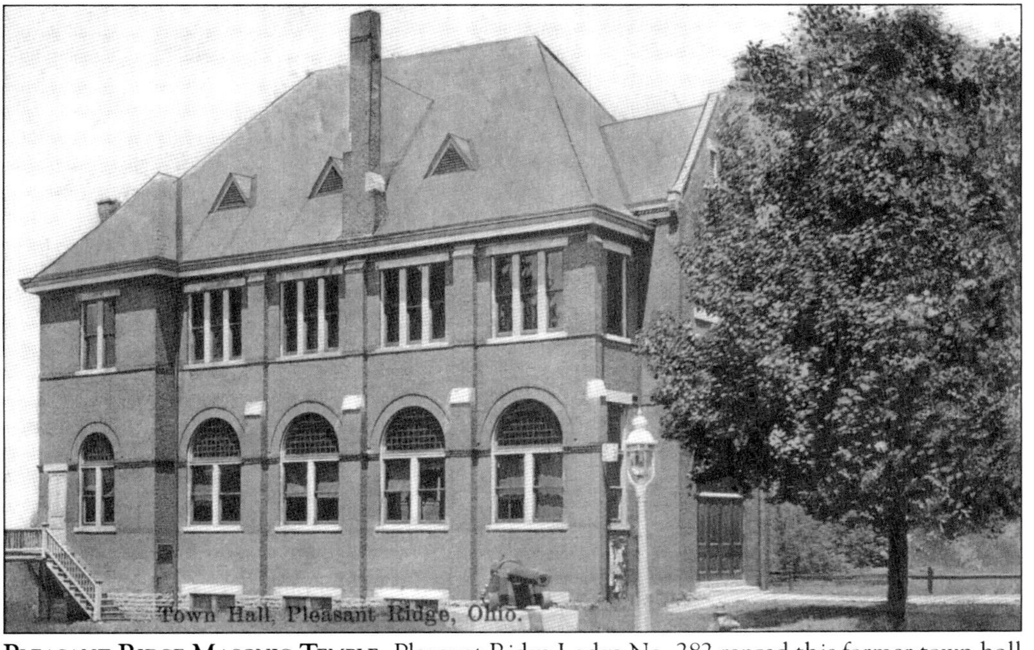

Pleasant Ridge Masonic Temple. Pleasant Ridge Lodge No. 282 rented this former town hall from the village of Pleasant Ridge and then from the city of Cincinnati from 1887. The lodge purchased the building in 1923. Royal Arch, Council, and Eastern Star bodies all called this building home. The lodge merged with Montgomery Lodge No. 94 in 1995. (Public Library of Cincinnati and Hamilton County.)

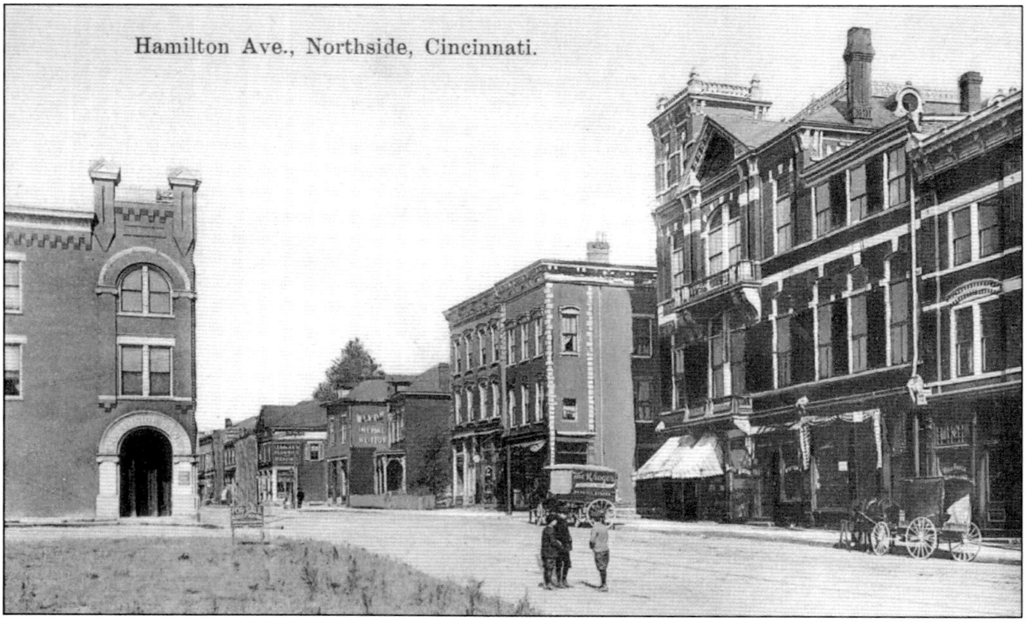

HOFFNER TEMPLE. Cumminsville Lodge No. 253, founded in 1854, changed its name to Hoffner Lodge in 1869 in honor of its very generous benefactor, Jacob Hoffner. A wealthy businessman and member of the lodge, he donated the land for this building (right), which opened in 1886. The temple was the first Masonic project of architects Hannaford & Sons. (Public Library of Cincinnati and Hamilton County.)

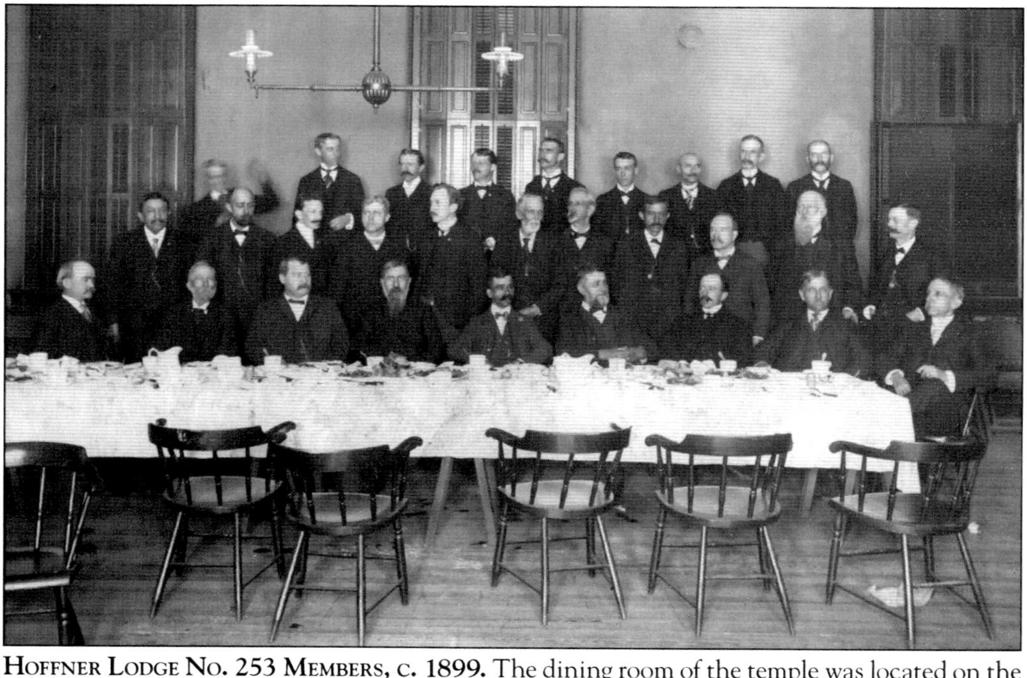

HOFFNER LODGE NO. 253 MEMBERS, C. 1899. The dining room of the temple was located on the second floor. The brother on the far left in the back row is thought to be Harry S. Johnson, future Grand Master. He apparently moved during the taking of the photograph. (GLofOH.)

JOHN HAYES GERARD. A native of Mt. Washington, Gerard (1802–1876) became a Mason in Milford Lodge No. 54 in 1829. The namesake of Gerard Lodge No. 428, he lived in Newtown, east of Cincinnati. He served in the Ohio senate, was county sheriff, editor at the *Cincinnati Daily Enquirer*, and owned a meatpacking business. He was one of the seven original members of the Scottish Rite in Cincinnati. (AASR.)

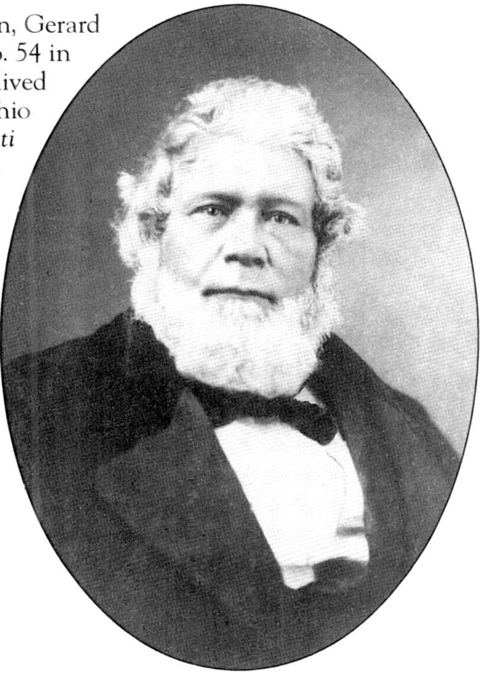

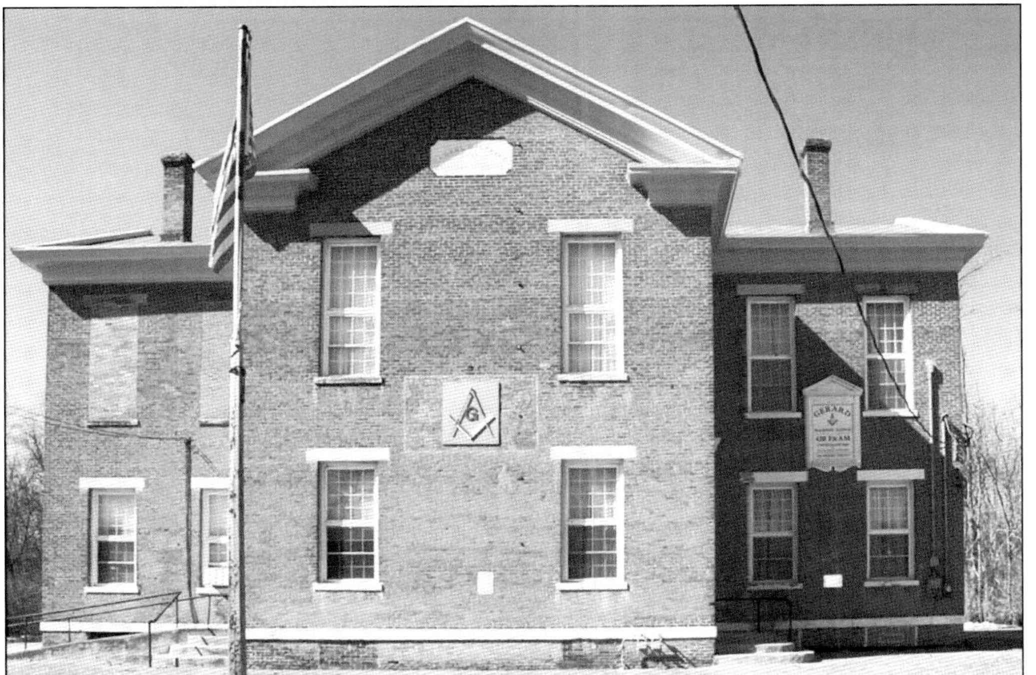

GERARD LODGE NO. 428. Gerard Lodge, founded in 1869, moved into this former school building in 1929. The lodge had met in several other places in Newtown. Grand Lodge forced the lodge to leave its first home when a saloon opened on the lower level. It then became a tenant in the Newtown Odd Fellows Hall.

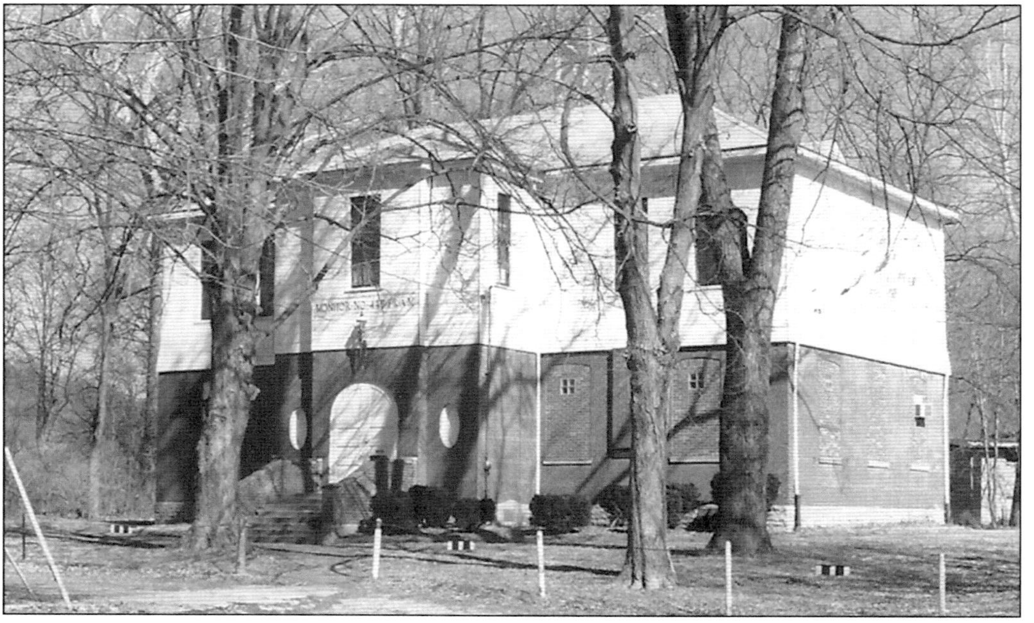

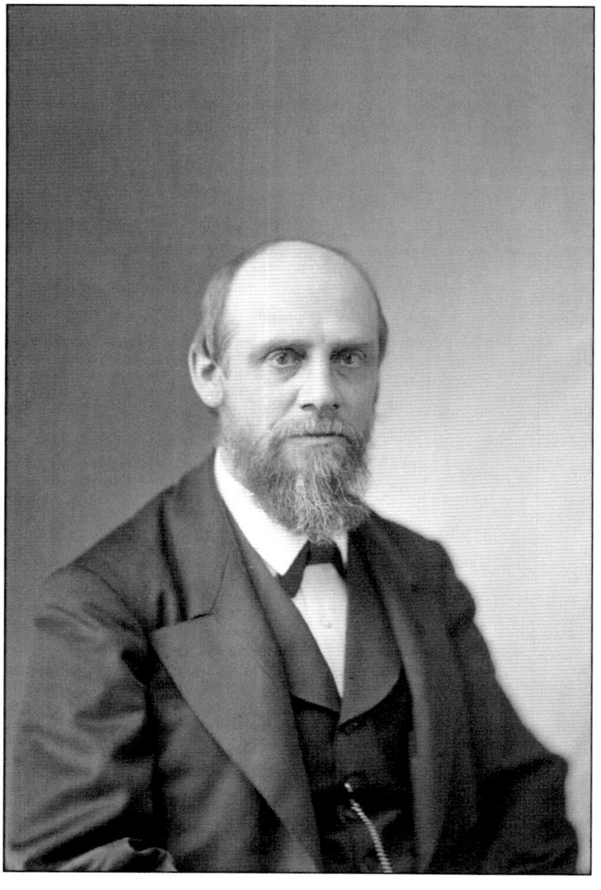

Fernbank Masonic Temple. Founded in 1870, Monitor Lodge No. 445 was originally located in Delhi Township. A fire destroyed the lodge's home there in November 1894. The lodge had at least two other locations before it acquired the old Fernbank School in Saylor Park and converted it into a temple. This was the final home of Monitor Lodge, which merged with North Bend Lodge No. 346 in 1987. (Saylor Park Historical Society.)

George Hoadly. A lawyer, politician, and judge, Hoadly (1826–1902) started his legal career with Salmon P. Chase, later chief justice of the US Supreme Court. Hoadly was elected governor of Ohio in 1883 as a Democrat. He was a charter member of Killwinning Lodge 356 and, later, Walnut Hills No. 483. He was the last surviving member of Cincinnati's seven founding Scottish Rite Masons. (Library of Congress.)

JOSEPH B. FORAKER. Foraker (1846–1917) joined Walnut Hills Lodge No. 483 in 1884. He was beaten for governor by George Hoadly in the election of 1883, but Foraker won against Hoadly in 1885. Thus, two members of the same Cincinnati lodge competed for the governorship against each other twice. Hoadly served from 1884 to 1886, and Foraker from 1886 to 1890. Foraker was also a US senator (1897–1909). (cincinnativiews.com.)

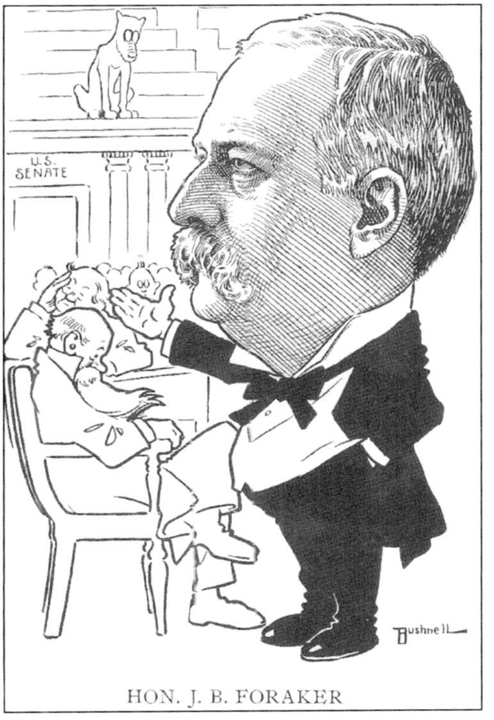

HON. J. B. FORAKER

FIRST HOME OF WALNUT HILLS LODGE AT PEEBLES CORNER. The third floor of the Taylor Building (since demolished), above Dow's Drugs, was the home of Walnut Hills Lodge No. 483 from its founding in 1874 until completion of its temple in 1924. E.T. Carson Lodge held its first meeting under dispensation here on March 1, 1907. Walnut Hills Lodge is now merged with Cincinnati-Lafayette. (E.T. Carson Lodge No. 598.)

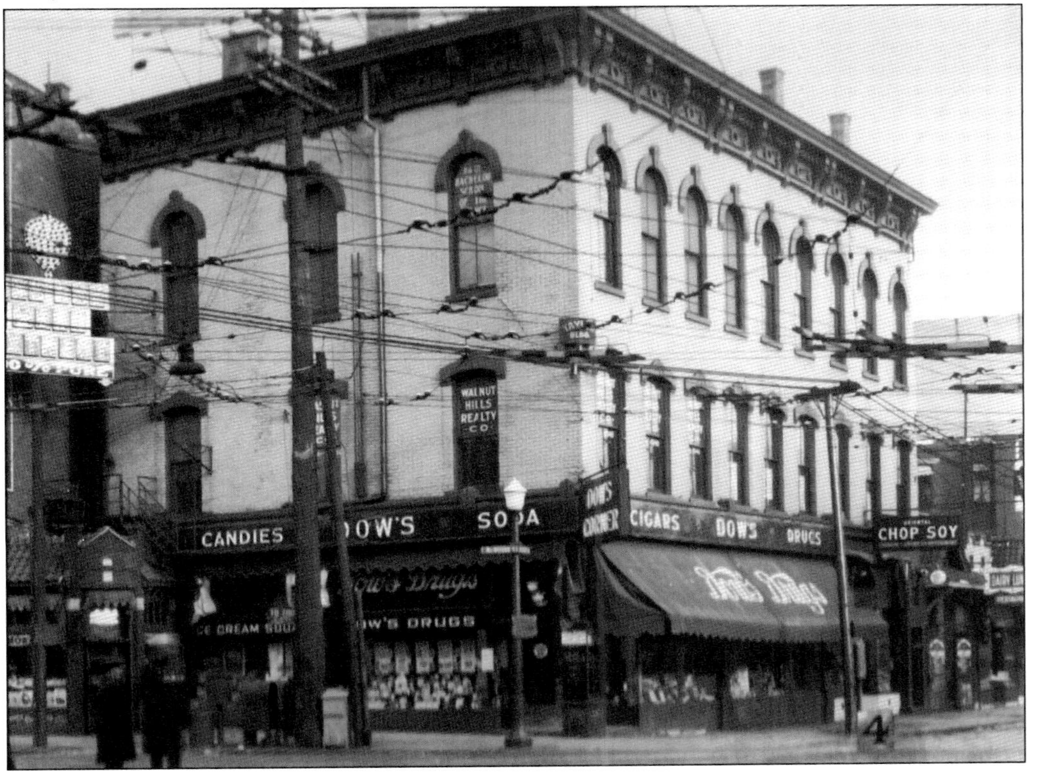

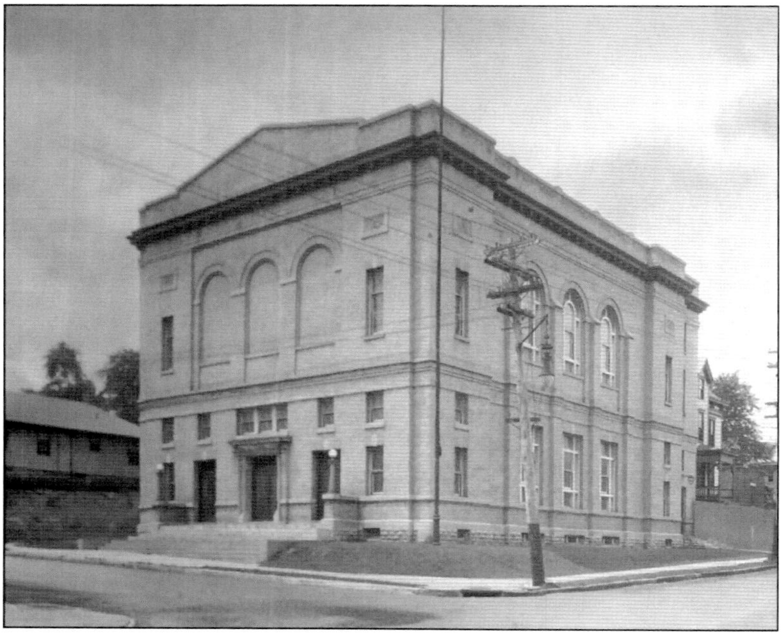

Price Hill Temple. Price Hill Lodge No. 524's temple was designed by the architectural firm of Hannaford & Sons. The building on Price Avenue in the East Price Hill neighborhood was dedicated on November 30, 1912. Several Cincinnati-area temples were built with similar design of a single lodge room on the second floor over a dining and reception space. (North Bend Lodge No. 346.)

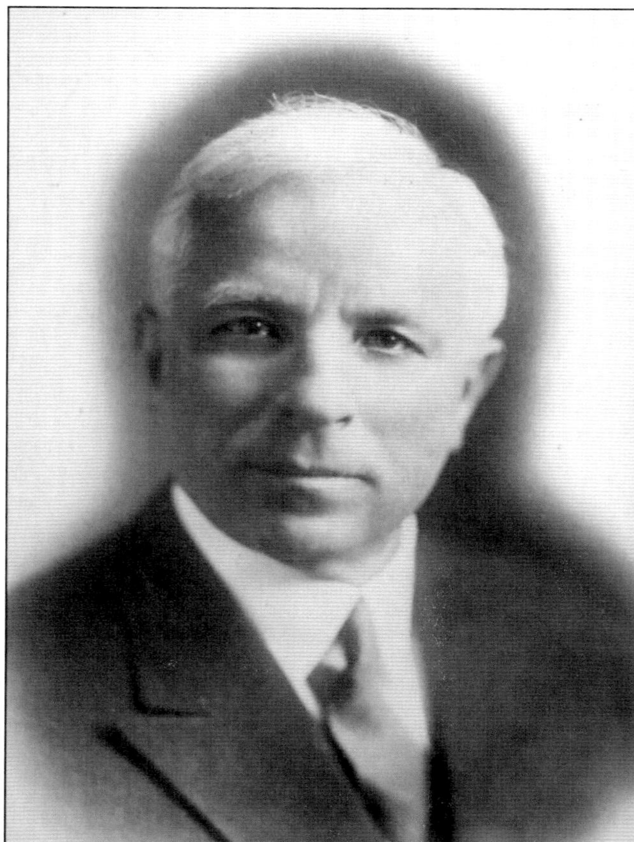

Albert D. Alcorn, 33rd Degree. Alcorn (1870–1946) was a member of Avon Lodge No. 542 and an officer in the Scottish Rite. He served in France in World War I as a major in the judge advocate general's department. His service in the Spanish-American War led to his election as commander in chief of the United Spanish War Veterans in 1923. (AASR.)

LINWOOD MASONIC TEMPLE. Chartered in 1892, Linwood Lodge No. 567 met here at the corner of Eastern and Linwood Avenues from 1910 until the lodge's merger with Norwood-Winton-Carthage Lodge in 2008. The lodge originally met in the third floor of a nearby firehouse. Many Masonic temples were built with rental space on the first floor, as seen here. (Norwood-Winton-Carthage Lodge No. 567.)

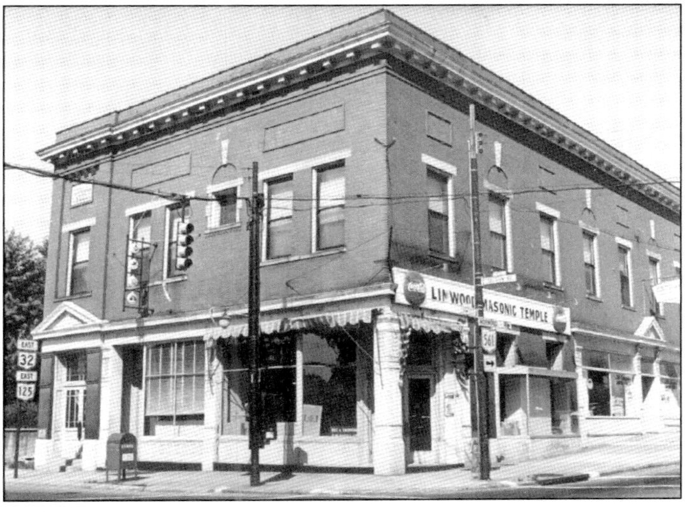

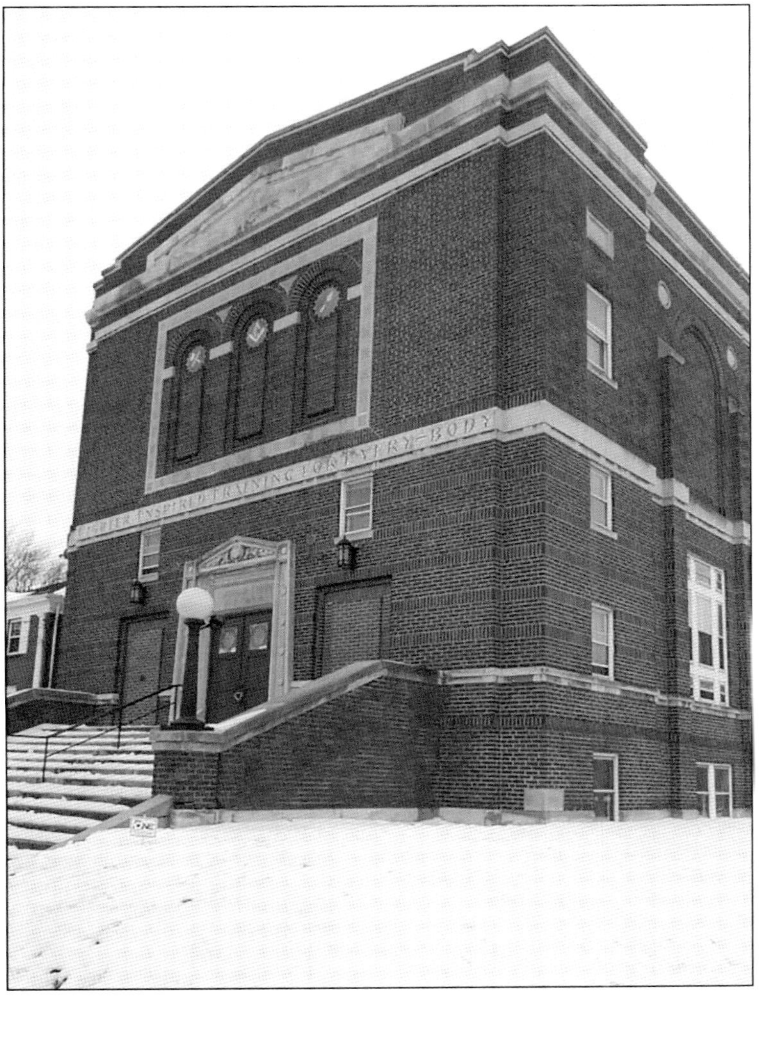

CARTHAGE MASONIC TEMPLE. The lot for this building at Vine and Sixty-ninth Streets in Carthage was acquired by the lodge in 1920. The cornerstone was laid on September 23, 1928, and the building was dedicated on June 9, 1929. The Depression hit almost as soon as the doors were opened. Minutes from the 1930s indicate that the mortgage was a burden. Carthage merged with Norwood Lodge in 2008.

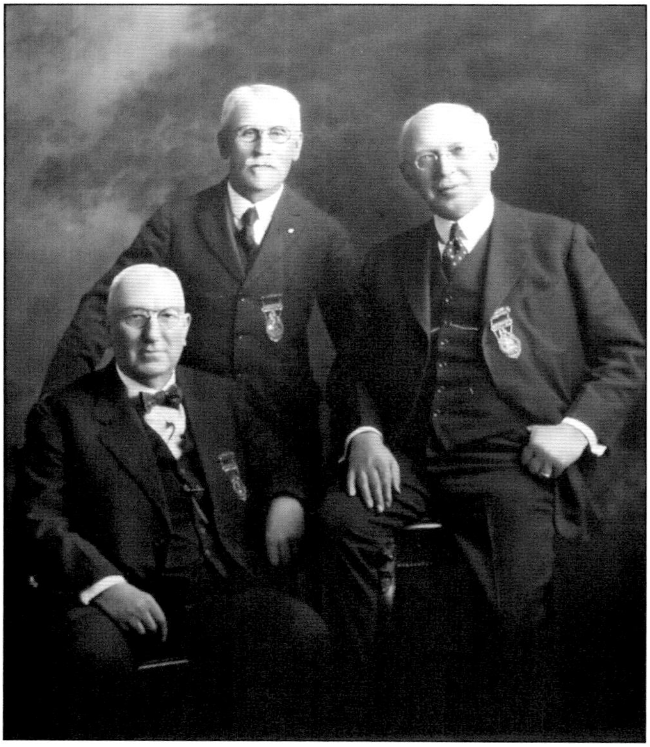

First Worshipful Master and Wardens of Norwood Lodge No. 576. The first Senior Warden, Master, and Junior Warden of Norwood Lodge were, respectively (from left to right), Dr. T.V. Fitzpatrick, William S. Cadman, and George Puchta. Each would also serve as Master. Cadman was superintendent of Norwood Schools, and Puchta was mayor of Cincinnati in 1916–1917. The lodge originally met in the Pleasant Ridge Masonic Temple. (Norwood-Winton-Carthage Lodge No. 567.)

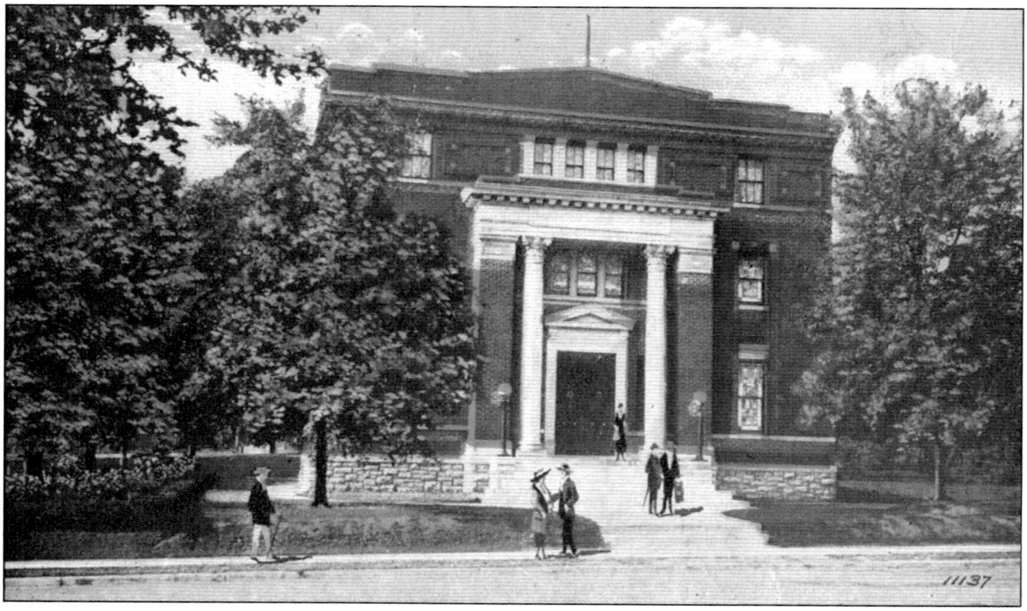

First Norwood Masonic Temple. After using the Norwood Knights of Pythias Castle since 1895, the members of Norwood Lodge built this Masonic temple on Weyer Avenue in Norwood. The building was dedicated in November 1918. This "permanent" home was very quickly outgrown, inducing the lodge to construct its current temple less than 10 years later. (Public Library of Cincinnati and Hamilton County.)

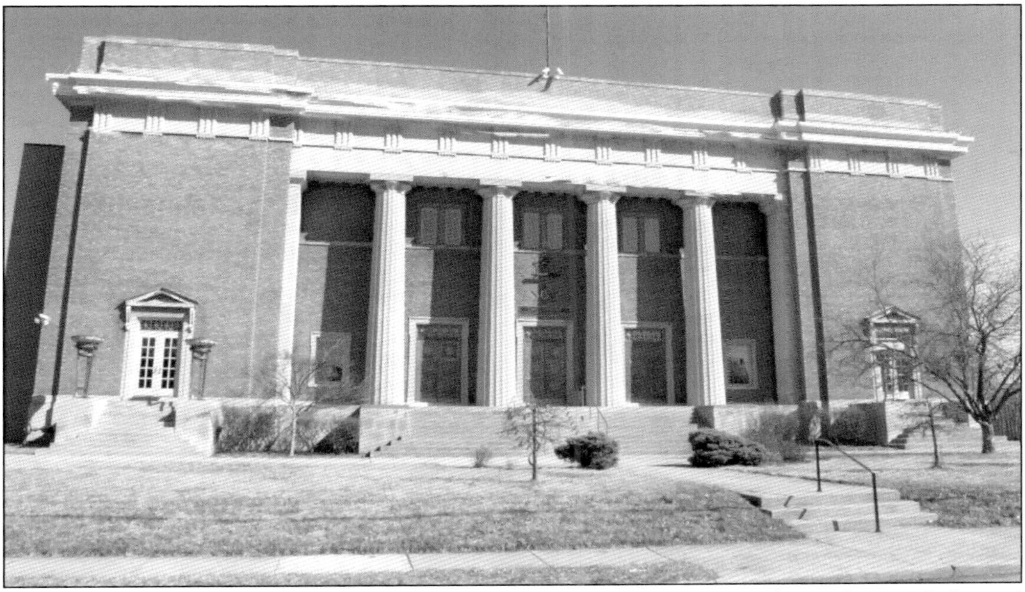

NORWOOD MASONIC TEMPLE, HOPKINS AVENUE. The current Norwood temple was dedicated on George Washington's birthday, 1927. The dedication was preceded by a parade from the old temple to the new one. The procession, consisting of 2,500 Masons, probably took a circuitous route, since the two buildings were only a few blocks apart. Norwood-Winton-Carthage Lodge No. 576, as the name reveals, is the product of the merger of several lodges.

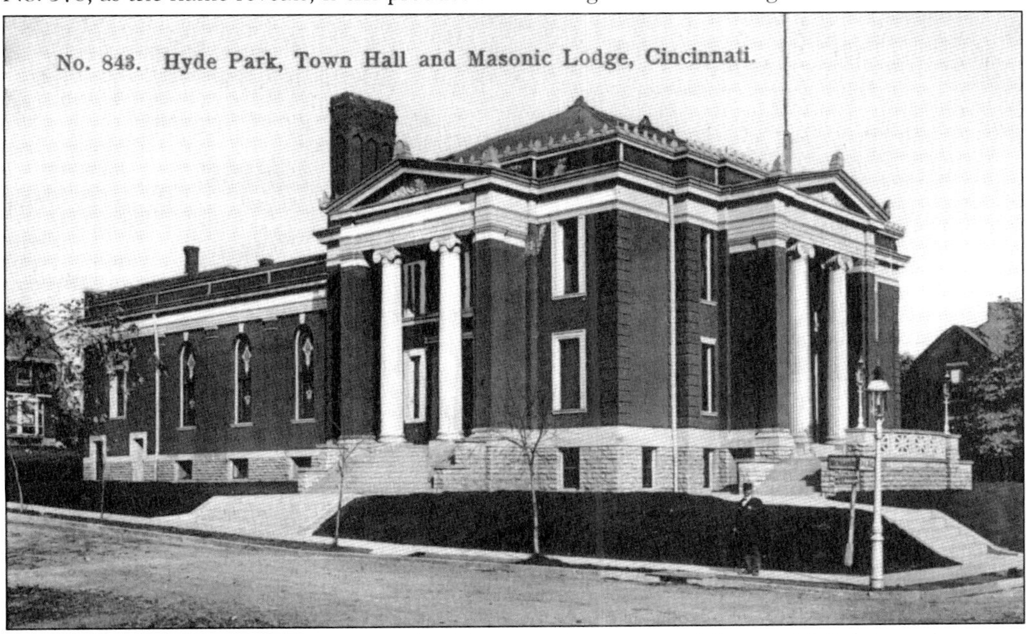

HYDE PARK MASONIC TEMPLE. This building, at the corner of Erie and Michigan Avenues, was Hyde Park Lodge No. 589's home until 1960. The lodge rented here and then bought the building in 1915. It had been the Hyde Park Town Hall for the short period that Hyde Park was an independent village, before annexation by Cincinnati. (Public Library of Cincinnati and Hamilton County.)

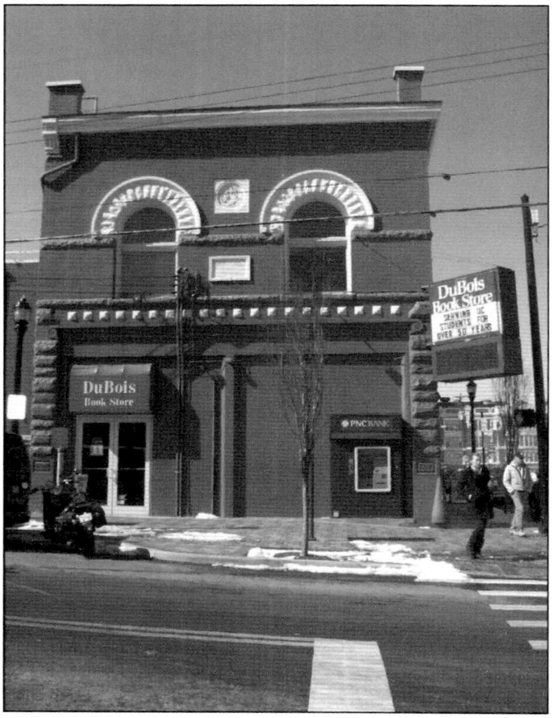

LIBERTY MASONIC TEMPLE. In 1922, Liberty Lodge No. 646 acquired this former Cincinnati fire station, located at Calhoun Street and West Clifton Avenue. The seal of the City of Cincinnati can be seen between the upper windows. Liberty Lodge, founded as World War I ended, originally met at the Peebles Corner home of Walnut Hills Lodge (see page 89).

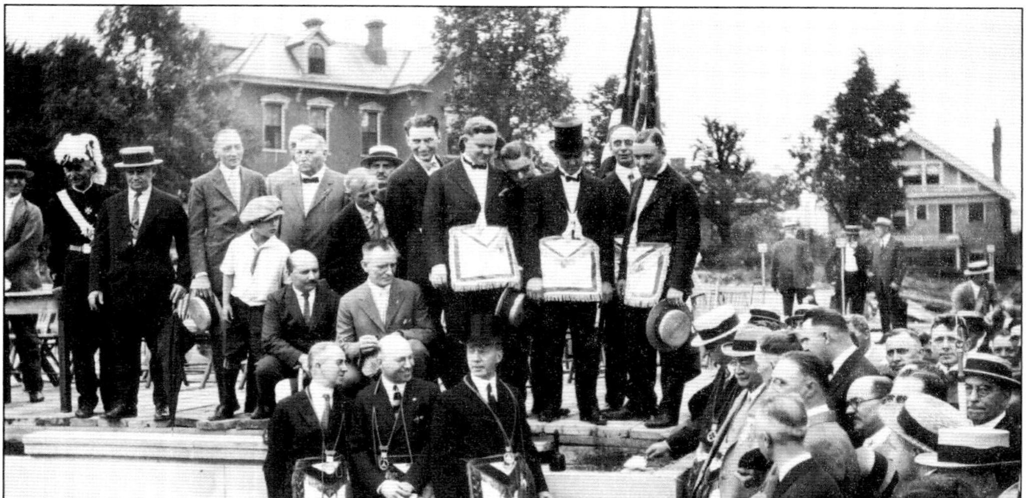

CORNERSTONE LAYING FOR E.T. CARSON TEMPLE, AUGUST 16, 1924. Chartered in 1907, E.T. Carson Lodge No. 598 bought its Ludlow Avenue property, across from Burnett Woods, in 1917. Standing in front of the foundation are, from left to right, Harry S. Johnson, Grand Secretary; Walter Linsey; and Harry Englehardt, Senior Grand Deacon. Standing on the upper level are August Nuernberger (right of Templar), H.P. Hoffman (left, wearing apron), Charles Frantz, Worshipful Master Robert J. Carroll III (top hat and apron), Bill Henke (in front of flag), and Bill Frantz (right, wearing apron). William B. Melish, Past Grand Master, wearing glasses, is on ground level (to the right of the man with the trowel at the corner of the foundation). (E.T. Carson Temple No. 598.)

E.T. Carson Temple. Gaining members quickly, Carson Lodge was at one time the largest lodge in Ohio. Carson had a very active Ladies Auxiliary, with its own officers and events. Starting in 1941, the Carson Corkscrew shows were an annual event of the Carson Club social group. Dorcas Chapter, Eastern Star; Carson DeMolay Chapter; Rainbow Girls; and other groups have all been a part of Carson. This temple was completed in 1925.

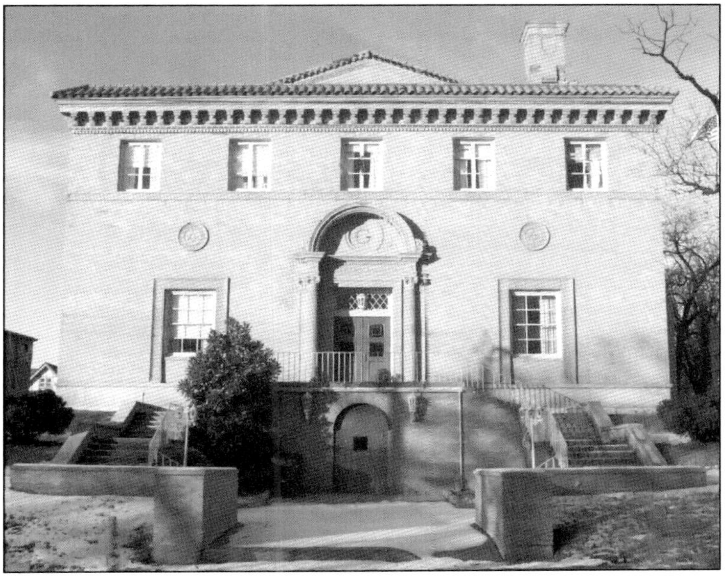

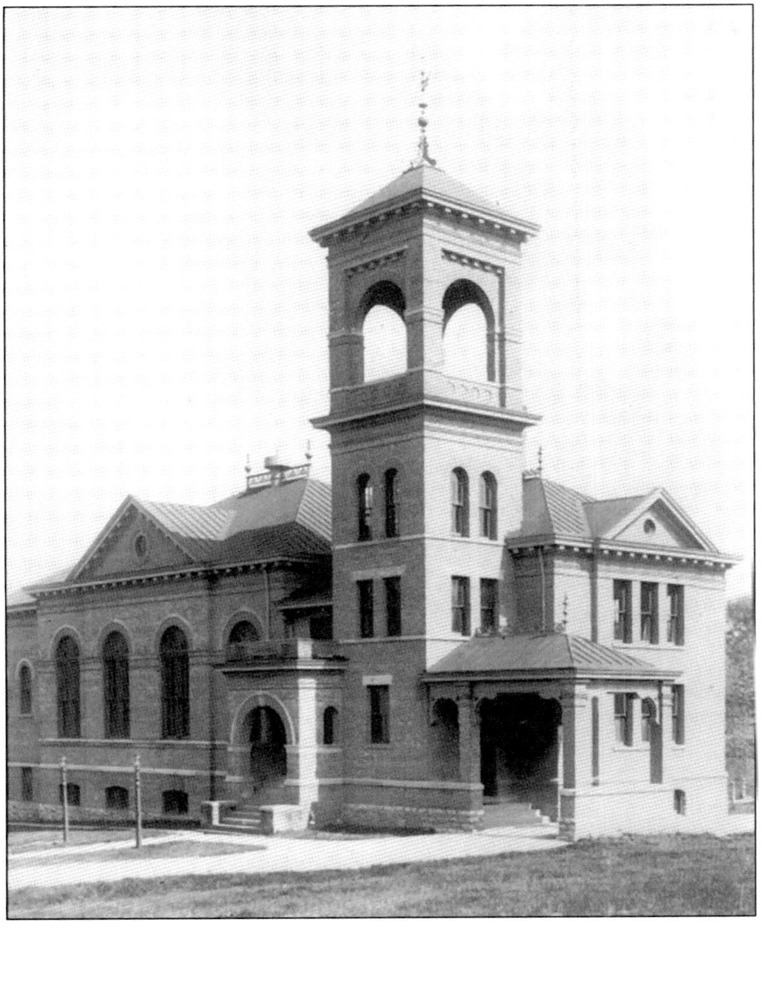

Old Town Hall, College Hill. This building served College Hill Lodge No. 641 as a lodge hall from 1918 to 1976. The lodge leased the building from the City of Cincinnati, which came to own it after the area was annexed into the city. (cincinnativiews.net.)

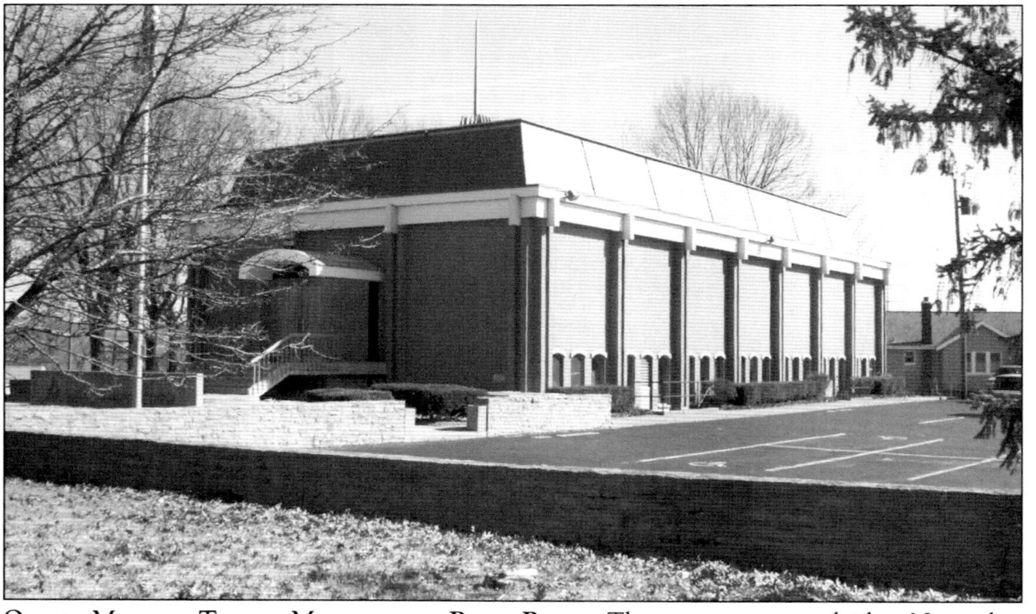

Oakley Masonic Temple, Madison and Ridge Roads. The cornerstone was laid on November 2, 1964, and the building was dedicated on September 12, 1965. Cincinnati annexed the eastside community of Oakley in 1913. The lodge was founded in 1920 and chartered in 1921. The temple has been home to an Eastern Star Chapter, DeMolay Chapter, Job's Daughters Bethel, Rainbow Girls Assembly, and Allied Masonic Degree Council. (Oakley Lodge No. 668.)

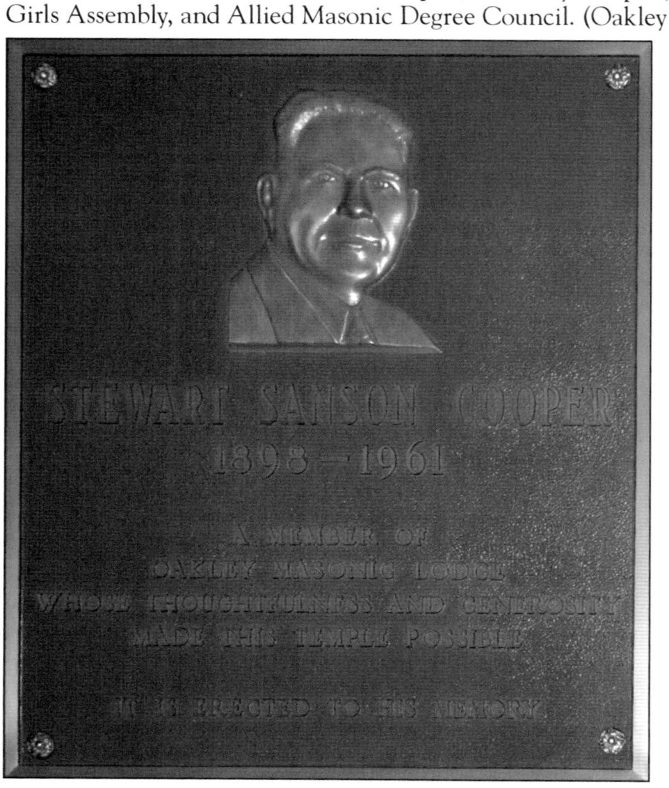

Stewart S. Cooper. A Cincinnati lawyer and member of Oakley Lodge No. 668, Cooper (1898–1961) generously left his brothers funds to construct and maintain a Masonic temple. Oakley met in temples belonging to Hyde Park and then Madisonville Lodges before buying the East Oakley School from the City of Cincinnati, demolishing it and building its midcentury modern home. (Oakley Lodge No. 668.)

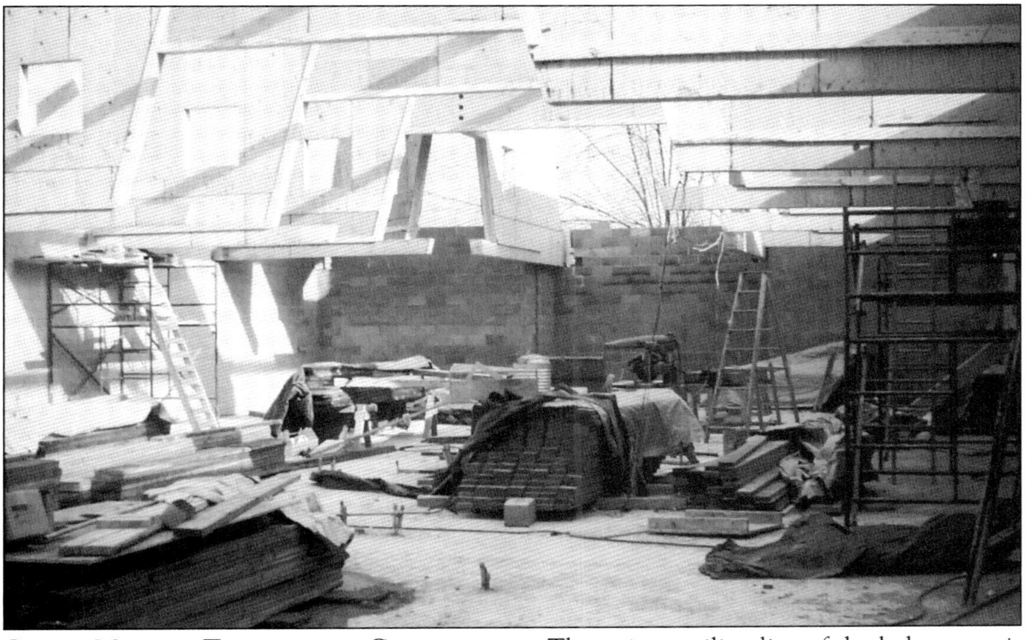

OAKLEY MASONIC TEMPLE UNDER CONSTRUCTION. The unique ceiling line of the lodge room is seen here during the building process. The finished product is shown on the opposite page. The temple is a split-level design. The lodge room and secretary's office are on the upper level, and the banquet room and kitchen are in the semi-basement. (Oakley Lodge No. 668.)

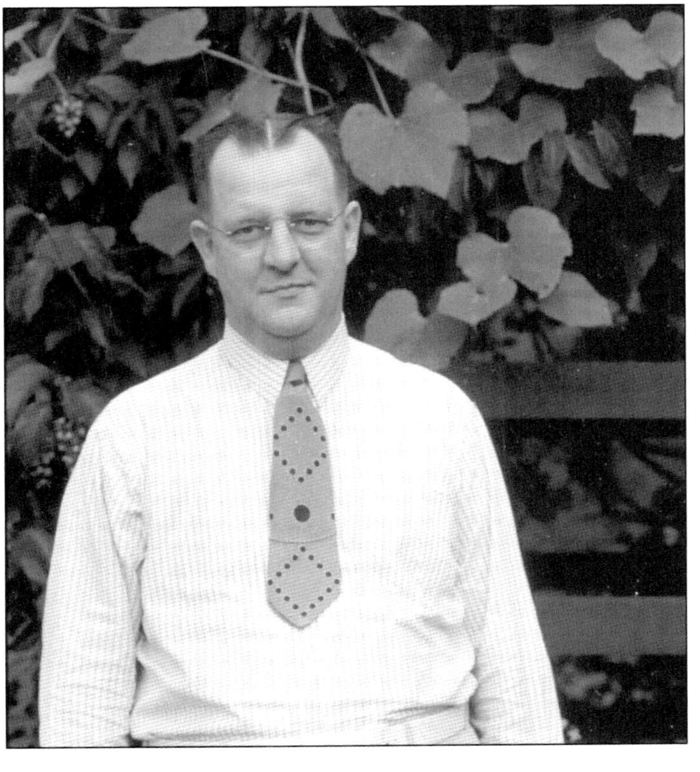

HARRY KELSO EVERSULL. A Christian minister was the namesake of Lodge No. 754, which ultimately merged with Melrose No. 671. Eversull (1892–1953) left Cincinnati in 1937 to become president of Marietta College, but returned in the 1940s. He was a member of Hyde Park Lodge No. 589. An author, his Masonic writings include *The Temples in Jerusalem* and portions of the 1942 version of the Scottish Rite 17th Degree. (Marietta College.)

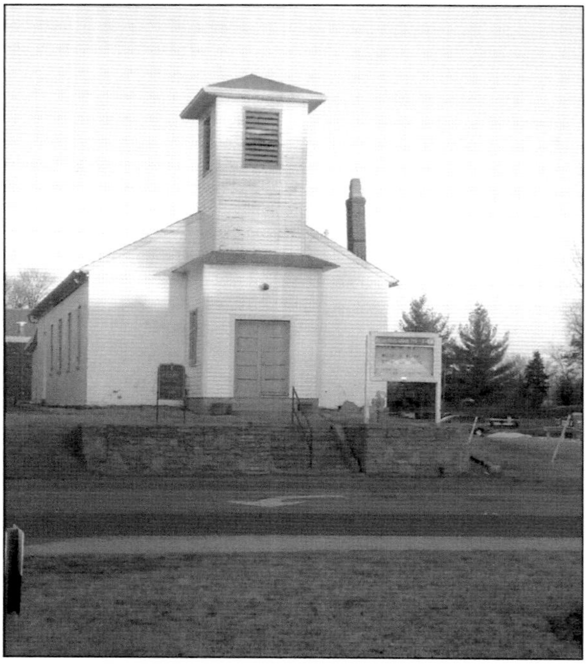

DELHI HILLS MASONIC TEMPLE. Delhi Hills Lodge No. 775, founded in 1973, is one of the youngest lodges in the First Masonic District. The lodge's home is the former Shiloh United Methodist Church building. Built in 1830, it is one of the oldest buildings in the village of Delhi.

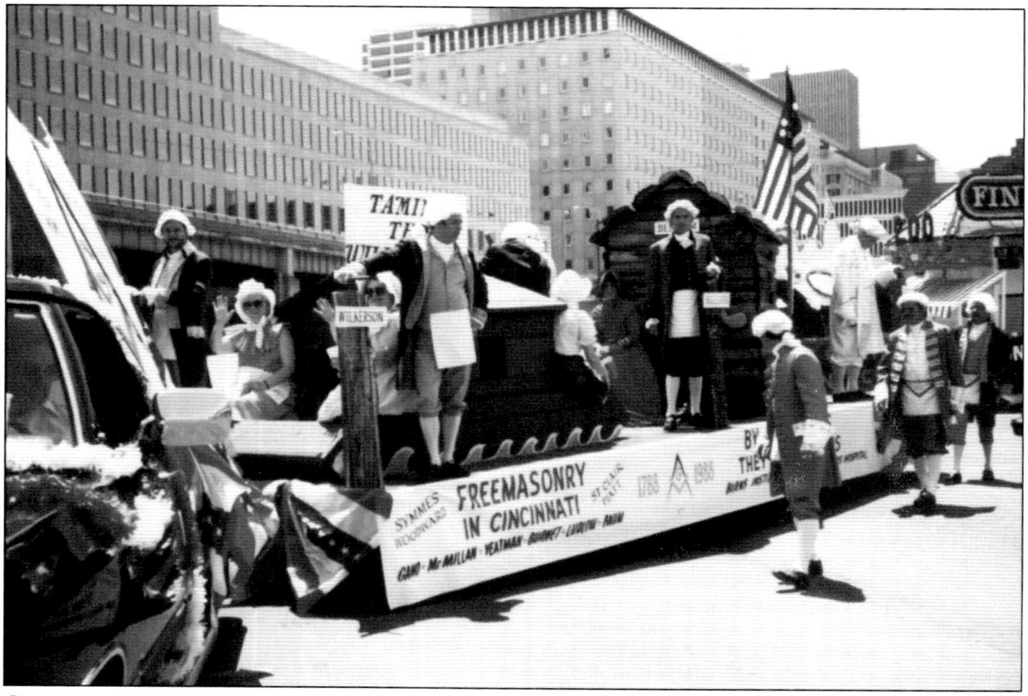

CINCINNATI BICENTENNIAL PARADE. Cincinnati Masonic lodges participated in Cincinnati's bicentennial celebration in July 1988. A float in the parade depicted a flatboat and a cabin. It was adorned with names of early settlers who were members of the fraternity, including William McMillan, Griffin Yeatman, Israel Ludlow, John Cleve Symmes, and William Woodward. Masons and their wives, wearing period costumes, accompanied the float. (NCH2.)

Six

The Bigger Circle of the Fraternity

Once a brother has become a Master Mason, he can, if he desires, join the York and/or Scottish Rite. The Ancient Accepted Scottish Rite confers 29 degrees or ceremonies. Locally, the Valley of Cincinnati oversees the work of this rite of Freemasonry. Ohio is a part of the Scottish Rite's Northern Masonic Jurisdiction. The York Rite is composed of three independent but interconnected bodies. A chapter of Royal Arch Masons (RAM) controls four degrees. The Council of Royal and Select Masons (R&SM) confers three degrees. Both are governed on a statewide basis. The Commandery of Knights Templar, a uniformed organization, confers three orders of knighthood (degrees). The Grand Commandery of Ohio, which oversees commanderies statewide, is subordinate to the national Grand Encampment.

In addition to these bodies, a number of "fun" organizations exist under the Masonic umbrella. The Shriners are well known for their fezzes, diminutive automobiles, and children's hospitals. Syrian Temple is the local body of this national order. The Tall Cedars of Lebanon and the Grotto each also have a local presence.

Freemasonry has a number of honorary organizations that recognize service, leadership, and participation. For example, those who have presided in each of the York Rite bodies are eligible to be considered for membership in the Knight York Cross of Honor. Other honorary groups with local presence include the Allied Masonic Degrees and Red Cross of Constantine.

The bonds of the fraternity stretch to encompass women and young people. Eastern Star and Amaranth are for female relatives of Masons, while youth organizations include the Order of DeMolay for young men and Rainbow Girls and Jobs Daughters for young women.

There is also a long and proud heritage of African American or Prince Hall Masonry in Cincinnati.

Ohio's southwest corner has contributed greatly to leading the fraternity in all its manifestations on the local, state, and national levels.

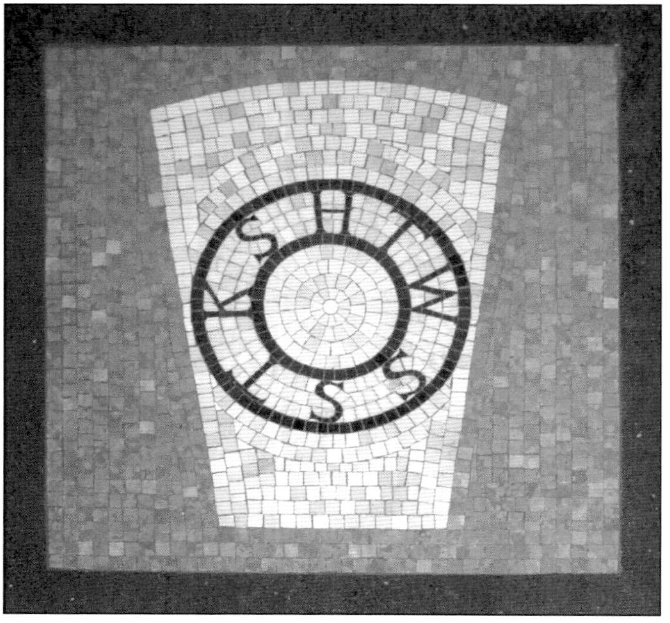

Royal Arch Keystone Emblem, Cincinnati Masonic Center. The Royal Arch is an appendant body to the Blue Lodge. The chapter, as bodies of Royal Arch Masons are called, controls four degrees elaborating on the tales of King Solomon's Temple presented in the lodge degrees. In keeping with the tradition of the time, the Royal Arch degrees were first conferred in Cincinnati in Nova Caesarea Lodge No. 10 in 1799. The emblem shown here appears on the elevator lobby floor, on the sixth floor of the Masonic Center.

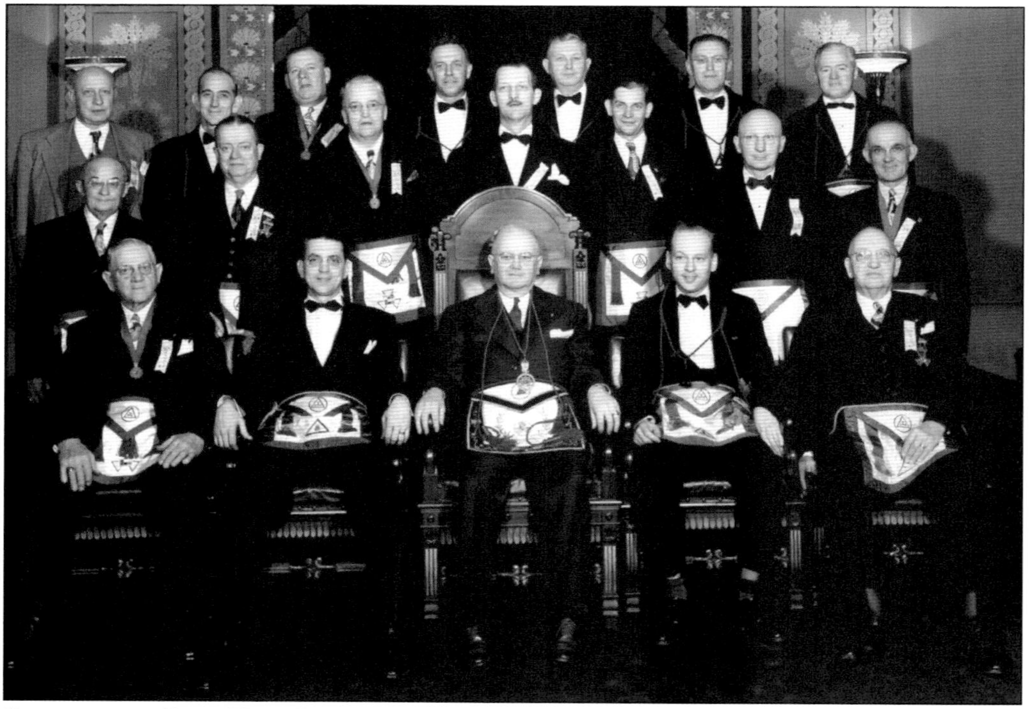

Officers and Past High Priests of Kilwinning Chapter, Royal Arch Masons No. 97, c. 1958. From left to right are (first row) Louis Botzing, Art Zoecklein, Earl Duesenberry, J.A. Eberhart, and Samuel Nicholson; (second row) William Grimm, ? Campbell, William Winans, Ralph Cove, Robert Herbig, George Kahler, and Louis Greber; (third row) William Meinders, Louis Schott, Carl Lutz, Chester Schiller, Walter Rardin, William Weintz, and Robert Benham. (Kilwinning Chapter No. 97.)

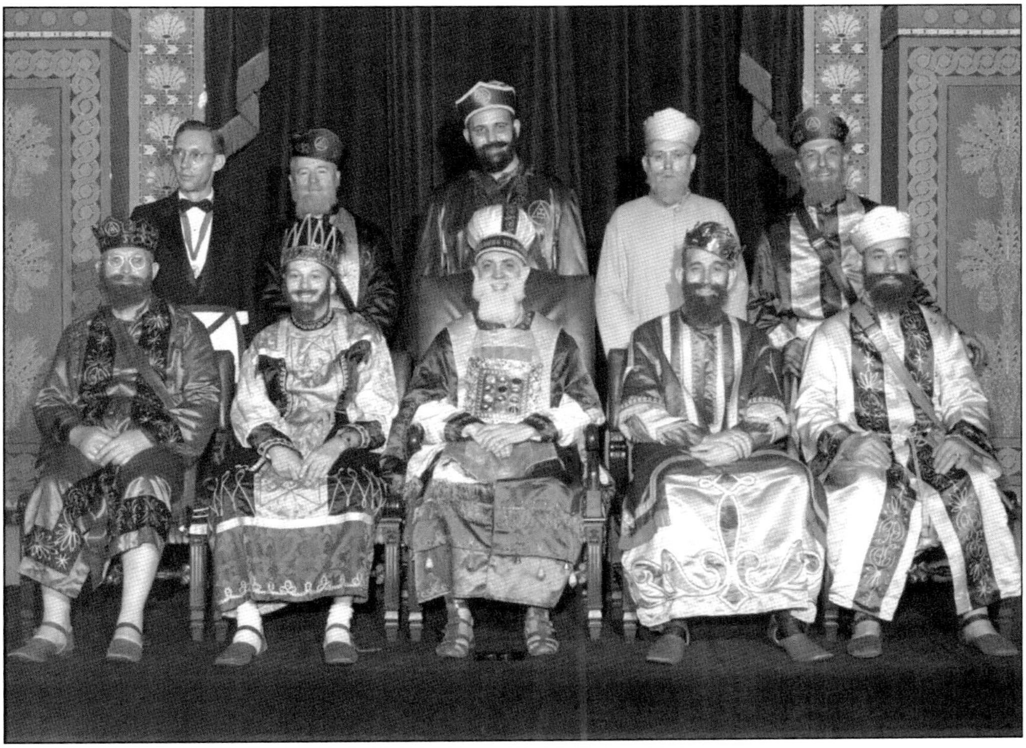

Degree Cast from Kilwinning Chapter No. 97. This photograph, taken in the Chapter Room at the Cincinnati Masonic Temple, includes some of the same "Companions" seen in the previous photograph. Masonic degrees tend to be participatory dramas, in which the candidate takes a role. Costuming and special effects are sometimes used to enhance the experience. (Kilwinning Chapter No. 97.)

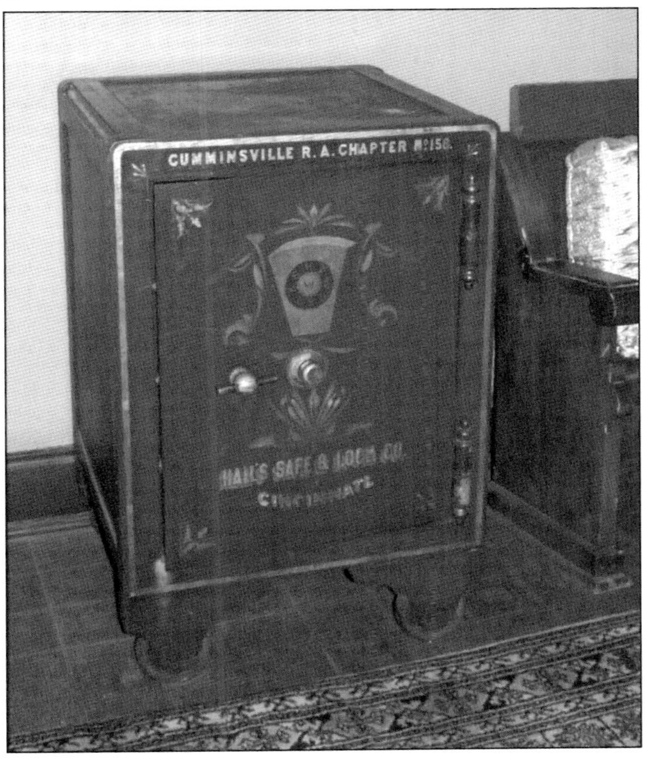

Safe Decorated with Royal Arch Emblems. Masonry has an iconography of emblems used as decoration as well as for teaching. Here, the keystone of the Royal Arch is adornment for a piece of 19th-century office equipment. (Maggie Kelley.)

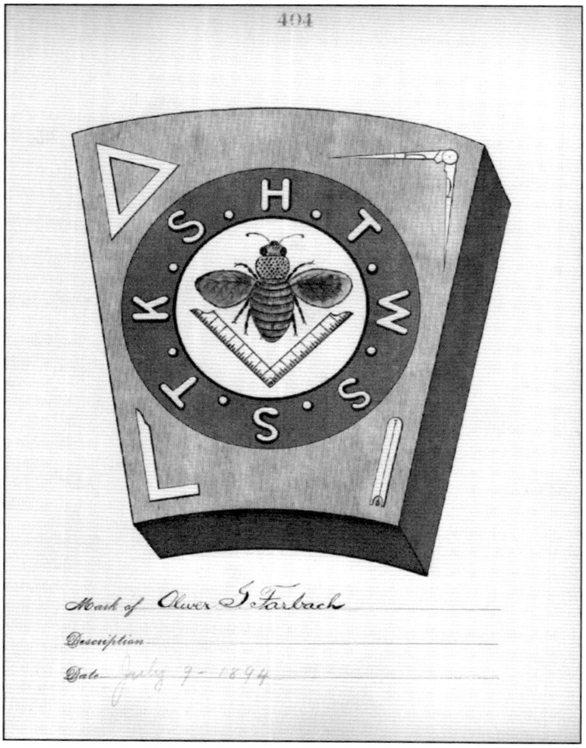

Mason's Mark. In the first degree of the Royal Arch, a new Mark Master is instructed to create his mark. Historically, an operative mason identified his work with his mark cut into stones on which he worked. Marks such as the one shown here are much more ornate than the ones operatives carved. (Wills Chapter No. 131, RAM.)

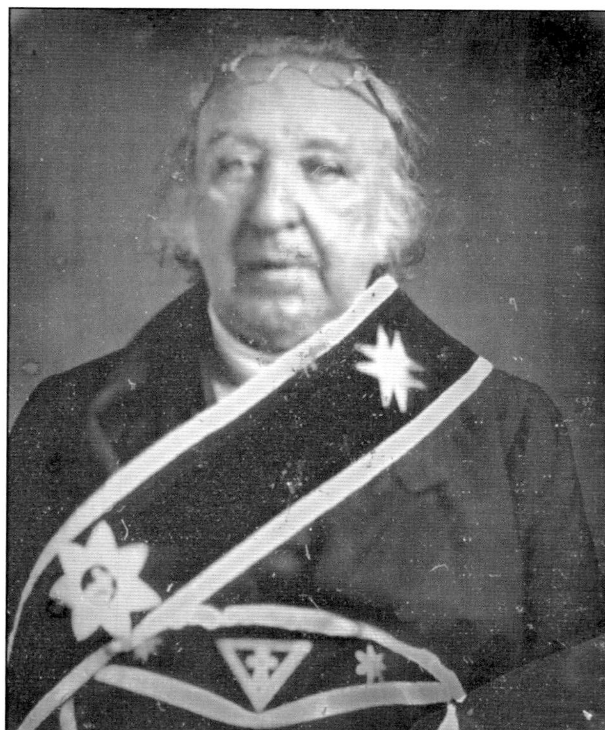

Robert Punshon, First Grand Puissant, Grand Council, Royal and Select Masters. Punshon, an English native, immigrated to America in 1802, reaching Cincinnati in 1822. He affiliated with Miami Lodge No. 46. Punshon (1777–1848) presided over Cincinnati Council No. 1, R&SM for 16 years and helped form the Ohio Grand Council in 1830. Councils of Royal and Select Masters (now Masons) work three degrees, which expound on the work of the Royal Arch. Punshon was also founding Commander of Cincinnati Encampment (now Commandery), Knights Templar, in 1839. (NCH2.)

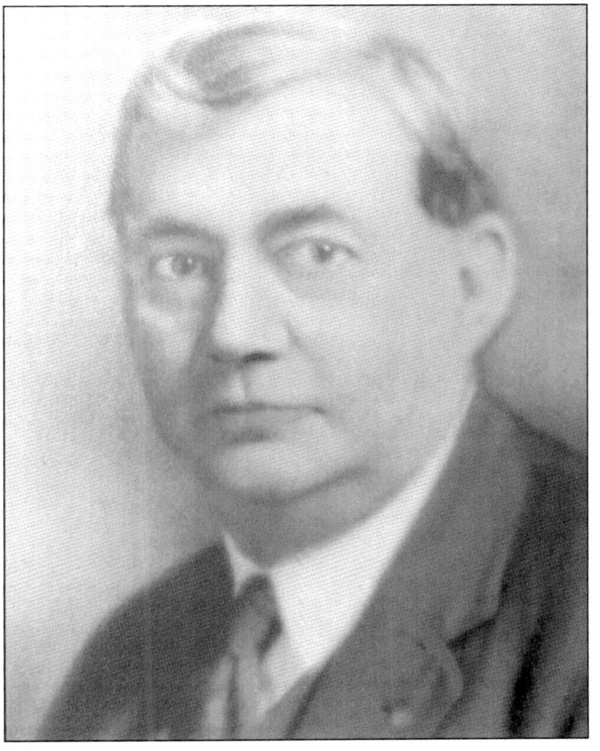

Henry Abraham Weeks. Grand Master of Grand Council Royal and Masters in 1923 and namesake of Henry A. Weeks Council No. 137, R&SM, Henry Weeks was a teacher and bookkeeper. He emigrated from Canada to Cincinnati in 1886. Weeks (1861–1925) affiliated with Pleasant Ridge Lodge No. 282, serving as Master in 1910. He was a charter member of Acacia Chapter No. 195, RAM and a member of Cincinnati Council No. 1, R&SM. (Henry A. Weeks Council No. 137.)

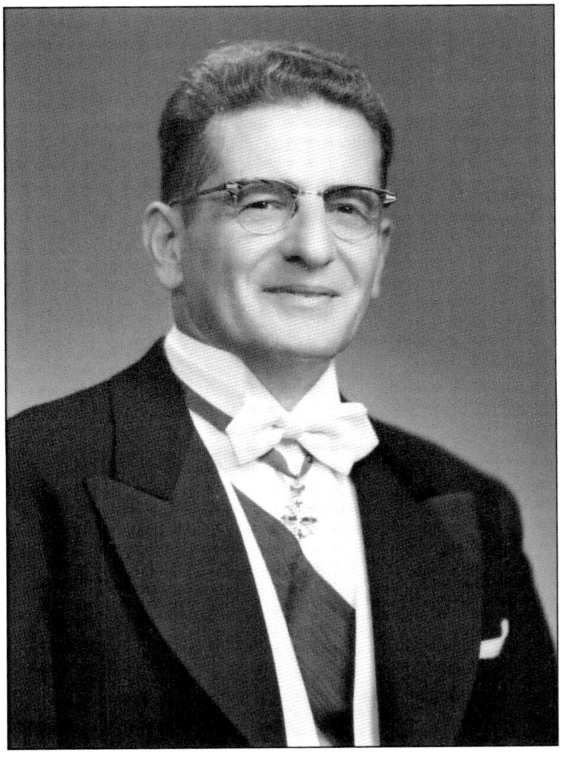

Hubert O. Auburn. Auburn (1907–1980) served McMakin Lodge No. 120 as Master in 1938. He was Illustrious Master of Cincinnati Council No. 1, R&SM in 1948. He is the namesake of Hubert O. Auburn Council No. 149, R&SM, founded in 1980. In this photograph, Auburn wears the regalia of the Red Cross of Constantine, which he presided over as Illustrious Sovereign. He also served the Scottish Rite. (AASR.)

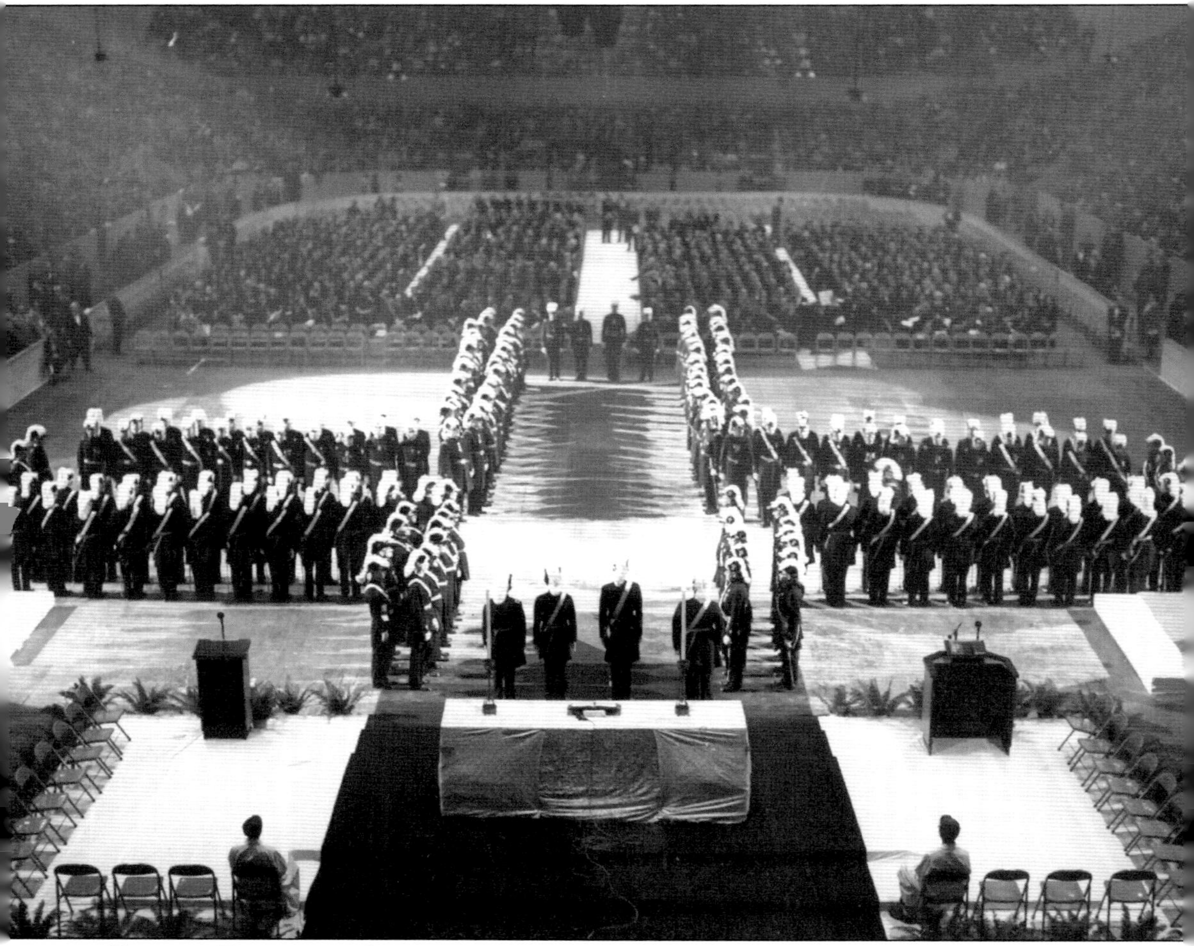

KNIGHTS TEMPLAR AT CINCINNATI GARDENS. On November 15, 1953, eight thousand people observed Affirmation Sunday at Cincinnati Gardens. Sir Knights from all over Ohio participated, forming a massive cross on the main floor of the arena. While the majority of bodies within the Masonic family require only a belief in a supreme being, the Commandery is overtly Christian. (Trinity Commandery No. 44.)

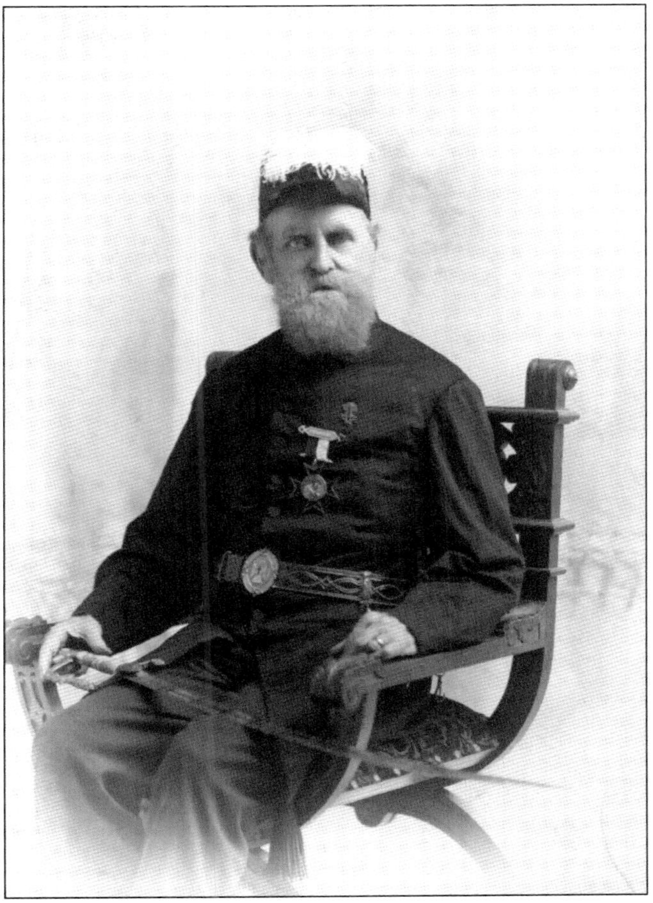

John D. Caldwell in the Uniform of a Knight Templar, mid-1890s. Templar uniforms became more consistent after the Civil War (see page 45). Aprons ultimately disappeared, and a military-style frock coat became standard. Baldrics or sashes were worn in full dress uniform at least through the 1920s. The chapeau, similar to a military officer's dress hat of this period, remains standard headgear today. (UC.)

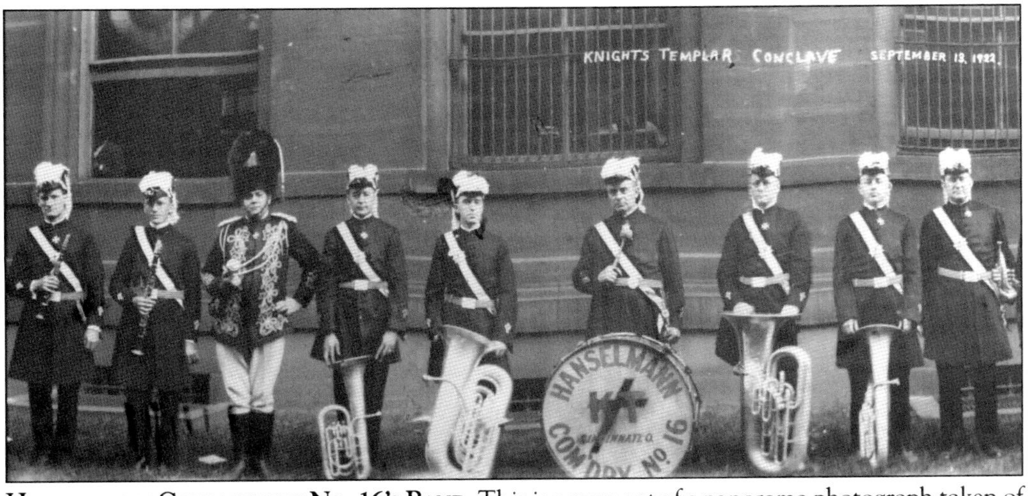

Hanselmann Commandery No. 16's Band. This is a segment of a panorama photograph taken of this Knights Templar Marching Band in 1922. Since drill and formation marching are an aspect of the ritual and public presentations of the Knights Templar, bands were part of many Commanderies, including all three of those in Cincinnati. (Hanselmann Commandery No. 16.)

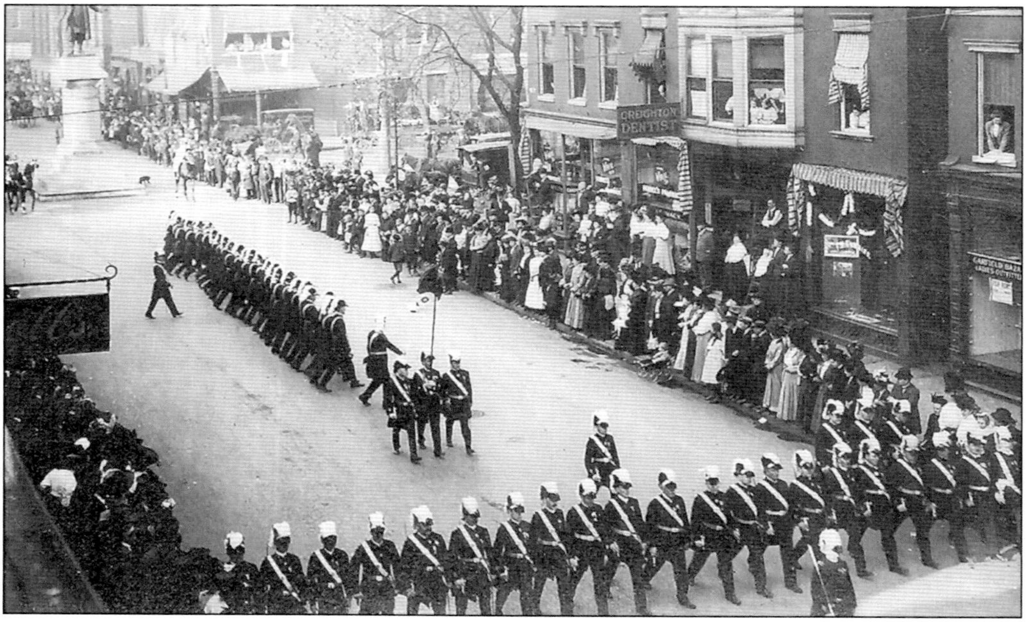

Templar Parade, 1908. The Grand Commandery of Knights Templar of Ohio held its annual session in Cincinnati in 1908. As part of that event, a large parade with Sir Knights from all over the Buckeye State marched through the downtown streets. Here, Knights perform a drill maneuver in the middle of Race Street, just past the intersection with Eighth Street. The statue of James A. Garfield, now at Eighth and Vine Streets, is visible at upper left. (cincinnativiews.net.)

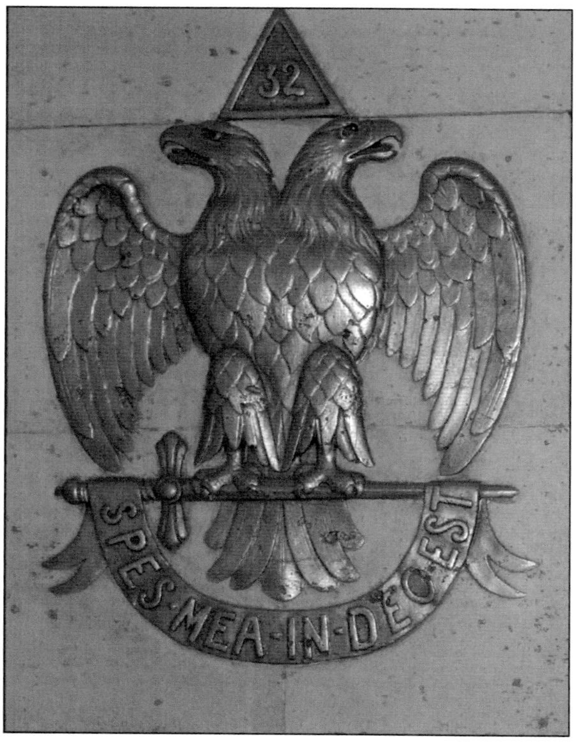

Emblem of the Ancient Accepted Scottish Rite. This wall decoration is near one of the Broadway doors to the Scottish Rite Cathedral. The Valley of Cincinnati, Ancient Accepted Scottish Rite was chartered in 1853 by the Supreme Council, AASR, Northern Masonic Jurisdiction. The Northern Masonic Jurisdiction refers to the supreme body of the Rite, given power in 1813 to control its workings in 15 states in the northeast United States, including Ohio.

KILLIAN VAN RENSSELAER. Van Rensselaer's efforts led to the creation of numerous Scottish Rite Valleys, including Cincinnati. He founded an informal Lodge of Perfection (4th Degree through 14th Degree) at Cambridge, Ohio, in 1852. This led to Columbus and Cincinnati becoming Valleys of the Rite. He served as Sovereign Grand Commander (Northern Masonic Jurisdiction's leader) from 1862 to 1867. Van Rensselaer (1801–1881) is buried in the Cincinnati neighborhood of Mt. Washington. (AASR.)

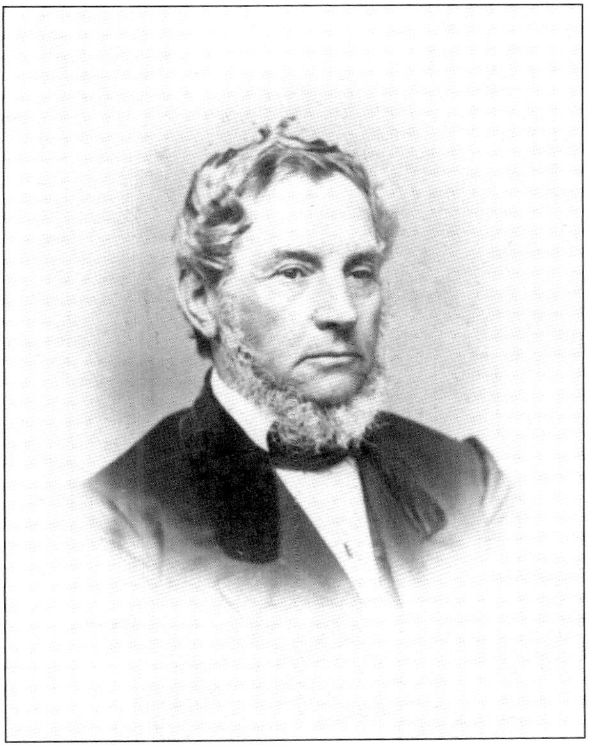

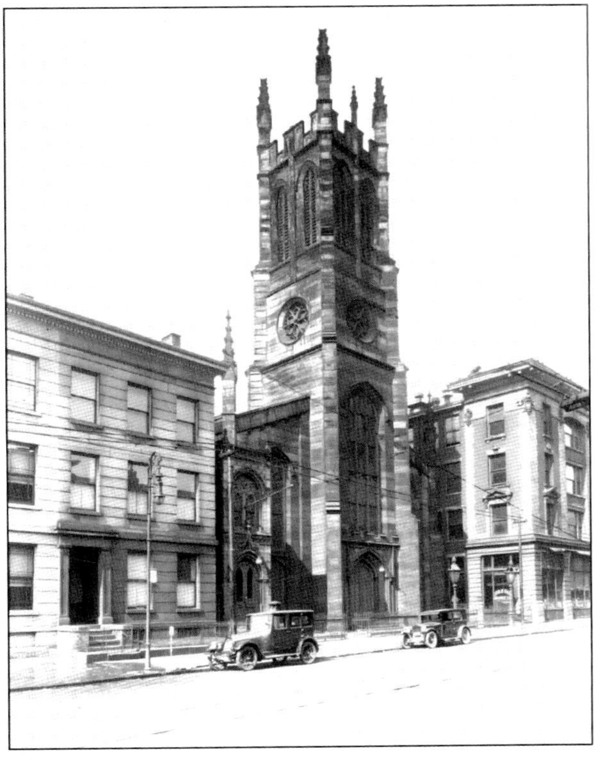

SCOTTISH RITE CATHEDRAL, 1885–1925. The Scottish Rite was hit particularly hard by the 1884 Masonic temple fire (see page 51), losing sets, costumes, paraphernalia, and charters. Long interested in having its own home, the Valley purchased the Seventh Presbyterian Church, on Broadway between Fourth and Fifth Streets, for $35,000. Its location would ultimately lead to the Cincinnati Masonic Center being situated there. (AASR.)

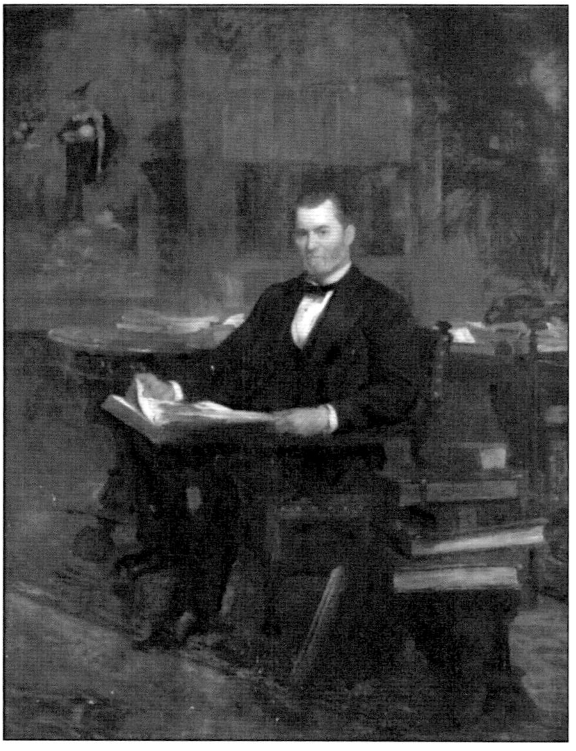

Enoch Terry Carson. Even though he was never Grand Master, Carson (1822–1899) was one of the most influential figures in Cincinnati Masonic history. His positions within the Scottish Rite gave him immense influence over that body and the Craft. The Valley of Cincinnati commissioned this portrait in 1884 by local artist C.T. Webber. The books depicted in the painting represent his extensive library of Masonic and Shakespearean works. Carson's Masonic collection went to the Grand Lodge of Massachusetts; his Shakespeare collection went to the University of Cincinnati. (AASR.)

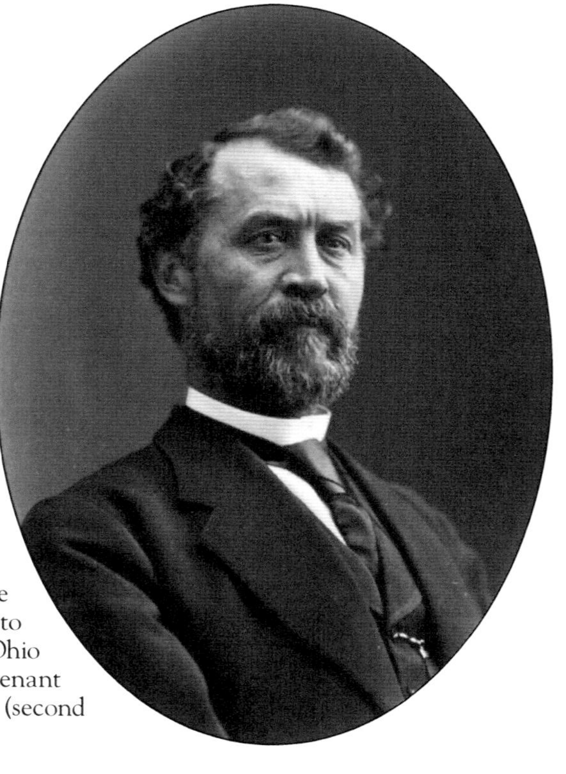

Most Influential of Original Seven. Of the seven original members of the Valley of Cincinnati who received the degrees in 1852–1853, Carson would exert the most influence. He was the Commander in Chief (presiding officer) of Ohio Consistory (19th Degree through 32nd Degree) from 1857 to 1894. In the Northern Masonic Jurisdiction, he was Deputy for Ohio and Indiana from 1860 to 1867 and Deputy of the Supreme Council for Ohio from 1867 until his death. Carson was Lieutenant Grand Commander of the Supreme Council (second in command) from 1870 to 1876. (UC.)

Carson's Other Careers. Carson was appointed by Pres. Abraham Lincoln as collector of the Port of Cincinnati, serving from 1861 to 1866, during the Civil War. In this role, Carson was frequently responsible for $10 million in a given day. Carson also sold gas fixtures, as shown in this advertisement. He was made a Mason in Marion (now McMakin) Lodge No. 120 in 1845. Carson was Master of Cheviot Lodge No. 140 in 1847, Cynthia Lodge No. 155 in 1857, and Kilwinning Lodge No. 356 in 1866. (E.T. Carson Lodge No. 598.)

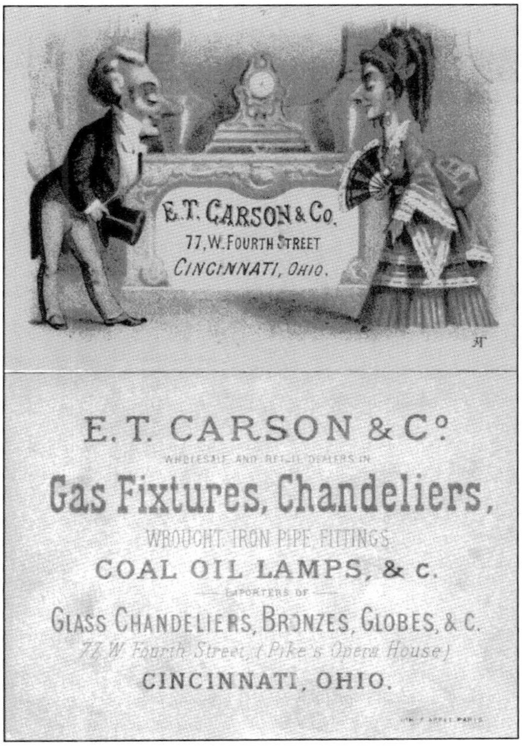

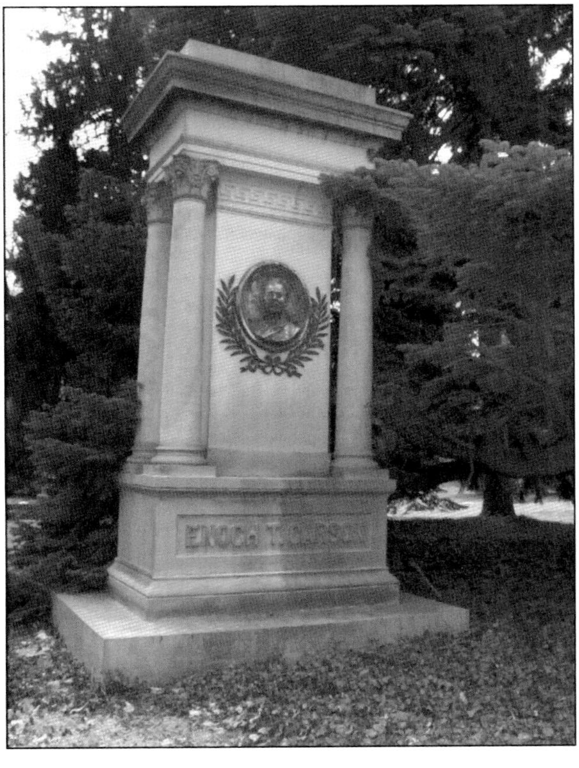

Scottish Rite to the End. On the day prior to Carson's death, during the 47th reunion of the Valley of Cincinnati, Carson had a telephone call placed to the Scottish Rite Cathedral to inquire how the degree work was going. Upon his death, Carson received a grand funeral in the old Scottish Rite Cathedral. He is buried in Spring Grove Cemetery. This 15-foot-tall monument was erected in October 1901.

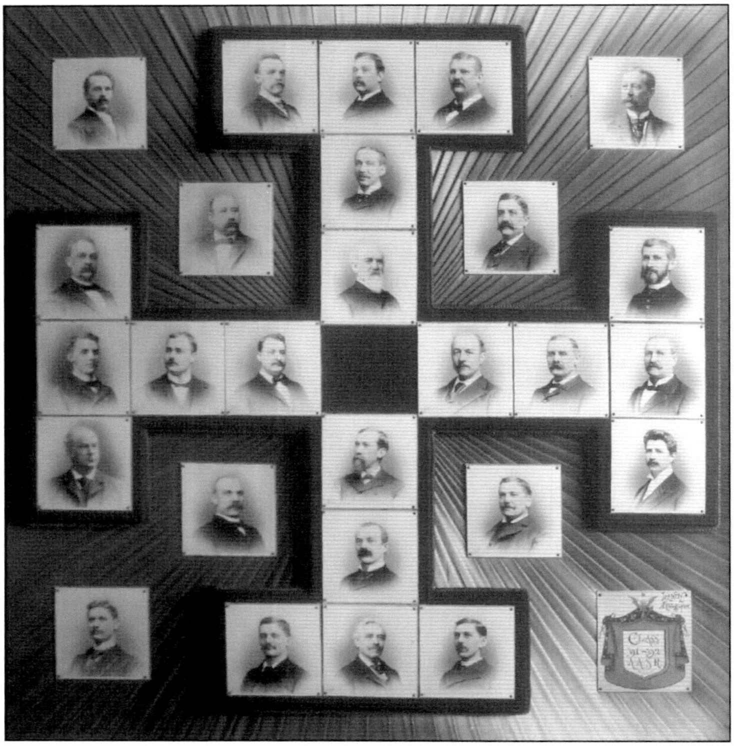

Class Photograph, Valley of Cincinnati, 1891–1892. The Valley of Cincinnati has photographs of members from its very beginning. In this example from the 1890s, the images of the class members are arranged in the form of the Teutonic cross of the 32nd Degree of the Scottish Rite. (AASR.)

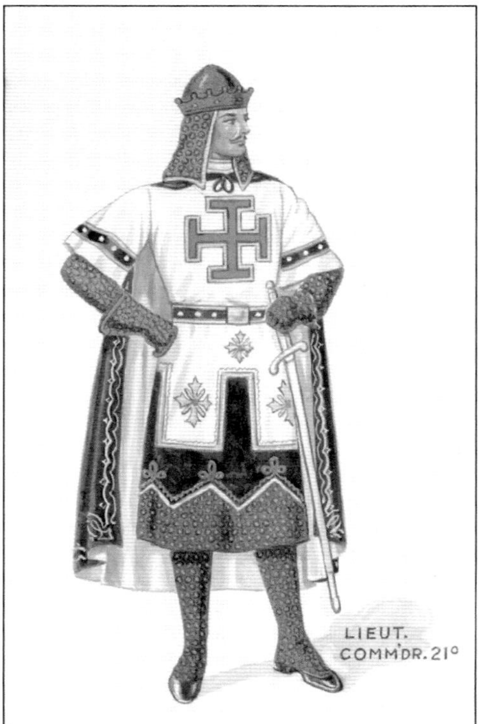

Scottish Rite Degree, Costume Study. The Valley is made up of four bodies, each controlling a number of degrees between 4th Degree and 32nd Degree. The 33rd Degree is an honor bestowed by the Supreme Council. The elaborate degrees of the Scottish Rite include biblical and chivalric allegories. Pettibone Brothers Manufacturing Company produced this costume design drawing. (AASR.)

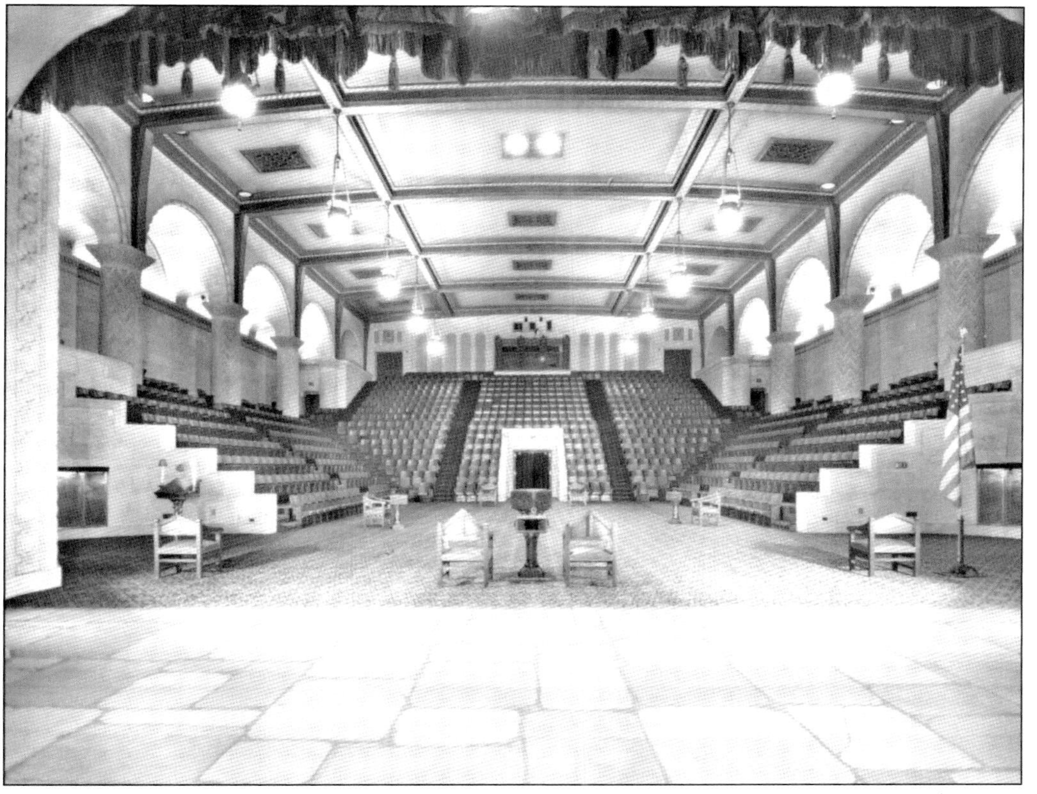

Scottish Rite Cathedral, Viewed from the Stage. The degrees of the Scottish Rite are dramatic and frequently include large casts. The vastness of the cathedral is evident in this photograph, taken from the vantage point of a brother doing degree work on the stage. (AASR.)

Carl Lindner, 33rd Degree, receives Van Rensselaer Medal, February 20, 1988. Al Rice, 33rd Degree (right), presents the Valley of Cincinnati's highest award to Cincinnati businessman and philanthropist Carl Lindner Jr. Other recipients have included Gen. Omar Bradley, Sen. Barry Goldwater, and Norman Vincent Peale, in addition to several Masonic dignitaries. (AASR.)

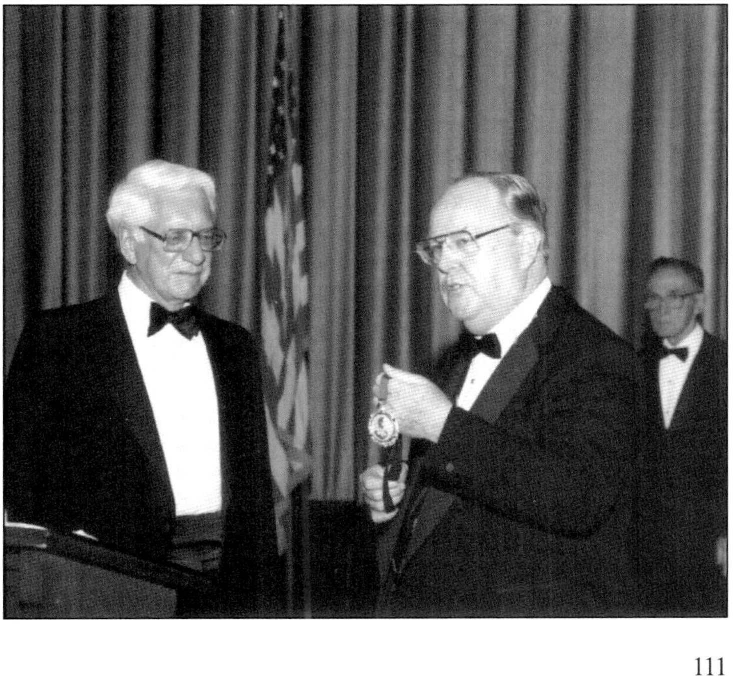

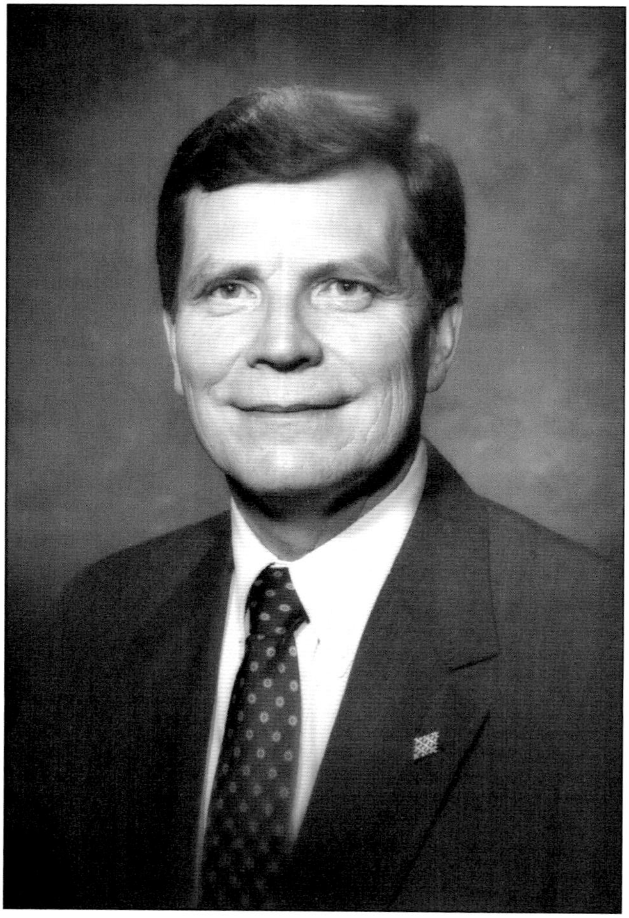

Robert O. Ralston, 33rd Degree, Sovereign Grand Commander, Northern Masonic Jurisdiction. Ralston (b. 1938) is the only Cincinnatian to have risen through the ranks to the top position in the Scottish Rite. Accomplishments during his term (1993–2003) include mutual recognition with the Prince Hall Scottish Rite and the establishment of the Children's Dyslexia Centers. He is a Past Master of Evanston-Eversull Lodge No. 695, which is now merged into Melrose Lodge No. 671. (AASR.)

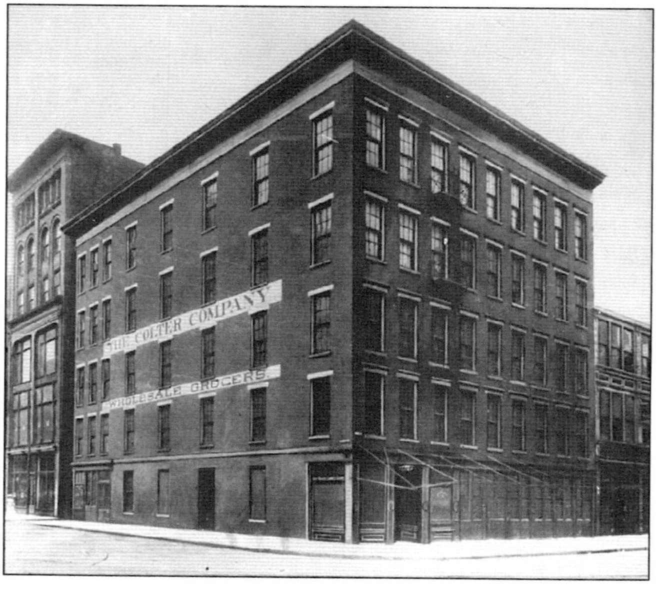

Prince Hall Masonry's Cincinnati Home from the late 1870s to mid-1880s. Local Prince Hall Freemasonry began in 1847, when seven African Americans traveled to Pittsburgh to become Masons and requested a charter to form a lodge in Cincinnati. That lodge, Corinthian Lodge No. 17 (now No. 1), with two others in Cincinnati, formed the Prince Hall Grand Lodge of Ohio in 1849. This building, formerly Allemania Hall, on the northwest corner of Sixth and Main Streets, had been the Valley of Cincinnati's home between 1853 and 1866. (AASR.)

JOHN D. CALDWELL'S *NEW DAY—NEW DUTY*, 1876. Grand Secretary Caldwell's findings, included in the Ohio Grand Lodge *Proceedings*, traced the origin of "colored Masonry" and the status of Masons of African descent elsewhere. He concluded that Worshipful Brother Prince Hall, a free black man, had legitimately been made a Mason and formed a lodge in the late 1700s in Boston, and that lodges descended from that lodge were legitimate. It would be almost 120 years before mutual recognition became a reality. (UC.)

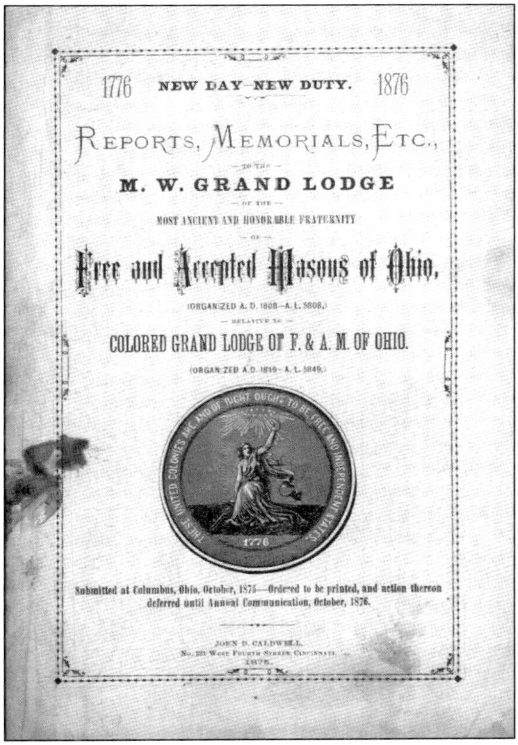

1776 NEW DAY—NEW DUTY. 1876

REPORTS, MEMORIALS, ETC.,

—TO THE—

M. W. GRAND LODGE

—OF THE—

MOST ANCIENT AND HONORABLE FRATERNITY

—OF—

Free and Accepted Masons of Ohio,

(ORGANIZED A. D. 1808—A. L. 5808,)

—RELATIVE TO—

COLORED GRAND LODGE OF F. & A. M. OF OHIO.

(ORGANIZED A. D. 1849—A. L. 5849.)

Submitted at Columbus, Ohio, October, 1875—Ordered to be printed, and action thereon deferred until Annual Communication, October, 1876.

JOHN D. CALDWELL,
No. 233 West Fourth Street, Cincinnati.
1876.

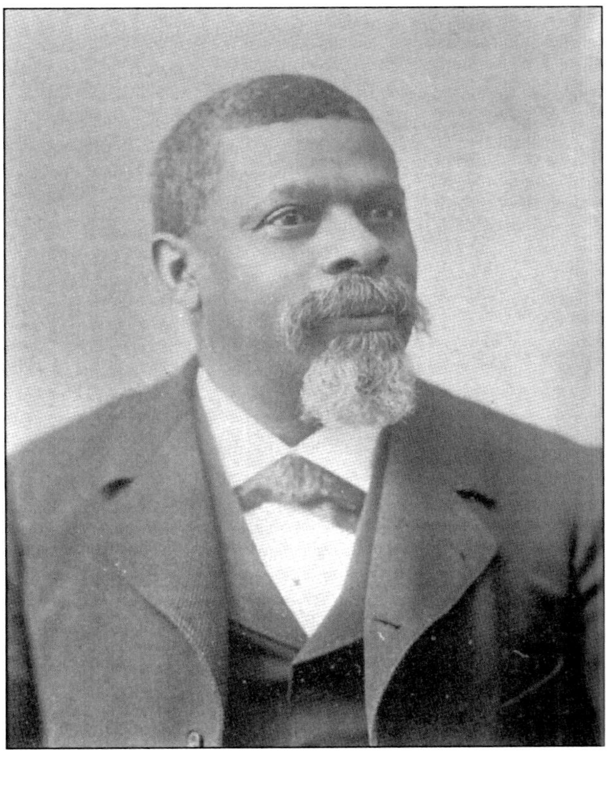

WILLIAM H. PARHAM, GRAND MASTER, PRINCE HALL GRAND LODGE OF OHIO, 1875–1879. An educator in the black public schools of Cincinnati, Parham (1839–1904) became the first African American graduate of the University of Cincinnati Law School, in 1874. He served in the Ohio legislature from 1896 to 1897. Much of the growth of Prince Hall Freemasonry sprung from Ohio. Twelve Prince Hall Grand Lodges originated from Ohio chartered lodges. This image is from *Representative Men of Ohio, 1896-97.*

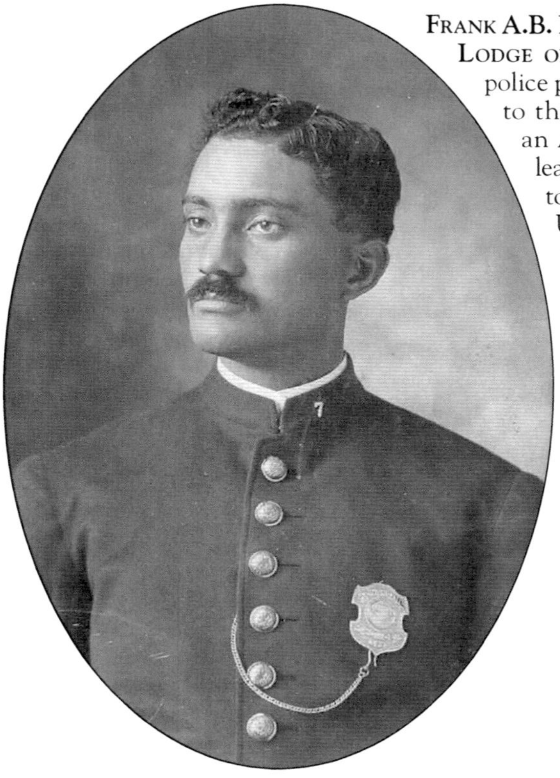

Frank A.B. Hill, Grand Master, Prince Hall Grand Lodge of Ohio, 1925–1930. Hill, a Cincinnati police patrolman, rose to detective and was elected to the Cincinnati City Council—all firsts for an African American. Like most Prince Hall leaders, Hill (1870–1934) was involved in efforts to advance his race, through groups like the Universal Negro Improvement Association, the Ancient United Knights and Daughters of Africa, and the National Association for the Advancement of Colored People. (Cincinnati Police Museum.)

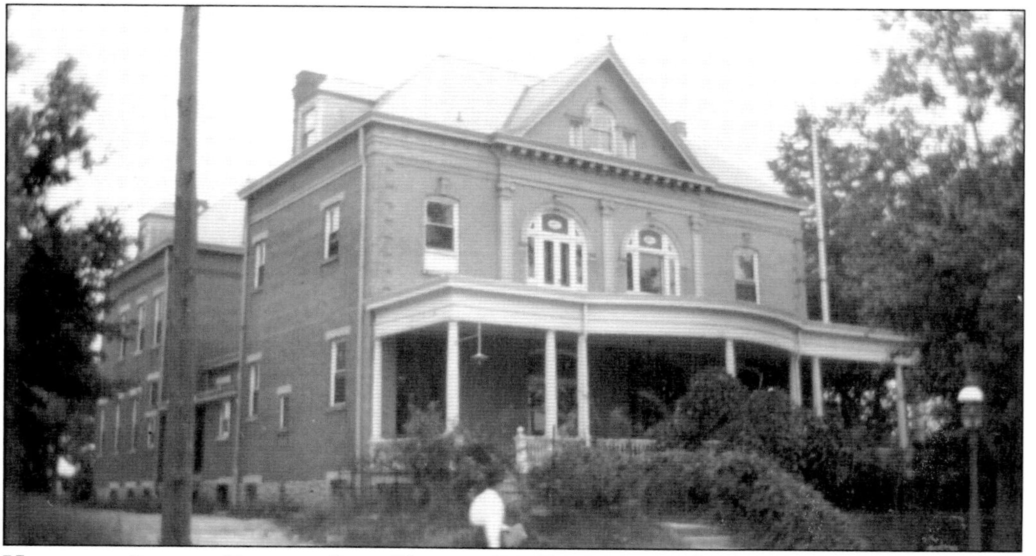

Hamilton County Eastern Star Home, 1922. Beginning with a hospital visitation program for Masonic-related patients in 1912, the Eastern Star created a rest home and hospital for aged members. The Park Hotel property, at the end of the College Hill trolley line, was purchased and remodeled. It received its first residents on October 21, 1923. Emma Engelhardt, a major force behind the project from its inception, served as president of the home's board from 1919 to 1939. (E.T. Carson Lodge No. 598.)

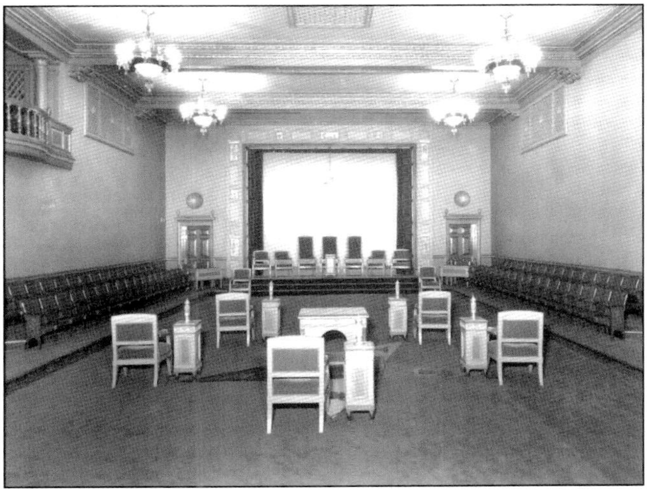

Order of Eastern Star Room, Cincinnati Masonic Temple. The second floor of the downtown temple was dedicated to the Eastern Star chapters, other "Adoptive" orders, and youth groups. OES had a tough time being accepted in Ohio, and their chapters were only allowed to meet in lodge rooms starting in 1895. The first chapter in Cincinnati was Violet Chapter No. 45, founded in 1895–1896. It met at Yeatman Lodge's Temple. (AASR.)

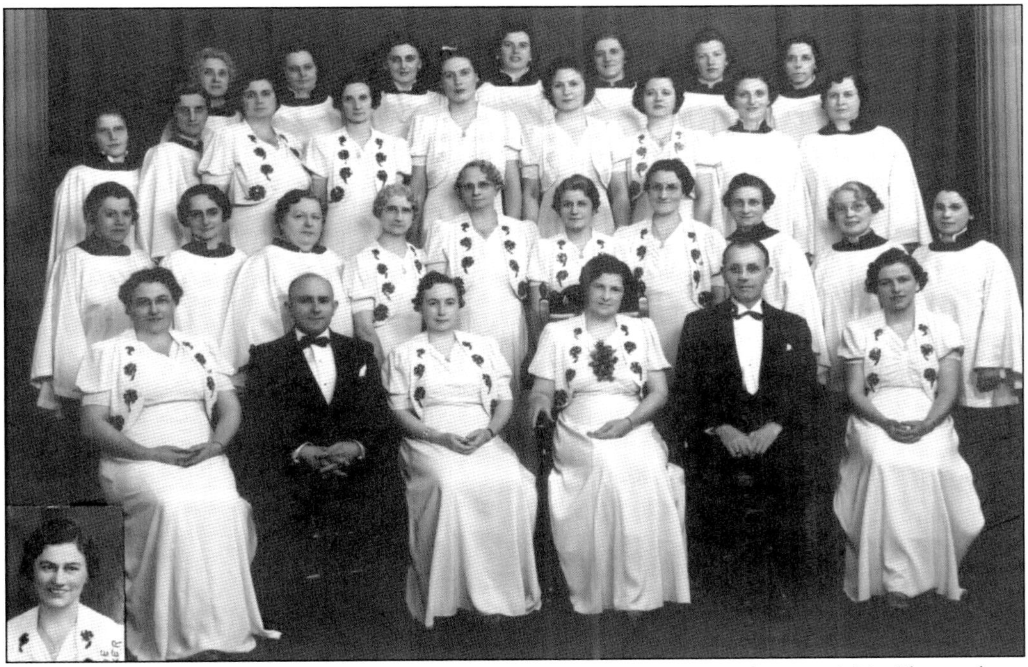

Officers of Dorcas Chapter No. 277, Order of the Eastern Star, 1940. Shown here are, from left to right, (first row): Marie Goebel, Associate Conductress; William Heidschuch, Associate Patron; Viola Heidschuch, Associate Matron; Helen Roeder, Worthy Matron; Edward F. Springmeier, Worthy Patron; and Virginia Toedt, Conductress; (second row) Mildred Franke, Organist; Frieda Ruttmueller, Choir; Eleanor Kirgan, Choir; Millie Holder, Treasurer; Louise Achepohl, Chaplain; Eva Gleason, Marshal; Alice H. Meyer, Secretary; Dorothy Boekcley, Choir; Stella Wittkamper, Choir; Myrtle G. Leffler, Choir Directress; (third row) Naomi Blum, Erwina Chandler, Choir; Irene Pitcher, Electa; Stella Koch, Martha; Helen Dahling, Esther; Martha Emigholz, Ruth; Marguerite Hassel, Adah; Alma Haefner, Choir; and Louise Goetz, Choir; (fourth row) Choir members Emma Knost, Margaret Gibka, Norma Haefner, Dorothea Niederhofer, Barbara Heareth, Allyne Goebel Wessel, and Dorothy Weber; (inset) Rose Baker, Warder. (Jean Watters.)

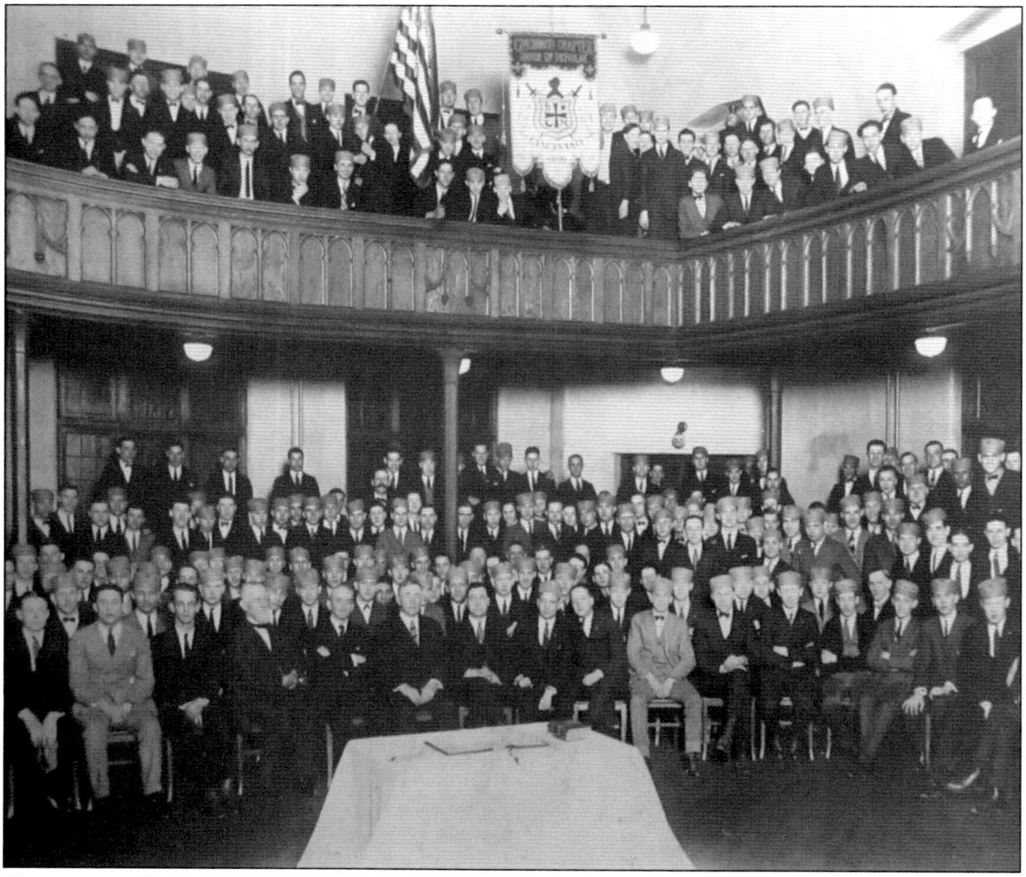

Cincinnati Chapter, Order of DeMolay, Early 1920s. DeMolay is a young men's organization, individual chapters of which are sponsored by a Masonic body. Founded in March 1919 by Frank S. Land in Kansas City, Missouri, it grew rapidly. Cincinnati Chapter, the first local chapter, was founded in February 1921. DeMolay was hugely successful in Cincinnati, with 16 chapters in the Seventh DeMolay District in 1967. (Earl Ross.)

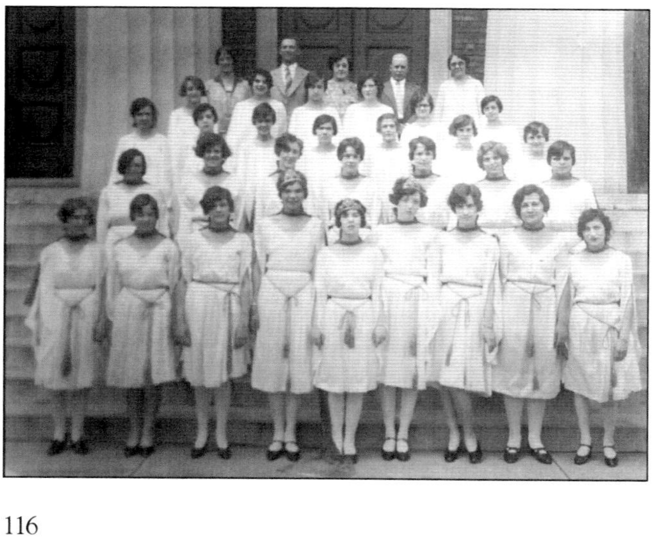

Job's Daughters, 1920s. Job's Daughters, an organization sponsored by the Masons, is for young women related to a Mason. It was founded in 1920. Job's Daughters meet in bodies called Bethels. These members pose on the steps of Norwood Masonic Temple. The girl at center in the first row is the Honored Queen, or presiding officer. (Norwood Masonic Temple.)

WILLIAM MELISH, TWICE ELECTED IMPERIAL POTENTATE. Melish revitalized Cincinnati's dormant Syrian Shrine Temple in 1881 and served as its second Potentate until 1897. He was elected Imperial Potentate (national leader) on two separate occasions, in 1892 and 1894. He stressed fiscal responsibility and charity. Extolling fun within the bounds of decency, he recommended the Shrine's mission be "Pleasure without intemperance, hospitality without rudeness, and jollity without coarseness." (Syrian Shrine.)

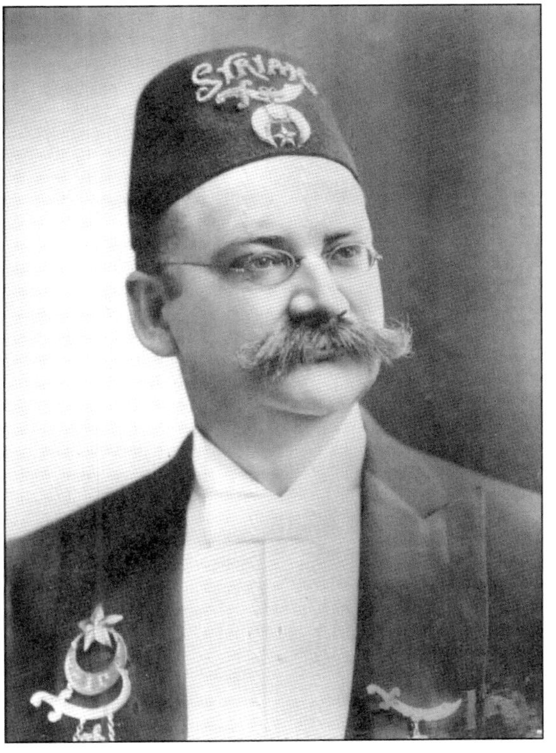

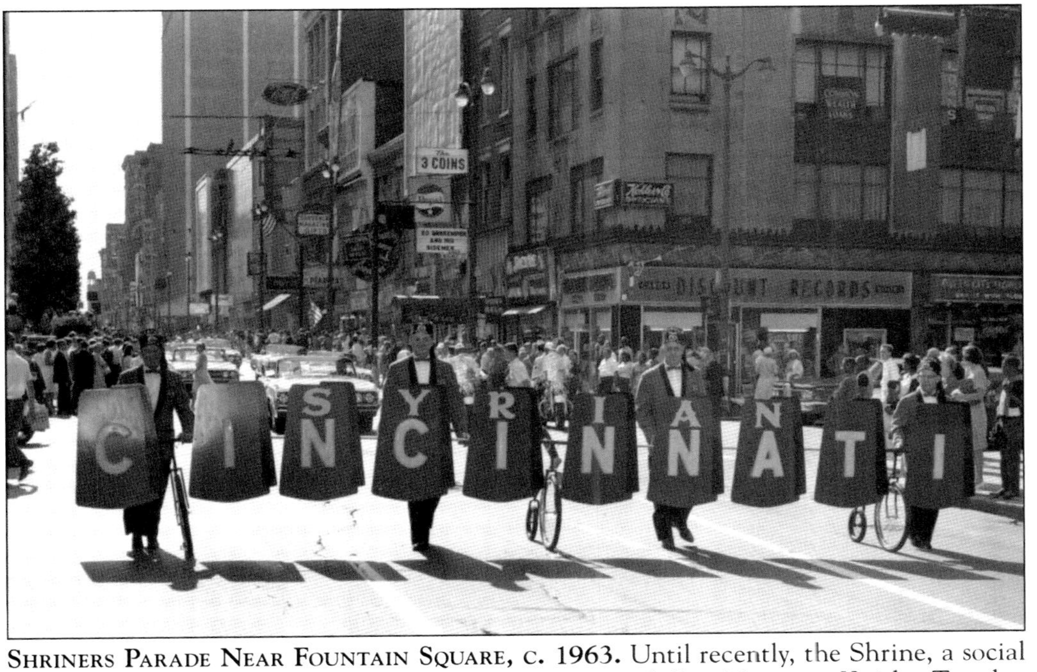

SHRINERS PARADE NEAR FOUNTAIN SQUARE, C. 1963. Until recently, the Shrine, a social organization, limited its membership to 32nd Degree Scottish Rite Masons or Knights Templar. Its ritual has an Arabian Nights flavor. The fez-shaped signs, spelling out the Syrian Temple's name, emphasize the importance of the red or maroon fez as a Shrine emblem. (Syrian Shrine.)

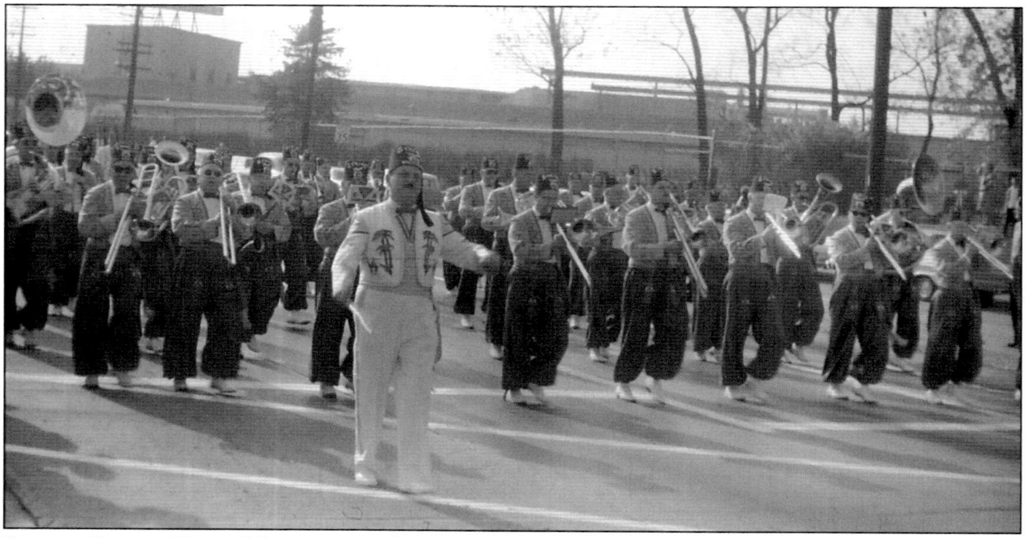

SYRIAN SHRINE BAND MARCHES TO CORNERSTONE LAYING AT OAKLEY MASONIC TEMPLE, 1964. The Shrine has traditionally been organized into units. The 1977 Syrian centennial book describes many musical units, including the Drum & Bugle Corps, Oriental Band, The Chanters singers, and a big band. Other units have included clowns, various small-car drivers, and the Hospital Hosts, who transport Shrine Burns Institute patients. (Oakley Lodge No. 668.)

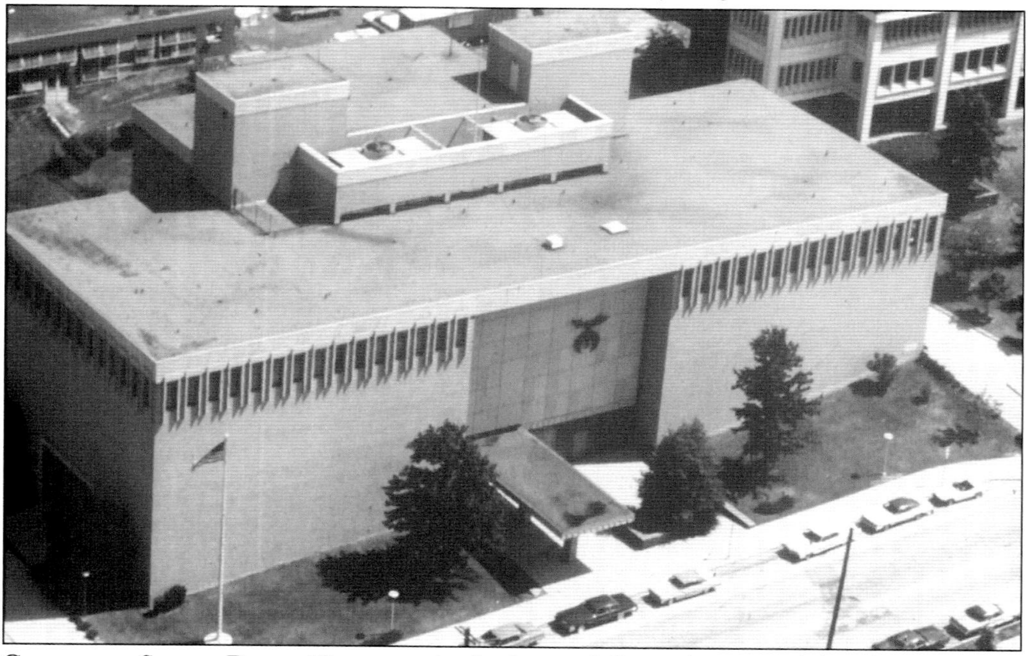

CINCINNATI SHRINE BURNS HOSPITAL. At the Imperial Council session of the Shrine in 1920, the Shriners Hospitals for Crippled Children (now Shriners Hospitals for Children) was born. The system has 20 hospitals in the United States and one each in Canada and Mexico. The hospitals provide free care to children. In the United States, three of the hospitals, like this one in Cincinnati, specialize in pediatric burns patients. The others specialize in juvenile orthopedics. (Shriners Hospitals for Children–Cincinnati.)

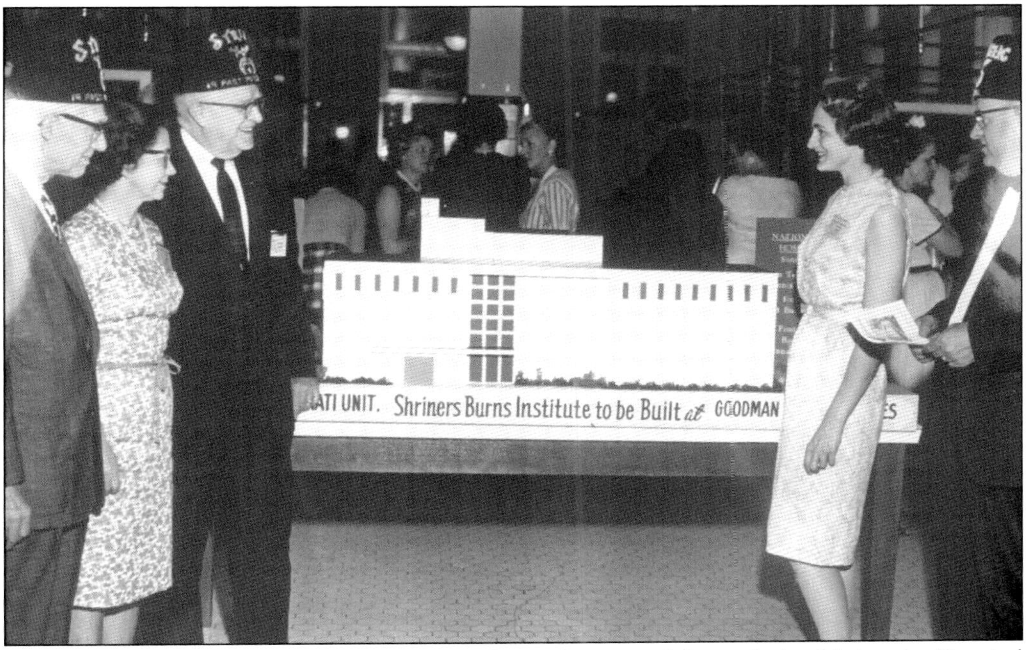

CINCINNATI, HOME TO THE BURNS INSTITUTE. In part because of the work that University Hospital was already doing with burns, Cincinnati was selected as the home for the Burns Institute. In this 1964 photograph, two past Potentates of the Syrian Shrine and an unidentified woman (left) view the model of the facility to be built on Burnet Avenue with Shriner and Dr. Bruce G. MacMillan, chief surgeon and chief of staff (far right), and Mary McErlane, executive secretary. (Shriners Hospitals for Children–Cincinnati.)

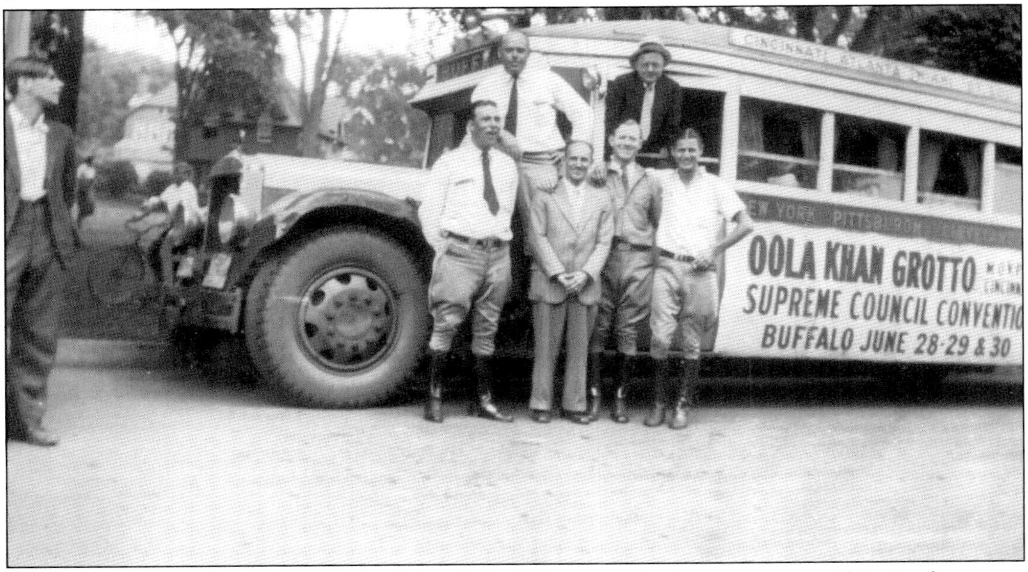

OOLA KAHN GROTTO. Founded in 1921, Oola Kahn staged a large ceremonial in its first year, initiating over 250 members. The Grotto, like the Shrine, is social in nature. It is organized into units, and its members even wear fezzes, black in their case. Here, members prepare to board a bus for the national convention in Buffalo.

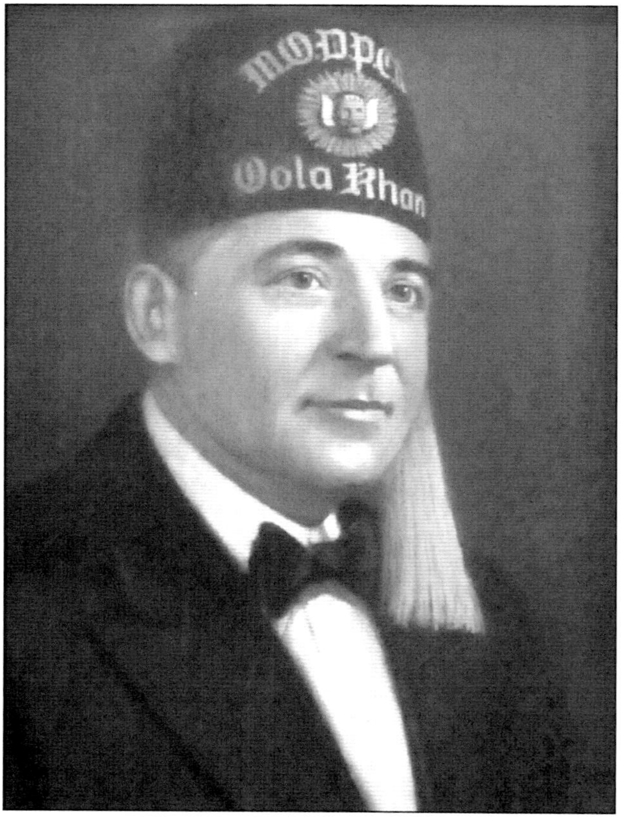

Harry H. Baker, Grand Monarch, MOVPER, 1944. Baker (1888?–1960) was elected the national presiding officer of the Mystic Order Veiled Prophets of the Enchanted Realm (Grotto's official name) in June 1944. He was a Past Master of Norwood Lodge No. 576 and Past Monarch of Cincinnati's Oola Khan Grotto. He served as the mayor of Norwood from 1926 to 1933. (Supreme Council, Grotto.)

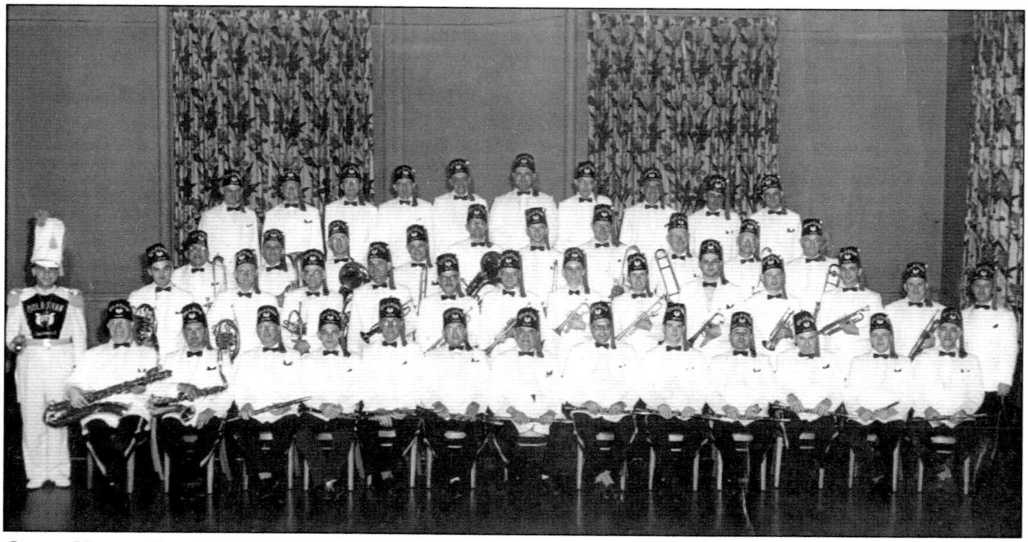

Oola Kahn Grotto Band, c. 1960. The Grotto has sometimes been pejoratively referred to as "the poor man's Shrine." This photograph puts such an idea into question. While similar in nature, the Grotto's members need only be a Master Mason, while the Shrine used to require Scottish Rite or Knights Templar membership. The only person identified in this photograph is George E. Gibbons Jr. (second row, eighth from left, holding trumpet). (Rodney Gibbons.)

Seven

Other Brotherhoods and the Business of Fraternity

The period from the second half of the 19th century to the Great Depression was a boom time for fraternalism during which Ohio's Masonic membership increased more than fourfold. The appendant and associated bodies discussed in the previous chapter also increased in terms of membership and number of groups.

Other fraternal groups multiplied in number and variety as well. Listings of secret or fraternal societies fill nine-and-a-half pages in *William's Cincinnati Directory* in 1900. Cincinnati's first lodge of the Independent Order of Odd Fellows (IOOF) was founded in 1830. Many more followed. The Knights of Pythias, founded in Washington, DC, near the end of the Civil War, was also popular. These organizations also centered on developing the character of their members, creating a network of brothers, and providing an outlet for theatrics and drama via the ritual. The Odd Fellows and the Knights of Pythias had uniformed groups equivalent to the Knights Templar. There were also Rebekahs and Pythian Sisters, for the ladies of Odd Fellows and Knights of Pythias members, respectively. As with the Freemasons, there were African American equivalents of these orders.

Lodges with animal names, like the Elks, were found in the Queen City. Temperance groups fought "demon rum" in several orders. Woodmen of the World and Modern Woodmen had lodges featuring stumps as altars. Their members conducted close-order drill with axes instead of swords. Some men belonged to one order. Others belonged to a collection of lodges, camps, and societies.

The growth and popularity of these orders led to an industry that supplied costumes, uniforms, paraphernalia, furniture, membership certificates, swords, and literature. Cincinnati was home to Pettibone Brothers Manufacturing, which produced fraternal goods as well as police, fire department, and military uniforms. Cincinnati Regalia was another firm specializing in the society goods business.

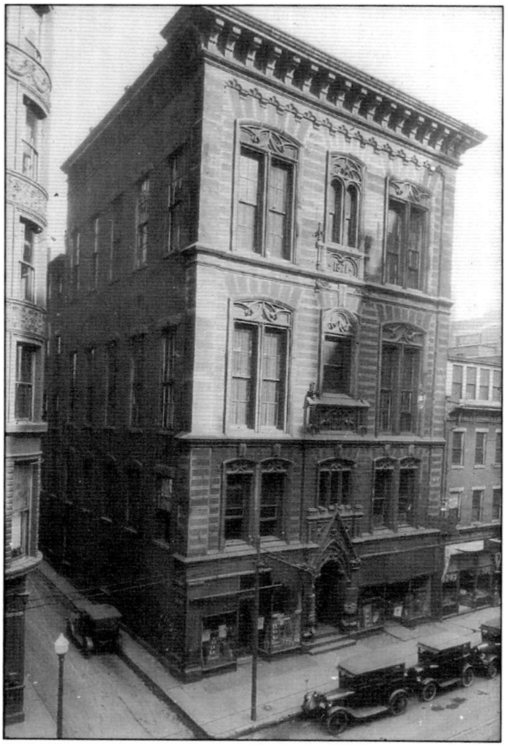

Odd Fellows Temple, 1872. This four-story building designed by architects Anderson and Hannaford at a cost of $75,000 stood at Fourth and Home Streets. It was dedicated on April 23, 1872. The uniformed Encampment occupied the fourth floor, and the lodge met on the third. A space for the Order of Rebekah occupied a half-story between. (Public Library of Cincinnati and Hamilton County.)

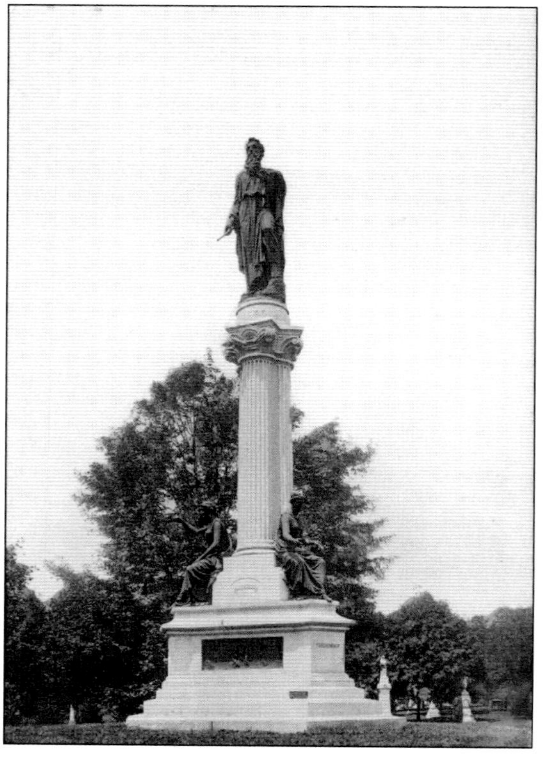

IOOF Memorial, Spring Grove Cemetery. Odd Fellows are commanded to "visit the sick, relieve the distressed, bury the dead and educate the orphan." In obedience to the third command, the order purchased an entire section of Spring Grove Cemetery. This monument, surmounted by a bronze figure of Moses, was dedicated in September 1884 by the national Sovereign Grand Lodge. (Public Library of Cincinnati and Hamilton County.)

Odd Fellows Temple. Dedicated on May 15, 1894, this temple at Seventh and Elm Streets stood seven stories tall. It included a theater, banquet rooms, eight lodge rooms of various sizes, plus stores and office space, mostly occupied by the Cincinnati Southern Railroad. Designed by Samuel Hannaford & Sons, it was built for $300,000. The building housed more than 13 IOOF groups. Many other non-IOOF fraternal groups were tenants, including Red Men and Royal Arcanum. (Public Library of Cincinnati and Hamilton County.)

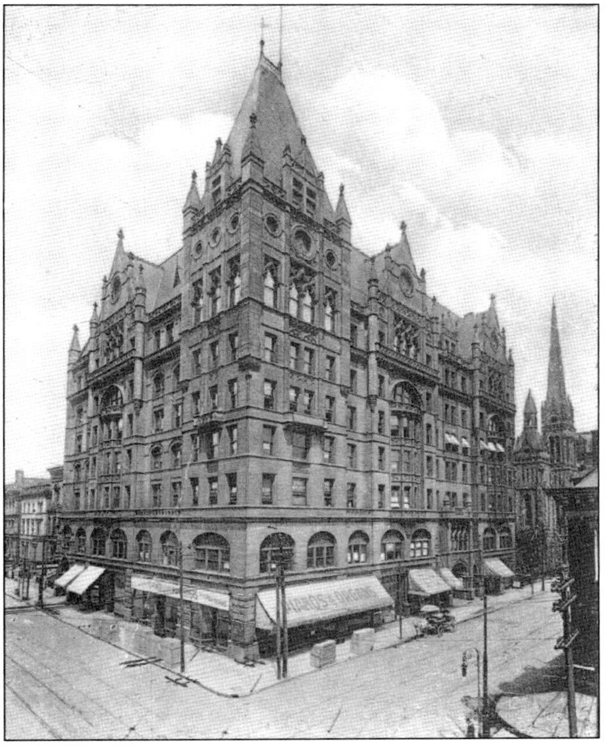

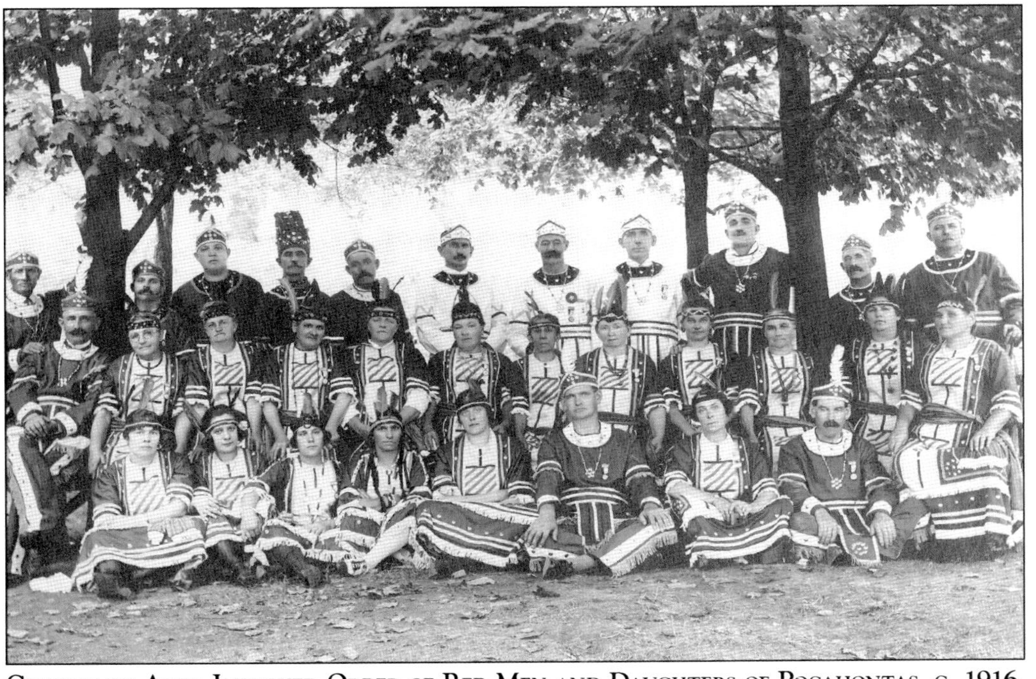

Cincinnati Area Improved Order of Red Men and Daughters of Pocahontas, c. 1916. Cincinnati's fondness for fraternalism ranged from groups like the American Indian–themed Red Men, to The Tribe of Ben Hur, which based its ritual on the popular 19th-century novel. (CHS.)

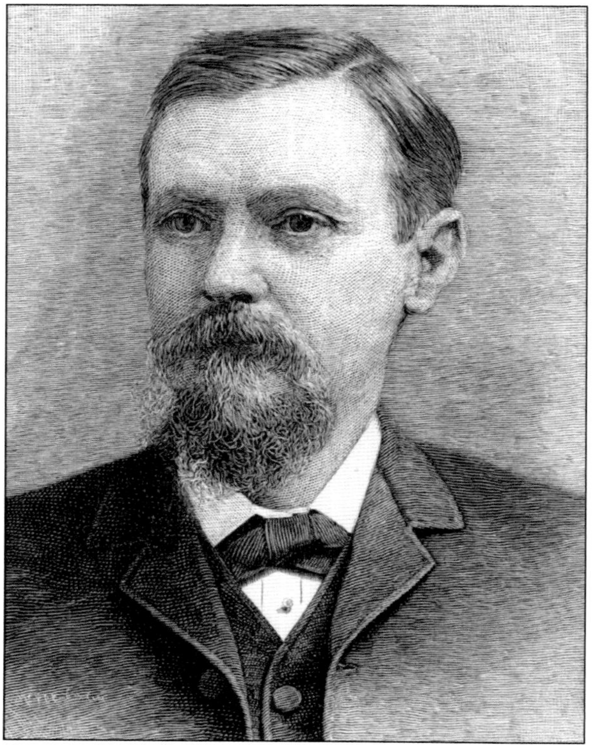

Howard Douglass, Supreme Chancellor, Knights of Pythias. Douglass (1846–1908), a Cincinnati attorney, was the Supreme Chancellor, or national leader of the Knights of Pythias, from 1886 to 1888. At his funeral on July 23, 1908, in the "old" Scottish Rite Cathedral, services were performed by the Pythians, Knights Templar, Lafayette Masonic Lodge No 81, the Elks, the Grand Army of the Republic, and the Episcopal Church. This image is from *Pythian Knighthood: Its History and Literature.*

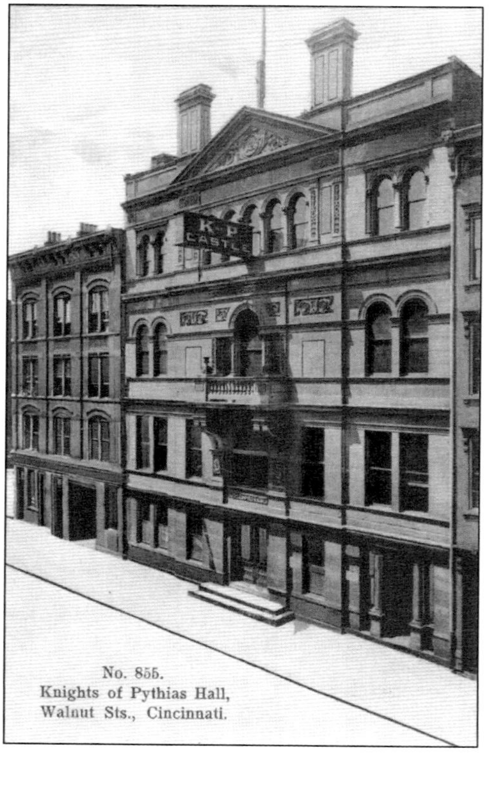

Knights of Pythias Castle. Samuel Hannaford designed the 1885 Musik Verein Hall. Lincoln Lodge No. 17, Knights of Pythias bought and converted the choir group's building, located on Walnut Street near the canal. Other Pythian lodges met at the Douglass Castle, at Walnut and Sixth Streets, and even at the Odd Fellows Temple. (Public Library of Cincinnati and Hamilton County.)

ELKS TEMPLE. The Benevolent & Protective Order of Elks, Cincinnati Lodge No. 5, erected this building in 1922. Harry Hake (see page 60) was the architect. It was acquired in 1942 by Powell Crosley to house WLW radio and took on the name Crosley Square. It was the home of WLWT-TV until 1999. (Public Library of Cincinnati and Hamilton County.)

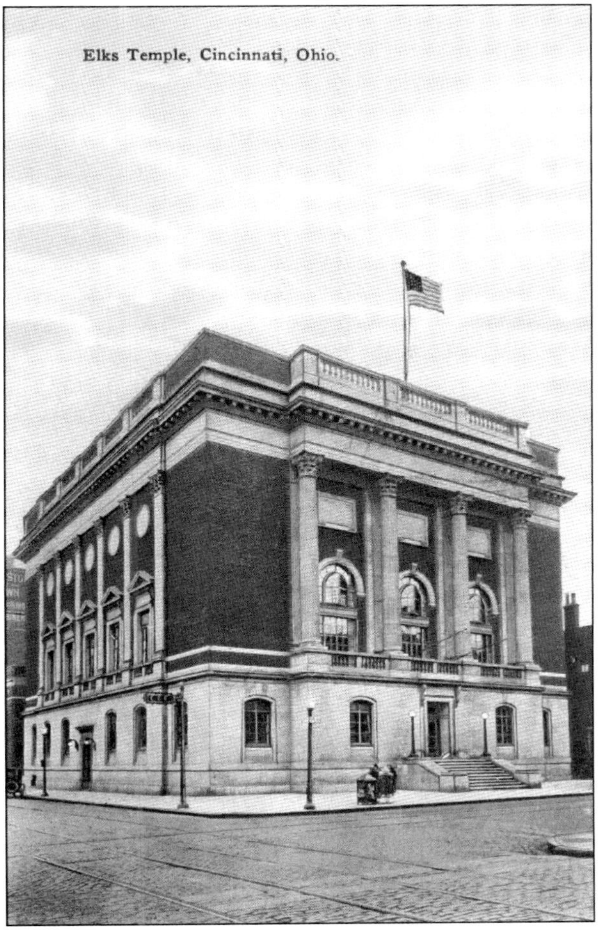

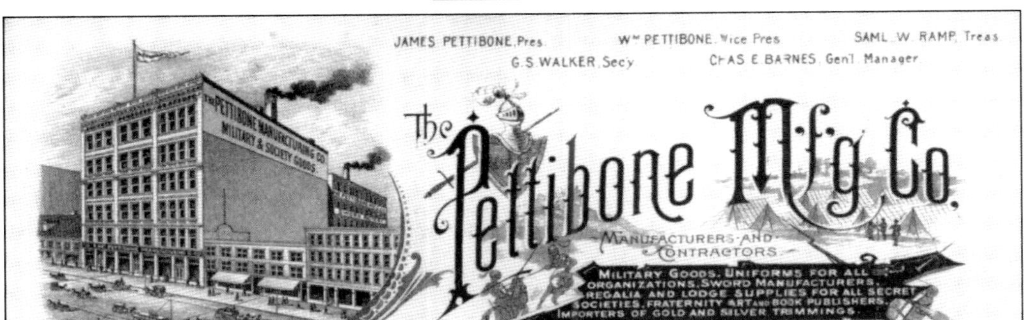

PETTIBONE BROTHERS MANUFACTURING. Fraternalism's growth at the end of the 19th century created a huge market for costumes, uniforms, regalia, jewelry, and furniture for the numerous brotherhoods throughout the United States. Among the largest of these concerns was Cincinnati's Pettibone Brothers, with a workforce of over 300 at the turn of the 20th century. The factory was located on the east side of Main Street, between Sixth and Seventh Streets. (Cumminsville Chapter No. 158.)

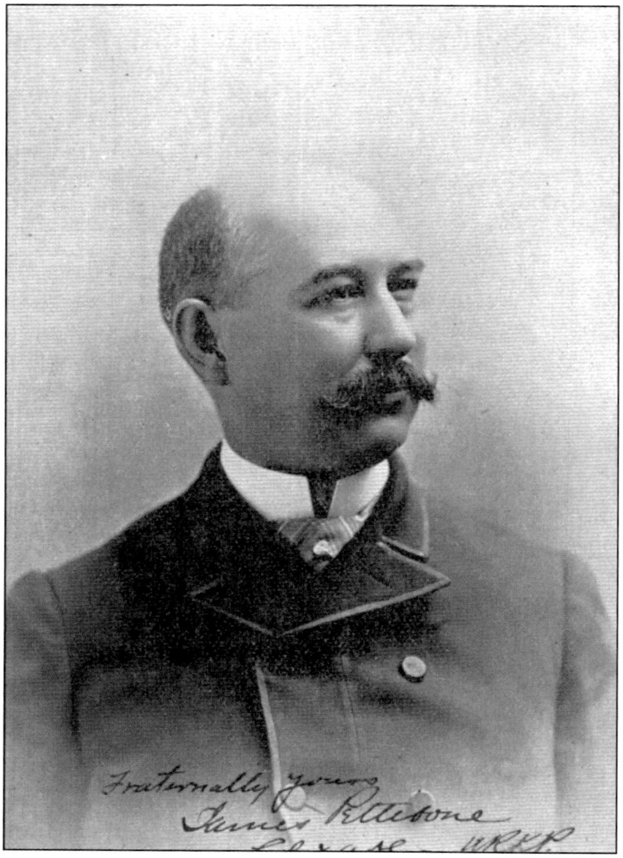

James Pettibone. President of Pettibone Brothers Manufacturing, James Pettibone was an active Mason. He was the Chief of Staff for the Grand Lodge of Ohio Centennial Parade in Cincinnati on October 21, 1908. The initials "URKP" on this photograph stand for Uniform Rank of the Knights of Pythias. This image is from *History of the Order of Knights of Pythias for the Jurisdiction of Cleveland, Ohio.*

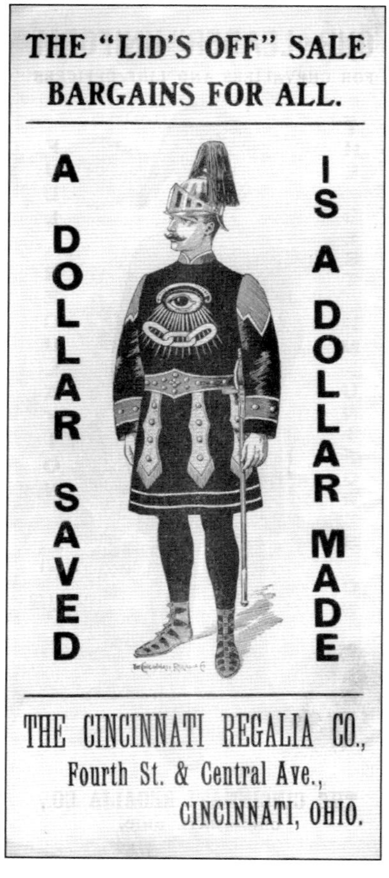

Cincinnati Regalia Company Catalog. *Williams' Cincinnati Directory 1900* had listings for six firms manufacturing regalia and society goods, including Pettibone and Cincinnati Regalia. Originally founded in hopes of taking over Pettibone while it was in receivership, Cincinnati Regalia instead became a competitor. It continued in business into the 1990s.

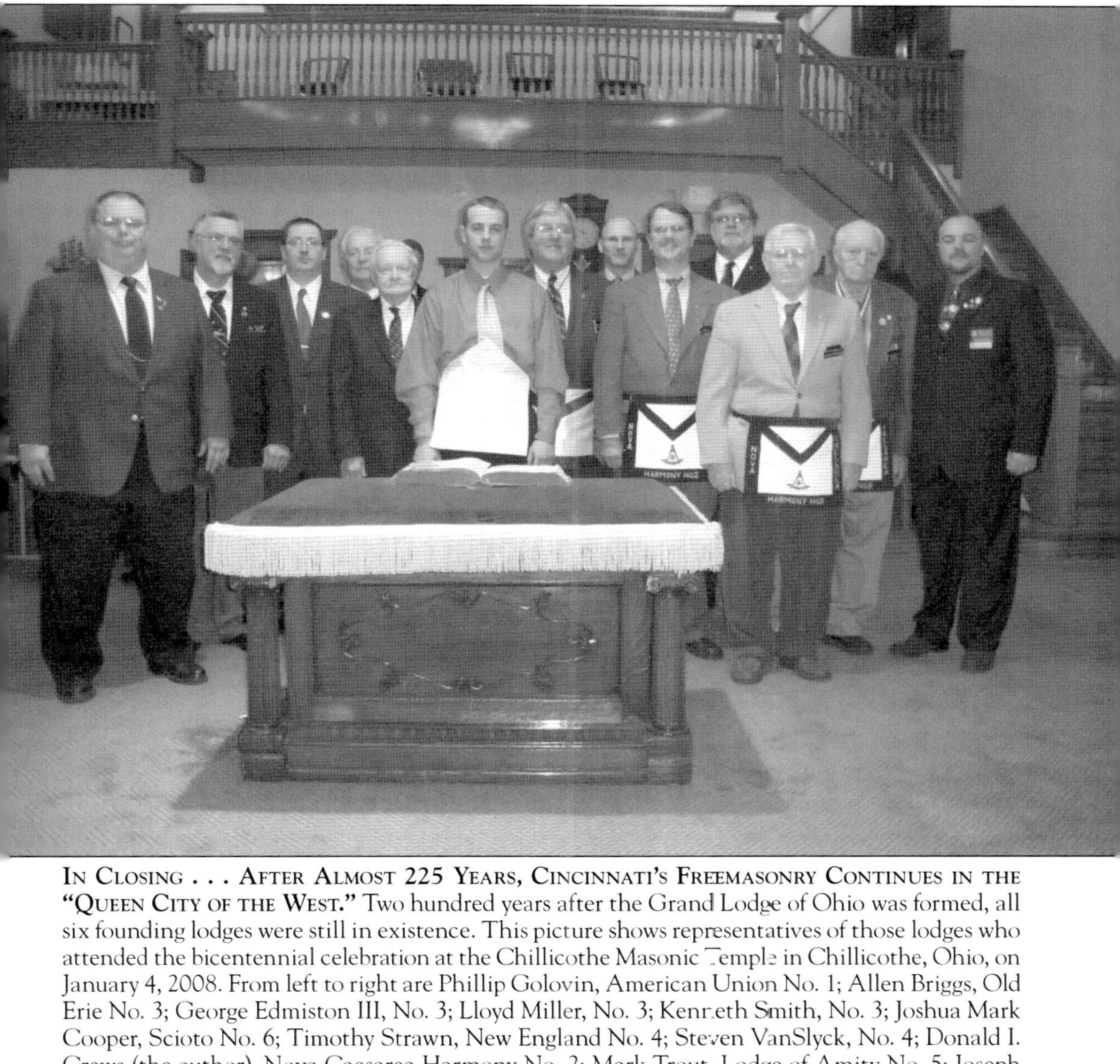

In Closing . . . After Almost 225 Years, Cincinnati's Freemasonry Continues in the "Queen City of the West." Two hundred years after the Grand Lodge of Ohio was formed, all six founding lodges were still in existence. This picture shows representatives of those lodges who attended the bicentennial celebration at the Chillicothe Masonic Temple in Chillicothe, Ohio, on January 4, 2008. From left to right are Phillip Golovin, American Union No. 1; Allen Briggs, Old Erie No. 3; George Edmiston III, No. 3; Lloyd Miller, No. 3; Kenneth Smith, No. 3; Joshua Mark Cooper, Scioto No. 6; Timothy Strawn, New England No. 4; Steven VanSlyck, No. 4; Donald I. Crews (the author), Nova Caesarea Harmony No. 2; Mark Trout, Lodge of Amity No. 5; Joseph Howell, No. 2; Cleve Cornelison, No. 2; and Chad Bonifield, No. 5. (GLofOH.)